JOANNE FLUKE'S LAKE EDEN COOKBOOK

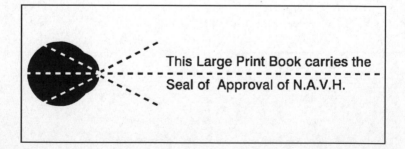

This Large Print Book carries the
Seal of Approval of N.A.V.H.

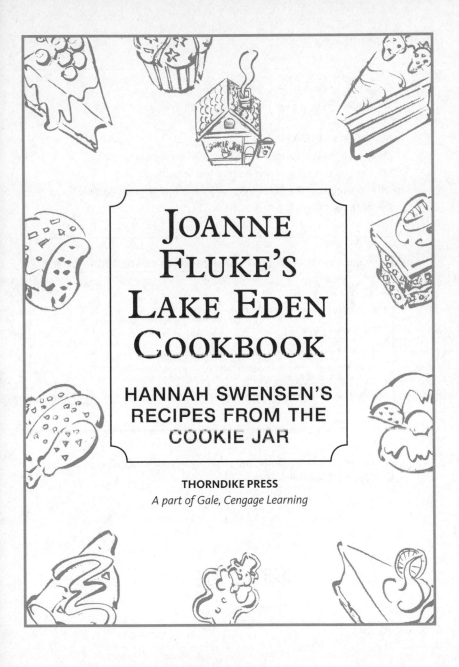

JOANNE FLUKE'S LAKE EDEN COOKBOOK

HANNAH SWENSEN'S RECIPES FROM THE COOKIE JAR

THORNDIKE PRESS
A part of Gale, Cengage Learning

GALE
CENGAGE Learning®

Detroit • New York • San Francisco • New Haven, Conn • Waterville, Maine • London

Copyright © 2011 by H.L. Swensen, Inc.

Thorndike Press, a part of Gale, Cengage Learning.

Thorndike Press® Large Print Health, Home & Learning.

The text of this Large Print edition is unabridged.

Other aspects of the book may vary from the original edition.

Set in 16 pt. Plantin.

LIBRARY OF CONGRESS CATALOGING-IN-PUBLICATION DATA

Fluke, Joanne, 1943-
    Joanne Fluke's Lake Eden cookbook : Hannah Swensen's recipes from the cookie jar / by Joanne Fluke. — Large print ed.
    p. cm. — (Thorndike Press large print health, home & learning)
    Includes index.
    ISBN-13: 978-1-4104-4445-5 (hardcover)
    ISBN-10: 1-4104-4445-7 (hardcover)
    1. Swensen, Hannah (Fictitious character) — Fiction.
2. Women private investigators — Minnesota — Fiction.
3. Cooking — Fiction. I. Title. II. Title: Lake Eden cookbook.
PS3556.L685J63 2012
813'.54—dc23

                                            2011041221

Published in 2012 by arrangement with Kensington Books, an imprint of Kensington Publishing Corp.

Printed in the United States of America
1 2 3 4 5 6 7 16 15 14 13 12

DEDICATION

This book is for Walter Zacharius.
And for Sheila Grimm, who would have
enjoyed baking
Andrea's Double Chocolate Puffs.

ACKNOWLEDGMENTS

Hugs to Ruel, my in-house editor, who's tasted every single recipe in this book.
(It's a tough job, but somebody's got to do it!)

And hugs to the kids who've helped so much along the way.

Big kisses for the grandkids who learned, early on, that a balanced diet is a cookie in each hand.

Big bundles of thanks for the cookbook advice I received from J.B., Gretchen, and the staff at **Seattle Mystery Bookshop**, Linda, Patrick, and MaryElizabeth at **Mysterious Galaxy** in San Diego, Barbara Peters and her staff at **The Poisoned Pen** in Scottsdale, AZ, the launch party crowd at **Mysteries to Die For** in Thousand Oaks, CA, and Mary Alice Gorman at **Mystery Lovers Bookshop** in Oakmont, PA.

7

Thank you to my friends and neighbors who don't seem to mind doing a taste test now and then: Mel & Kurt, Lyn & Bill, Lu, Gina & Fiona, Adrienne, Jay, Bob, Laura & Mark, Amanda, John B., Judy Q., Dr. Bob & Sue, Richard & Krista, Mark B., Angelique, Daryl and her staff at Groves Accountancy, and everyone at First Private Bank.

Special thanks to my superb Editor-in-Chief and valued friend, John Scognamiglio.

Hugs all around to Steve, Laurie, Doug, David, Adam, Robin, Karen, Adeola, Lesleigh, Vida, Darla, Rosanna, and all the other folks at Kensington Publishing who keep Hannah sleuthing and baking up a storm.

Thanks to Hiro Kimura, my talented cover artist, who's drawn scrumptious desserts for the covers of every Hannah Swensen mystery.

Grateful thanks to Lou Malcangi at Kensington for designing all of Hannah's incredibly gorgeous dust jackets and paperback covers.

Thanks to John at Placed4Success.com for Hannah's movie and TV spots.

And even more thanks for handling my social media.

Thanks to Kathy Allen for testing most of the new recipes in this cookbook and organizing taste tests.

Thank you to Sally Hayes *(and Gary, too)* for sharing oodles of her wonderful recipes.

And hugs to my friend, Trudi Nash, who comes up with some of the best homemade treats I've ever tasted.

Thank you to Angie Sherwood of SherwoodsForest.com for making deliciously scented candles of the title desserts. Angie's candles look so real and smell so tasty, several have ended up on dinner tables by mistake!

Thanks to Ken Wilson, friend, media guide in L.A., and an excellent cook.

Hugs to superb food stylist Lois Brown, for making my recipes look yummy on KPNX-TV in Phoenix. And thanks to a second fantastic food stylist, Judy Krug, for making things easy for me on WGN-TV in Chicago.

Thank you to Dr. Rahhal, Dr. and Kathy Line, and Dr. Wallen.

Thanks to Jamie Wallace for keeping my

Web site, **MurderSheBaked.com** up to date and looking great.

Thank you to all the readers who love to cook and share their favorite recipes with me. You'll find some of them in this cookbook.

Special thanks to Mom, Gammie, Kitty, Myrt, Bert, and all the resourceful Minnesota cooks who know how to make do with what's in the pantry and still come up with something delicious.
(You can't run to the store in a blizzard, don'cha know?)

AUTHOR'S NOTE

You will notice that there are two types of recipe titles in this book. Those that are written in mixed case letters and are preceded by an asterisk are new recipes, never before published. They are debuting in this book.

Recipe titles written in uppercase letters (all caps) are for recipes that have been published before in one of the following Hannah Swensen mystery novels: *Chocolate Chip Cookie Murder* (special edition), *Strawberry Shortcake Murder, Blueberry Muffin Murder, Lemon Meringue Pie Murder, Fudge Cupcake Murder, Peach Cobbler Murder, Cherry Cheesecake Murder, Key Lime Pie Murder,* and *Carrot Cake Murder.*

BAKING TIPS

If eggs are called for in a recipe, use large eggs, the kind they label "large" at the grocery store.

11

If one of the ingredients in a recipe is butter, that refers to salted butter, not unsalted or sweet butter.

If a recipe calls for flour, you should use all-purpose white flour such as Pillsbury or Gold Medal. Be careful about substituting wheat flour, soy flour, bread machine flour, or any of the other specialized flours out there.

Most of the time you can substitute any common nut for any other common nut in a recipe, especially if chopped nuts are called for. Be careful with peanuts. Some people have peanut allergies.

If you're baking cookies, it's always wise to bake one cookie first as a test cookie. If it spreads out too much on the cookie sheet, add 1/3 cup flour to the cookie dough left in your mixing bowl. Mix that in thoroughly (you may have to knead it in with your hands if the cookie dough is stiff) and then try another test cookie. If that second cookie passes muster, write a note on the bottom of the recipe so you'll mix in the extra flour right away the next time you bake those cookies.

When you're baking anything, it's a good idea not to open the oven door very often. Every time you do, the oven loses heat and it takes time for it to come back up to temperature.

If you come from a cold climate, you probably already know that baking is a great way to warm up the kitchen. You probably also know that if a recipe calls for softened butter or butter at room temperature, they're not talking about the butter dish on the counter of a Minnesota farm kitchen at the crack of dawn in the winter.

Hannah Swensen frowned as she turned a slow circle in the center of the kitchen at The Cookie Jar, her bakery and coffee shop in Lake Eden, Minnesota. The timer had just sounded a one-minute warning, the latest batch of cookies was about to come out of the oven, and this had all the earmarks of a baking disaster. Every available surface was filled with various kinds of Christmas cookies.

"There's no more room!" Hannah complained, not expecting an answer since she was the sole occupant of the kitchen. But just then her partner, Lisa Beeseman, came in through the swinging restaurant-type door that separated the kitchen from the coffee shop.

"I can fix that. No problem." Lisa held up two of the giant glass jars they kept behind the counter in the coffee shop to display their daily cookie offerings. "I'll just fill up these jars and you'll have lots of room. And if you need more room than that, I've got three more jars that are running low."

By the time the oven timer sounded for the second time, Lisa had cleared cookies from several tiers of the baker's rack. Hannah filled them up again with trays of fresh, hot cookies, and then she slipped more cookies into the oven. The thing to do while this new batch was baking was to clear more space.

Her mother's cookies were cool, and Hannah arranged them in individual boxes. Delores Swensen was hosting her fourth annual Christmas cookie exchange this afternoon, and Hannah and Lisa were catering the luncheon at the event. Each lady Delores had invited would arrive with a dozen cookies for each of the other ladies attending, plus an extra dozen for charity. That meant everyone went home with a lovely assortment of Christmas cookies and this year's charity, the Winnetka County Children's Home, would have homemade cookies for the children.

Hannah picked up the boxed cookies intending to stash them in her cookie truck to clear even more counter space, but all it took was one step outside to cause her to change her mind. It was the second Wednesday in December, and according to Rayne Phillips at KCOW Radio, Lake Eden, Minnesota's news and weather station, the temperature would dip to minus double-digits today. It seemed that Rayne was right for a change. Turning on her heel, Hannah stepped back into her warm kitchen. The day was cold and blustery, it was already well below zero, and her mother's cookies would freeze in a matter of minutes if she stored them in the back of her cookie truck.

Hannah had just re-stacked the cookie boxes in a safe corner of the kitchen when the phone rang. She grabbed the phone on the wall so that Lisa wouldn't have to leave the customers to answer it. "The Cookie Jar," she said. "Hannah spreading."

"Hello, Hannah. It's Bertie." Hannah could hear the high-pitched whine of hair dryers in the background and she knew that Bertie was calling from her beauty shop, the Cut n' Curl. "You'll be at your mother's cookie exchange, won't you?"

"I'll be there. Lisa and I are catering the luncheon."

"Perfect! I was wondering if you'd share something with me."

"Share what, Bertie?"

"A recipe."

Hannah began to smile. To her, *share* meant dividing something tangible into pieces, and she couldn't help forming a mental picture of Bertie grasping one side of a printed recipe while she held on to the other and awaited the signal to tear it in half. Of course that's not what Bertie meant, and Hannah didn't mind giving out her recipes to anyone who asked. The chances of Bertie refusing to order something Hannah sold at The Cookie Jar just because she could go home and bake it herself were negligible. "Which recipe would you like?" she asked.

"The one for that appetizer you made for the film shoot. It was on a round cracker and you said it had cream cheese in it."

"Cream Cheese Puffs?"

"That's it. I'd like that one. You said it was easy."

"It is, but you have to serve it hot out of the oven."

"I can do that. Will you bring the recipe to your mother's luncheon?"

"Sure," Hannah promised. "I'll see you there, Bertie."

"Marge and Dad are here early," Lisa announced, entering the kitchen only seconds after Hannah had hung up the phone. "I came to relieve you so that you can make the morning deliveries."

"That's great. This last batch of cookies

has five minutes to go. Do you want me to stay until they're out?"

"You go. I'll take care of it."

"Okay." Hannah retrieved the steno pad they kept by the phone, flipped to the right page, and jotted a note about the recipe Bertie wanted.

"Another cookie order?" Lisa guessed.

"No, it's a list of all the recipes I have to print out before we go to Mother's cookie exchange. Everybody wants something."

"Like who? And what do they want?"

"Like Carrie Rhodes. She's supposed to bring a pie to a Christmas party and she needs a recipe. I'm going to bring all of my pie recipes so she can choose. And then there's Mother. She wants a recipe for shrimp bisque that she can make in a crockpot."

"Your mother's going to cook?" Lisa looked horrified.

"I doubt it. She'll probably ask me to mix it up so all she'll have to do is plug in the slow cooker. They're having a potluck at the hospital, and shrimp bisque is Doc's favorite soup."

"Who else is on your list?"

"Claire. She wants to make homemade candy for the church Christmas packages."

"But Grandma Knudson makes great

candy! Why doesn't Claire just ask her for recipes?"

"She did, but Claire read them and she said they all mentioned stages like soft ball, and hard ball, and crack. Grandma told her not to worry about it, that all Claire had to do was use a candy thermometer, but Claire just started learning how to cook and she didn't think she could handle anything that complicated."

"Okay. I guess that makes sense." Lisa pointed to a name on Hannah's list. "Rose McDermott wants a cake recipe? And she bakes some of the best cakes in town?"

"She told me she's looking for something new. Almost everyone Mother invited wants me to bring some type of recipe."

"Then you'd better go home right after you make the deliveries and start printing out those recipes. Print out enough sets for everyone there. That way you won't have to do it again the next time they ask you."

"Good idea. But can you get along without me for a couple of hours?"

"Of course I can. I already told Herb I'd need some help, and he's going to move all our supplies to the community center kitchen. And Andrea's doing the tables, so we don't have to worry about that. The pies are all ready, and you made the chicken salad this morning. What else is there?"

"The champagne cocktails, but I'll bring everything I need for those."

"Then we're all set." Lisa glanced over as the oven timer gave a one-minute warning. "Did you print out the luncheon menu so I can put one by each place setting?"

"They're in a blue folder on the passenger seat of your car. You really ought to lock it, Lisa. Your husband's going to give you a ticket."

Lisa laughed. Everyone in town knew that Herb took his job as the Lake Eden marshal, the only law enforcement officer hired directly by the mayor, very seriously.

The timer started to ring for the second time and Lisa hurried to the oven. But she looked up as Hannah slipped into her parka and picked up the stack of cookie boxes set aside for delivery. "Your recipes are really popular, Hannah. Doesn't that make you happy?"

"Yes, and no."

"Why *no*?"

"Because I've got so many recipes to print. And that means I'll have to run out to the mall on my way home to buy more paper and ink cartridges."

Delores Swensen's 4th Annual Christmas Cookie Exchange Luncheon

Appetizer Course
Razzle Dazzle Champagne Cocktails
(or Faux Razzle Dazzle Champagne Cocktails)
Razzle Dazzle Baked Brie

Main Course
Hannah's Chicken Salad
Herb's Herb Biscuits

Dessert Course
Tapioca Cheesecake
Peanut Butter and Jelly Pie

Delores Swensen's 4th Annual
Christmas Cookie Exchange Luncheon

Appetizer Course
Razzle Dazzle Champagne Cocktails
Razzle Dazzle Baked Brie
Assorted Crackers

Main Course
Hannah's Chicken Salad
Herb's Herb Biscuits

Dessert Course
Tapioca Pie with Toasted Coconut
Peanut Butter and Jelly Pie
Swedish Plasma Coffee

"Ready or not, here they come!" Hannah said, giving a relieved sigh. She'd just dipped the rim of the last champagne flute in red decorator sugar when she'd heard the sound of women's voices and the clatter of high heels on the stairs.

"We're ready," Lisa answered, removing a baked brie from the oven. She carried it to the counter they'd designated as their staging area and placed it next to a second baked brie and several baskets of assorted crackers. "Do you want me to put the appetizers out on the table now?"

"Yes. They'll need something to munch on while I mix the cocktails. Do you have the individual appetizer knives?"

"They're on the table."

Hannah glanced over at the long table in the banquet room. Before she'd gone upstairs to wait for their mother to arrive, Hannah's sister Andrea had decorated it with a red and green tablecloth, several small Christmas trees with colored lights, and some stylized gold deer that were frozen in the act of browsing on faux evergreen and holly centerpieces. The appetizer knives were there, one at each place setting.

Bertie Straub was the first one to enter the room, and she rushed over to Hannah. "Did you bring my recipe, Hannah?"

"Yes, and I also brought the recipe for the appetizer we're having today," Hannah answered, gesturing toward the small card table she'd set up in the corner. "I'll pass them out just as soon as I serve the Razzle Dazzle Champagne Cocktails."

"That sounds heavenly," Bertie declared. "Addie Borgia had to tell me all about her grandson's wedding while I colored her hair this morning, and she's told me the exact same stories three times before!"

Hannah hurried to the kitchen when Bertie left to stack her boxes of cookies on the long table against the wall. She found Lisa assembling several pans of biscuits. "Those should be wonderful," she said, eyeing the melted butter in the bottom of the pan.

"They will be. It's Marge's recipe, but she gave Herb the credit. She loved calling them

Herb's Herb Biscuits." Lisa gave a little smile when she mentioned her mother-in-law's name. "Marge is wearing the new beaded sweater Herb and I got her for her birthday. Does your mother have a new outfit?"

"Do bears . . . uh . . . *growl* in the woods?" Hannah sanitized the popular saying for her young partner. "I'm sure Mother will have a new outfit. She always does."

"Welcome, ladies!" Hannah watched as her mother took her position at the head of the table. "I'm so glad you could come to our annual cookie exchange. Please find your place card and be seated. I understand my daughter, Hannah, will be making champagne cocktails for those of us who want to indulge and faux champagne cocktails for those who don't. And while we're waiting for our libations, let's take a look at the appetizer and beverage recipes that Hannah has printed out for us. And then we'll start in on this lovely baked brie."

That was Hannah's cue to carry out the champagne flutes rimmed in red sugar and play her part as the bartender. She picked up the tray, took a deep breath, and walked out to pour the bubbly.

Appetizers

CREAM CHEESE PUFFS

Hannah's Note: If you're not going to serve these right away, you can mix up the cream cheese part and refrigerate it until it's time to spread it on the crackers.

**8-ounce package cream cheese *(the firm kind, not the whipped)*
2 Tablespoons *(1/8 cup)* mayonnaise *(We used Hellmann's***)*
3 Tablespoons minced green onion
OR 3 Tablespoons minced dried onion
OR 3 Tablespoons minced shallots
1 beaten egg**

A box of salted crackers *(We used Ritz Crackers and they were great!)*

Unwrap the cream cheese and put it in a microwave-safe bowl. Nuke it on HIGH for 30 seconds, or until it begins to soften.

Mix in the mayonnaise and stir until the mixture is smooth.

Mix in the onion. *(If you use green onion*

***Hellmann's Mayonnaise is also known as Best Foods Mayonnaise in some parts of the country.

instead of shallots or dried onion, you can use up to one inch of the stem.)

Mix in the beaten egg.

Lay out the crackers on a broiler pan, salt side up. *(We used a disposable broiler pan so we could trash it at Granny's Attic and we wouldn't have to carry it back to The Cookie Jar.)*

Spread the cream cheese mixture on top of the crackers in a circle that reaches the edges of the crackers. If you don't cover the crackers completely, they tend to burn under the broiler. Use about 2 teaspoons of cheese mixture per cracker and mound it slightly in the center.

Position the rack approximately three inches below the coil of the broiler and turn it on HIGH. Wait until the coil gets hot and then put in the cheese puffs. Broil the crackers *(with the oven door open to the first latch so the broiler doesn't kick on and off)* until the cream cheese puffs up and is just starting to turn golden. This should take about 90 seconds if the rack is correctly positioned. Remove them from the oven immediately.

Let them cool for a minute or two, so

your guests won't burn their tongues. Then transfer the Cream Cheese Puffs to a platter and serve.

Yield: Approximately 2 dozen hot and yummy hors d'oeuvres.

Another Note from Hannah: I haven't actually tried this, but I'm willing to bet a dozen of my best cookies that you could also add a quarter cup chopped smoked salmon to the cream cheese mixture.

*Razzle Dazzle Baked Brie

Preheat oven to 350 degrees, rack in the middle position.

- 1 cup salted cashews, finely chopped*** *(measure after chopping)*
- 2 large eggs
- 2 Tablespoons heavy cream *(that's 1/8 cup)*
- 1 small wheel of Brie with rind all over it *(I used a 13-ounce baby Brie that was approximately 5 inches in diameter)*
- 1/4 to 1/3 cup seedless raspberry jam *(I used Knott's Berry Farm)*

a basket of assorted crackers
small appetizer knives and spoons for serving

Chop the salted cashews in a food processor or by hand. The pieces should be no larger than coarse grains of sand.

Place the finely chopped cashews in a glass pie plate sprayed with Pam or another non-stick cooking spray. *(A flat-bottomed, oven-safe dish with sides will also work just as long as it's several inches larger than your wheel of Brie.)*

***I've also used pistachios.

Whisk the eggs and the heavy cream *(that's whipping cream)* together in a small bowl until they're thoroughly blended. Pour the resulting mixture into a second shallow dish or bowl *(or pie plate)*.

Unwrap your wheel of Brie. Leave the rind on. You need the rind intact so that the cheese will hold its shape.

Dip the bottom of the Brie into the egg and cream mixture. Then pick it up by its sides and set it in the finely chopped cashews. Move it around a little so that the nuts will adhere to the egg and cream mixture.

Lift the Brie and take it back to the dish with the egg and cream mixture. Tip the cheese on its side and roll it in the mixture until the sides are coated with egg and cream.

Carry the Brie to the dish with the finely chopped nuts and roll it around in there so that the nuts adhere to the sides. You can press the nuts on with your hands to make them stick even better. When you're through, position your Brie in the center of the dish with the chopped cashews, the bottom side down and the top side *(without any nuts)* up.

Heat the raspberry jam for 5 to 10 seconds in the microwave on HIGH until it's easily spreadable. Then spoon it on top of the Brie, right in the middle. Use a rubber spatula or a frosting knife to spread it out to the edges.

Use a small spoon or your impeccably clean fingers to scoop up some chopped cashews and sprinkle them on top of the raspberry jam. Put on as many as you like as long as a bit of the red raspberry color shows through.

Leave the rest of the chopped cashews right there in the pie plate or ovenware dish.

Bake your Razzle Dazzle Baked Brie at 350 degrees for 15 to 20 minutes or until the cheese is beginning to melt inside.

Hannah's Note: I've also made this with other double and triple cream cheeses and with other flavors of jam. Mother loves it with apricot jam and Andrea is crazy about Brie with peach jam.

FAKE ORANGE JULIUS

3 cups orange juice *(you'll need 6 cups in all)*

1 envelope dry Dream Whip *(the kind that makes 2 cups)*

1 package dry vanilla pudding mix *(the kind that makes 2 cups)****

3 more cups orange juice

Pour the 3 cups of orange juice into a blender. Add the envelope of dry Dream Whip and the dry pudding mix. Blend for one minute on LOW and then for another minute on MEDIUM speed.

Pour the mixture in a 2-quart pitcher. Add the remaining 3 cups of orange juice and stir well.

Serve over ice.

Yield: Makes almost 2 quarts.

***Since this recipe is not cooked, you can use sugar free vanilla pudding mix if you wish.

*Razzle Dazzle Champagne Cocktail

red decorator sugar
one lime, or one lemon
one small bottle of Chambord *(raspberry liqueur)*
one bottle of good champagne, chilled***
red maraschino cherries with stems *(optional — to decorate)*

champagne flutes
one shallow, flat-bottomed dish that's an inch or two wider than the top of the champagne flutes

Pour approximately a quarter-inch layer of red decorator sugar in the flat-bottomed dish.

Cut a lime or lemon into pieces and run the cut part around the rim of a champagne glass. The object is to wet the rim with the citrus juice.

Hannah's 1st Note: Hank Olsen down at the Lake Eden Municipal Liquor Store told

***Use a good grade of champagne. It doesn't have to be awfully expensive, but do choose a medium-priced brand that has a good reputation. I used Korbel.

me that real bartenders use Rose's Lime Juice to wet the rim of a glass before they sugar it for sweet drinks.

Turn the champagne glass upside down and dunk the rim into the dish of red sugar. Roll it around until sugar adheres all around the outside of the rim. Do this for all of the champagne glasses. This is a step that can be done in advance.

When you're ready to assemble the cocktails, pour 1/4 inch of Chambord in the bottom of your champagne flute. Then carefully fill the champagne glasses with champagne. You'll have to pour slowly because champagne can foam up very quickly. *(There's a reason some people call it "bubbly" instead of "champagne".)*

There's no need to stir *(and you don't want to break down those pretty bubbles anyway)* because this drink will mix itself.

Top off your creation with a maraschino cherry if you wish. A fresh, plump raspberry speared with a little cocktail pick would also be nice if raspberries are in season.

Hannah's 2nd Note: To make a non-alcoholic version of this drink, follow the directions for Razzle Dazzle Faux Champagne Cocktail.

*Razzle Dazzle Faux Champagne Cocktail

red decorator sugar
one lime, or one lemon
one large bottle of sparkling apple-
   raspberry juice, chilled***
red maraschino cherries with stems *(optional — to decorate)*

champagne flutes
one shallow, flat-bottomed dish that's an
   inch or two wider than the top of the
   champagne flutes

***I used Martinelli. If you can't find that where
you live, use sparkling apple juice and add raspberry concentrate, raspberry juice, or raspberry
syrup until the resulting cocktail is a pretty pink
color.

Pour approximately a quarter-inch layer of red decorator sugar in the flat-bottomed dish.

Cut a lime or lemon into pieces and run the cut part around the rim of a champagne glass. The object is to wet the rim with the citrus juice so that the sugar will stick to the rim.

Hannah's 1st Note: You could also use Rose's Lime Juice to wet the rim of the glass. Just pour it on a paper towel and wipe the rim.

Turn the champagne glass upside down and dunk the rim into the dish of red sugar. Roll it around until sugar adheres all around the outside of the rim. Do this for all of the champagne glasses. This is a step that can be done in advance.

When you're ready to assemble the faux cocktails, carefully fill the champagne glasses with sparkling apple-raspberry juice. You'll have to pour slowly so that it won't foam up and melt the red sugar you've put around the rims.

Top off your creation with a maraschino cherry if you wish. A fresh plump raspberry speared with a little cocktail pick would also be nice if raspberries are in season.

Hannah's 2nd Note: Kids just love these. Andrea and I both think it's because they're served in a "grownup" champagne glass.

"This cocktail is wonderful!" Carrie declared, turning to Hannah. "Could I please have another?"

"Better be careful, Carrie," Delores smiled to show she was teasing her best friend. "You know what happened to Winnie Henderson the night she had too much dandelion wine, don't you?"

Carrie looked puzzled. "But Winnie doesn't drink. I offered her a glass of wine when we had lunch at the Lake Eden Inn last week and she told me that."

"She doesn't drink . . . now," Delores gave a little chuckle. "Actually, she didn't drink then. And that was part of the problem. Poor Winnie was just following Doc's orders."

"Doc Knight told Winnie to drink?" It was obvious that Carrie was still confused.

"Not exactly, but Winnie came to see him because she was having trouble sleeping."

"That was over twenty years ago,"

Grandma Knudson explained, "when Winnie was married to that awful third husband of hers, the one who sold aluminum siding and was gone for weeks at a time."

"Right," Delores took up the story again. "Winnie told Doc that she just couldn't fall asleep. And if she did, she startled awake after only a couple of minutes. Doc could see that she was at her wit's end and he suggested a mild form of sleeping pill. But Winnie didn't want that, so Doc told her to drink a jigger of brandy right before bedtime and that would do the trick."

"That would work," Marge Beeseman agreed. "Jack sleeps better if he has a little blackberry brandy before bedtime."

There were several nods around the table and then Delores went on. "Well, Winnie was a complete nondrinker. She had no idea how big a *jigger* was. But her second husband used to drink Jack Daniel's in a water glass so she figured that was probably what Doc meant."

"Oh, good heavens!" Florence, who was still wearing her Red Owl Grocery nametag gave a little groan. "Poor Winnie must have been as drunk as a skunk."

"Oh, she was. A few minutes after she drank it, her head started to spin and she decided that she needed some air. She made it all the way down her driveway and almost out to the country road. But then she decided it was time to take a little nap and she stretched out right there at the foot of her driveway."

"Poor Winnie!" Ellie Kuehne gave a little shiver. She'd taken the afternoon off from her managerial duties at Bertanelli's Pizza, and she looked happy to have some free time. "Did she have a terrible hangover?"

"Yes, but she was already in the hospital. But we're getting ahead of ourselves. There Winnie is, stretched out on her gravel driveway, so drunk she's not moving a muscle, and a car comes along. The driver's a lady who's visiting someone down the road. She gets out to see what's wrong and she can't rouse Winnie, so she rushes back home and calls for an ambulance."

"So Doc sent the paramedics out to get Winnie?" Carrie guessed.

"Not exactly. Doc didn't have his own ambulance back then. He contracted with Digger to use the hearse as an ambulance. It worked just fine. Digger took down the *Gibson Funeral Home* signs, removed the velvet curtains on the windows in the back, and put a gurney in the place where the casket would be. He even had a light like the deputies have on their squad cars that attached

41

to the roof of the hearse with a suction cup."

"So Digger went out to pick Winnie up?" Carrie leaned forward slightly, waiting for the answer to her question.

"Actually . . . Digger wasn't home, but he'd arranged with Cyril Murphy to take any ambulance calls that came in. Brigit answered the phone and rather than bother Cyril, who was working late at the garage, she called. . . ."

"Me," Alice Vogel interrupted, and Hannah, who was watching from the pass-through window in the community center kitchen, noticed that Alice was blushing with embarrassment. "I was living back at home after my divorce, and I told Brigit I'd be right over to help her."

"So Brigit and Alice went out in Digger's ambulance," Delores continued. "Except they never even thought to take down the Gibson Funeral Home signs and the curtains."

"We put the gurney in, though," Alice volunteered.

"That's right. Brigit drove and Alice rode next to her in the passenger seat."

Alice nodded. "The lady who called said she thought that Winnie was dead, so we didn't hurry that much. Brigit seemed okay about going to pick up a . . . a deceased person, but I wasn't exactly comfortable."

"When they got there, Winnie was still passed out cold on her driveway. She's not very big, so Brigit and Alice didn't have any trouble loading her on the gurney and lifting it into the back of the ambulance." Delores paused and gave a little smile. "Or perhaps I should say . . . hearse."

"We thought the lady was right and Winnie was dead," Alice said, sounding a bit defensive. "I was okay when we loaded her on the gurney, but after we got in the front again and started driving out to the hospital morgue, I started thinking about how there was a dead person riding in back of me. I kept telling myself that it was the living who could hurt you, not the dead, but I was still really jumpy. I made sure that glass panel between the front of the hearse and the back was shut tight, and that made me feel a little better. And then I asked Brigit to turn on the radio to distract me. Brigit must have been nervous too, because she found a country western station and turned it up really loud. That helped a lot until I heard a screech from the back of the hearse."

There were several gasps from the ladies, even though most of them had heard this story before.

"Winnie came to," Carrie breathed, shivering slightly.

Delores gave a little nod. "That's right. Winnie regained consciousness and the first thing she saw was the funeral home sign in the hearse window. And the next thing she saw was that the curtains were still up. Winnie's a bright woman. She said, *Hello? Is anybody there?* but the glass panel was closed and the radio was so loud that Brigit and Alice didn't hear her. Winnie put two and two together, but unfortunately, she came up with the wrong answer. She thought she must be dead, and it scared her so much she screamed."

"So that's why Winnie doesn't drink," Carrie concluded.

"That's right. And that's why Doc never prescribes a jigger of brandy for insomnia. Now he says, 'an ounce,' or 'half an inch in the bottom of a water glass.'"

"I never heard that one before," Lisa said to Hannah.

"Maybe your folks thought you were too young. Let's dish up the soup, Lisa. I think they're almost ready."

Lisa headed for the slow cooker sitting on the counter. "Okay. Maybe they'll tell more stories. This is really fun!"

Soups

TRUDI'S SHRIMP BISQUE

Hannah's 1st Note: You can also make this bisque with crabmeat, or with a combination of shrimp and crab.

10 and 3/4 oz. can condensed tomato soup *(I used Campbell's)*

11 and 1/4 oz. can condensed green pea soup *(I used Campbell's)*

3 cups whole milk *(or light cream, if you want it richer)*

2-pound package salad shrimp, roughly chopped

1/2 cup sherry *(optional)*

Hannah's 2nd Note: Trudi revised her original recipe. You CAN use split pea soup. If it has bits of ham in it, make sure you process it in a blender or food processor to smooth it out.

Mix the tomato soup and the green pea soup together. The green pea soup is lumpy, so use a blender if you have one.

Add the milk or light cream.

Heat the soups and the milk in a saucepan over low heat, stirring occasionally, while you thaw and chop the shrimp. When the mixture is warm, add the chopped shrimp and stir it in.

When the soup is heated thoroughly, add the sherry and serve.

Yield: Makes approximately six servings.

Lisa said this bisque is even better than the bisque she had at the very fancy, very expensive restaurant in Minneapolis where Herb took her last year on Valentine's Day. Herb agreed, and not just because it's a whole lot cheaper.

*Lobster Bisque with Sour Cream and Red Caviar

This soup is a variation of Trudi's Shrimp Bisque and it's just as easy to make. Everyone who's ever tried it has been very impressed.

10 and 3/4 oz. can condensed tomato soup *(I used Campbell's)*

11 and 1/4 oz. can condensed green pea soup *(I used Campbell's)*

3 cups whole milk *(or light cream, if you want it richer)*

2-pound package of frozen lobster meat, roughly chopped

1/2 cup sherry *(optional)*

---

8 ounces of sour cream

small jar of red caviar *(or a sprinkling of paprika)*

Mix the tomato soup and the green pea soup together. *(I just found out that you CAN use split pea soup if you process it in a blender or a food processor until it's smooth.)*

Add the milk or light cream. *(You can even use heavy cream if you want to be decadent.)*

Heat the soups and the milk in a saucepan over low heat, stirring occasionally, while you thaw and chop the lobster. When the mixture is warm, add the chopped lobster and stir it in.

When the soup is heated thoroughly, you can "hold" it in a crockpot set on LOW for several hours if necessary.

Add the sherry right before you're ready to serve your Lobster Bisque.

Dish up your soup and decorate each bowlful with a dollop of sour cream.

Sprinkle the sour cream with a bit of red caviar or sprinkle it with paprika and serve.

Yield: Makes approximately six servings.

"That was a lovely soup, Hannah," Delores said as Hannah approached to remove her soup bowl.

"Thank you, Mother."

"Will mine be like that?" she asked in a lower voice.

"Yes. The only difference is that you'll be using shrimp and this is lobster."

"Oh, good! Can I garnish mine the way you garnished yours?"

"Of course. The garnish is a matter of personal taste. Since I don't like caviar, I usually garnish mine with sour cream and several ripe olive rings."

"Isn't this Marguerite and Clara Hollenbeck's recipe for Mexican Hotdish?" Grandma Knudson asked, paging through the Quick and/or Easy Meals section of the thick binder that Hannah had given to each of her mother's guests.

"That's right."

"It's a wonderful recipe. Clara brought it to my Bible Study group and everyone enjoyed it. And that reminds me . . . she called me this morning. You met her niece Gladys the last time she was in town, didn't you?"

"I think so," Hannah said, trying to remember. "Isn't she the niece that lives up in Duluth?"

"That's Gladys. How about the rest of you? Does anyone know Gladys Hollenbeck?"

Almost everyone around the table nodded. Gladys had driven down to Lake Eden several times to visit her aunts.

"Didn't she drive to California to a friend's wedding last month?" Florence asked.

"Yes. All by herself. Gladys didn't even have one of those life-size male dolls that some women prop up in the passenger seat to fool everyone into thinking they're not alone."

"Marguerite told me she hoped that Gladys would meet a nice man in California and decide to stay there. The poor girl really hates the winters up in Duluth."

"That's exactly what happened," Grandma Knudson informed them, and Hannah noticed that her eyes were twinkling the way they always did whenever she had a good story to tell.

"Is she going to marry him?" Bertie asked, clasping her hands.

"Yes."

Edna Ferguson looked pleased. "I lived in Duluth for three years, and the cold wind blowing off Lake Superior never seemed to stop. This is wonderful for Gladys! Now she'll be able to live in sunny California."

"It's wonderful, but she won't be living in California."

"She won't?" Bertie looked puzzled.

"No, they'll be moving. Gladys told Marguerite that he seemed to be really interested in hearing about her life here. It's one of the reasons she fell in love with him. And now it turns out he was sincerely interested, but there was another reason he wanted to know more about Minnesota. He'd just accepted a job at the University of Minnesota in Duluth and they'll be living up there!"

AUNT KITTY'S COTTAGE CHEESE PANCAKES (POOR MAN'S BLINTZES)

2 cups cottage cheese
4 eggs
1/2 teaspoon salt
1/2 cup flour

Mix cottage cheese, eggs, salt and flour together in a small bowl. Let the mixture "rest" in the refrigerator for an hour *(overnight is fine, too).*

Heat a nonstick griddle to 350 degrees F., or use a frying pan that's been sprayed with non-stick cooking spray. *(The frying pan is ready when a drop of water sizzles and "dances" across the surface.)*

Spoon pancake batter in pan or on griddle and fry until the bubbles on the surface of the pancake remain open. *(You can check to see if the bottom side is done by lifting the edge with a spatula.)* When the bottom side is a nice golden color, flip the pancake over and cook until the bottom color matches the top.

Place the finished pancakes on a plate, sprinkle artificial sweetener over the tops, and add sliced fruit of your choice.

FOR POOR MAN'S BLINTZES:

Mix up the pancakes as directed and fry them. When they're done, spread each pancake with butter and sprinkle with sugar. Top with spoonful of jam, add a generous dollop of sour cream, and enjoy.

BREAKFAST OMELET

Do not preheat the oven — this breakfast dish needs to be refrigerated before it can be baked.

Hannah's 1st Note: I didn't have the heart to tell Michelle that this dish wasn't technically an omelet. What's in a name anyway? It's like Shakespeare said, Would a rose by any other name smell as sweet? — or in this case, as savory?

1 and 1/2 pounds skinless sausage links or breakfast sausage patties

8 slices white bread *(white, sourdough, French, country, etc.)*

3/4 pound grated cheddar cheese *(the sharper the cheddar, the better)*

1/4 cup grated onion

1/4 cup finely chopped green peppers

6 eggs

1/4 teaspoon salt

2 cups milk

1/4 cup half and half, or cream

1 Tablespoon prepared mustard *(I used stone ground)*

1 can *(10 and 3/4 ounces)* **condensed cream of mushroom soup, undiluted**

1/4 cup sherry***

1 can *(5 ounces)* sliced mushrooms, drained

Spray the inside of a 2-quart casserole dish with Pam or other nonstick cooking spray. A 9-inch by 13-inch cake pan will also work well for this recipe.

Cut the sausage links into thirds and sauté them over medium heat on the stovetop until they're lightly browned. If you used patties instead of links, cut each one into four parts and sauté them until they're lightly browned.

While your sausage is browning, cut the crusts from the slices of bread. *(You can either save the crusts to feed to the birds, or throw them away, your choice.)* Cut the remaining bread into one-inch cubes. Toss them into the bottom of your casserole or cake pan.

Drain the fat from your sausage. Put the drained sausage on top of the bread cubes in the casserole. *(Mother used to save the fat*

***If you don't have sherry, dry white wine will work just fine. Dry vermouth is also an option. If you don't want to use liquor of any type, you can simply add another 1/4 cup milk.

from sausage or bacon for Dad — he used it for frying eggs when he had one of his poker nights.)

Sprinkle the grated cheese over the top of the sausage.

Sprinkle the grated onions over the cheese.

Sprinkle the chopped green peppers on top of the onions.

Whisk the eggs with the salt, milk, half and half or cream, and prepared mustard in a bowl by hand, or beat them with an electric mixer.

Pour the egg mixture over the top of the casserole, cover it tightly with plastic wrap and refrigerate it overnight.

(Michelle says that now you can sleep soundly because you know you've got breakfast almost ready to go in the morning.)

The next morning, 2 hours before you want to serve breakfast:

Preheat the oven to 350 degrees F., rack in the middle position.

Take the casserole from the refrigerator

and remove the plastic wrap. Place it on a baking sheet with sides, if you have it. A jellyroll pan will work beautifully.

Mix the condensed cream of mushroom soup, the sherry *(or equivalent)*, and the drained sliced mushrooms in a mixing bowl.

Pour the mushroom mixture over the top of the casserole.

Bake the casserole for 1 1/2 hours at 350 degrees F.

Remove the casserole from the oven and let it stand for 10 minutes to set up before serving.

Hannah's 2nd Note: Michelle told me that she once used some of her roommate's leftover champagne instead of the sherry and it was really good. I didn't ask her how her underage roommate got the champagne in the first place.

FUNERAL HOTDISH
(ANNIVERSARY HOTDISH)

Preheat oven to 350 degrees F., rack in the middle position.

OR

Use an 18-quart electric roaster set to 350 degrees F.

Recipe courtesy of Joyce and the Swanville Funeral Committee

Hannah's 1st Note: Joyce says this is easiest with three people helping: one person to chop and sauté the celery and onions, one person to brown the hamburger, and one person to cook the pasta and mix the sauce.

Start by spraying the inside of your pan or the electric roaster with Pam or another nonstick cooking spray. *(I used a great big disposable turkey roaster sprayed with Pam.)*

1 bunch of celery *(approximately 10 stalks)*

3 large onions *(We used four because we love onion)*

6 pounds lean hamburger *(We used 8 pounds because we like it beefier)*

2 two-pound boxes elbow macaroni *(for*

a total of four pounds — Joyce uses Creamettes Elbow Macaroni)
- 1 large can *(50 ounces)* Campbell's tomato soup, undiluted
- 2 large cans *(46 ounces each)* Campbell's tomato juice
- 1 large bottle *(46 ounces)* catsup *(the Swanville Funeral Committee uses Heinz Ketchup)*
- 1 Tablespoon brown sugar
- 1 teaspoon ground black pepper *(freshly ground is best, of course)*

Clean and chop the celery into bite-sized pieces. Put them in a frying pan with a little butter and start cooking them over low heat, stirring occasionally.

Peel and chop the onions into bite-sized pieces. Add them to the frying pan with the celery and continue to cook them, stirring occasionally, until they're translucent.

Brown the hamburger over medium heat. Be sure to "chop" it with a spoon or heat-resistant spatula so it browns in bite-sized pieces. *(Joyce and her committee do this in a pan in the oven.)*

Drain the browned hamburger, and rinse off the fat by putting the meat in a strainer and spraying it with warm water. *(We drained the hamburger, but we forgot to rinse it off with warm water — it was good anyway.)*

Cook the elbow macaroni according to the directions on the box. DO NOT OVER-COOK. *(Joyce's committee does not salt the water, but we did.)* Drain it and set it aside.

Combine the undiluted tomato soup, the tomato juice, and the catsup. Mix in the brown sugar and the pepper. *(Joyce's committee does this right in the electric roaster and then heats it before they add the other ingredients. We mixed up our sauce in the bottom of the disposable turkey roaster and didn't heat it before we added the other ingredients.)*

Add the cooked celery and onions to the sauce and stir them in.

Stir in the hamburger.

Add the cooked, drained macaroni and mix well.

Once everything is thoroughly mixed, cover the disposable roaster with heavy duty foil and put it into a 350 degree F. oven for 2 hours, stirring occasionally so that it heats evenly and doesn't stick to the bottom. *(If you used an electric roaster, put on the lid, turn it up to 350 degrees F., and cook it for 2 hours, stirring occasionally so that it heats evenly and doesn't stick to the bottom of the roaster.)*

Joyce's Note: Joyce says to tell you that cooking the hotdish for 2 hours is mainly to blend the flavors since everything is pre-cooked.

Hannah's 2nd Note: When we made this for the family reunion, we sprinkled shredded Parmesan cheese on the top before we served it. Marge says if she ever makes it at home, she's going to add pitted black olives to the sauce, because Herb and Jack like them so much. She's also going to make garlic bread to go with it.

Yield: Joyce says this recipe will serve 75, but they always serve plenty of other side dishes with it. If you plan to use Funeral Hotdish as your only main course, I wouldn't expect it to serve more than two dozen people, especially if they're really hungry.

GRILLED CREAM CHEESE SANDWICHES

(Hannah Swensen's Very Best Mistake)

For each sandwich you will need:
2 slices of bread *(white, egg, whole wheat,*
take your pick)
1 package of chilled block cream cheese
(not softened or whipped)
Softened butter

Butter two slices of bread. Place one slice buttered side down on a piece of wax paper. Cut slices of cream cheese approximately 1/2 inch thick to cover the surface of the bread. Put the other slice of bread on top, buttered side up.

Preheat a frying pan on the stove. Using a spatula, place your sandwich in the pan. Fry it uncovered until the bottom turns golden brown. *(You can test it by lifting it up just a bit with the spatula.)* Flip the sandwich over and fry the other side until it's golden brown. Remove the sandwich from the frying pan, cut it into four pieces with a sharp knife, arrange it on a plate, and serve it immediately.

This sandwich goes well with piping hot mugs of tomato soup.

You can turn this into a dessert sandwich by using slices of banana bread or date-nut bread and sprinkling the sandwich with a little powered sugar. If you really want to go whole hog, top it with a scoop of ice cream. It's delicious that way!

*Hannah's Chicken Salad

4 cups cubed chicken

4 peeled and chopped hard-boiled eggs

1/2 cup crumbled cooked bacon *(make your own or use real crumbled bacon from a can — I used Hormel Premium Real Crumbled Bacon)*

1 Tablespoon chopped parsley *(it's better if it's fresh, but you can use dried parsley flakes if you don't have fresh on hand)*

1/4 cup grated carrots *(for color and a bit of sweetness)*

1 cup well-drained, pitted black olives

4 ounces cream cheese

1/4 cup sour cream

1/2 cup mayonnaise *(I used Best Foods, which is Hellmann's in some states)*

1/2 teaspoon garlic powder *(or 1/2 teaspoon freshly minced garlic)*

1/2 teaspoon onion powder *(or 1 teaspoon freshly minced onion)*

salt to taste

freshly ground black pepper to taste

---

curly leaf lettuce leaves, red lettuce leaves, butter lettuce leaves, or spinach leaves (with the stems removed) to form a bed for Hannah's Chicken Salad

1/4 cup salted sunflower nuts for a garnish***

Place the cubed chicken *(approximately the size of bouillon cubes)* in a large mixing bowl.

Peel and chop the hard-boiled eggs. A rough chop is fine. You want people to recognize them as eggs. Add them to the bowl with the chicken cubes.

Add the crumbled bacon, the parsley, the grated carrots, and the black olives to the bowl. Mix well.

Put the cream cheese in a small, microwave-safe bowl and microwave for 30 seconds on HIGH to soften it. If it can be easily stirred with a fork, take it out of the microwave and add the sour cream and mayonnaise. Mix well.

If the cream cheese is too solid to stir, give it another 10 seconds or so on HIGH in the microwave before you add the other ingredients.

***If you can't find salted sunflower nuts, use chopped salted cashews, or even crushed potato chips.

Stir in the garlic powder and onion powder.

Add the cream cheese mixture to the bowl with the chicken mixture and stir it all up. Add salt and freshly ground pepper to taste, and chill until ready to serve.

You can serve this salad on a large platter so that everyone can help themselves, or on individual plates. Line the platter or individual plates with lettuce leaves or spinach leaves and cover them with mounds of chicken salad.

Sprinkle the top of your salad with salted sunflower nuts, chopped salted cashews, or crushed potato chips to add crunch.

Yield: 6 entree-sized portions.

Hannah's Note: You can cut the egg and the chicken in smaller pieces and use this salad as sandwich filling. This recipe will make about a dozen chicken salad sandwiches.

HOLE IN ONE

One slice of bread *(any kind)*
One egg
Softened butter
Biscuit cutter or juice glass

Spray a frying pan with nonstick spray and set it aside.

Butter the piece of bread on one side. Put it butter-side-down in the frying pan. Butter the side on top. *(Using a rubber spatula makes this easier.)*

With a biscuit cutter or the rim of a juice glass, stamp a hole in the center of the slice of bread. Put the circle you've cut out next to the slice of bread in the pan.

Put the pan on medium heat and wait until the bread starts to fry. Then crack an egg and drop it into the hole in the bread. *(If you're really hungry, you can use two eggs.)* Add salt and pepper to the egg if you wish. When the egg has cooked on the bottom, flip the whole thing, bread and all, with a pancake turner. Also flip the cutout circle of bread. Fry until the egg is done the way you want it.

Tracey loves these for breakfast. She pre-

fers a runny yolk so that she can dip the fried bread in it. Now she's teaching Bethie how to do it.

MEXICAN HOTDISH

Preheat oven to 350 degrees F., rack in the center position.

- **4-ounce can Ortega diced green chilies** *(with the juice)*
- **2 cups shredded Monterrey Jack cheese** *(approx. 8 ounces)*
- **2 cans** *(14 ounces each)* **diced tomatoes** *(with the juice)*
- **1 medium onion, chopped**
- **2-ounce can sliced black olives** *(with the juice)*
- **1 large green bell pepper, seeded & chopped**
- **2 cups UNCOOKED white rice**
- **2 packages** *(approx. 1-ounce each)* **Taco seasoning** *(Clara buys Lawry's)*
- **3 cups cubed cooked chicken**
- **1 can** *(14.5 ounces)* **chicken broth**
- **1/2 cup cold butter** *(1 stick, 1/4 pound, 4 ounces)*
- **2 cups Fritos corn chips**
- **2 cups** *(approx. 8 ounces)* **shredded Mexican cheese*****

***If the cheese selection at your grocery store is limited, just use shredded Monterrey Jack for the first cheese, and shredded sharp cheddar for the second cheese to melt on top of the Fritos. If you

(I used the kind with four cheeses mixed together)

Spray a 6-quart roaster with Pam or other nonstick cooking spray. *(Clara buys disposable half-size steam table pans at CostMart and uses one of those. She says to be careful to set it on a cookie sheet before you fill it, though. The disposable foil could buckle and you could end up with uncooked Mexican Hotdish all over your kitchen floor!)*

Hannah's 1st Note: This hotdish is easy to make because once you've got the cubed chicken, all you have to do is open a bunch of cans. You don't even have to drain them. Just dump them in your baking pan, juice and all!

In the bottom of the pan or roaster, mix together the diced green chilies, the Monterrey Jack cheese, the two cans of diced tomatoes, the chopped onion, the can of sliced black olives, the chopped bell pepper, and the UNCOOKED white rice. *(Marguerite told Norman that she washes her hands and then just mixes everything up with her fingers, but that's only if Clara's not around.)*

---

can't find Monterrey Jack, use mozzarella or Swiss.

Sprinkle the Taco seasoning over the top, add the chicken cubes, and mix again.

Add the chicken broth and stir everything up with a wooden spoon. *(You can also get in there with your impeccably clean hands and mix it up that way.)*

Cut the cold stick of butter into 8 pieces and put the pieces on top of the hotdish.

Cover the pan with heavy duty foil (or a double thickness of regular foil) and turn down the edges to seal them.

Bake the hotdish for 1 and 1/2 hours *(90 minutes)* at 350 degrees F.

Take the baking pan out of the oven BUT DON'T TURN OFF THE OVEN YET. Remove the foil carefully as steam may escape.

Sprinkle the Fritos on top of the hotdish, spreading them out as evenly as you can.

Sprinkle the cheese on top of the Fritos as evenly as you can.

Don't cover the hotdish. Return it to the oven to cook for another 10 minutes, uncovered, or until the cheese has melted.

Let the baking pan or roaster sit for at least 10 minutes so the hotdish can firm up before you serve it.

Hannah's 2nd Note: When I first had this hotdish at Clara and Marguerite's condo, they served it with white wine margaritas. If you don't want to serve alcohol, it would also be good with ice cold lemonade.

Hannah's 3rd Note: Norman served this with sour cream on the side for those who wanted to put a dollop on top of their serving. **(I really liked it that way.)** I think it would also be good with guacamole on the side for those who want to add that.

SALLY'S SUNNY VEGETABLE SALAD

5 cups chopped broccoli florets

5 cups chopped cauliflower florets

2 cups shredded cheddar cheese *(the sharper the cheddar, the better the salad)*

1/2 cup golden raisins *(Sally says to tell you she's used sweetened dried cranberries as a substitute for the raisins)*

2/3 cup minced onion *(Sally uses chopped green onions)*

1/2 cup white *(granulated)* sugar

1 cup mayonnaise *(Hannah uses Hellmann's — it's called Best Foods west of the Rockies)*

2 Tablespoons red wine vinegar *(I used raspberry vinegar)*

---

6 bacon strips, cooked and crumbled *(or 1/2 cup bacon bits)*

1/4 cup **SHELLED**, salted, toasted sunflower seeds

Chop the broccoli and cauliflower florets into tiny bite-sized pieces.

Combine the broccoli and cauliflower in a large salad bowl. Add the shredded cheese and mix it up with your fingers.

Mix in the raisins and the minced onion.

In a small bowl, combine the sugar, mayonnaise, and red wine vinegar. Mix it with a rubber spatula, or a whisk until it's smooth.

Pour the dressing you just mixed over the top of the salad. Toss it, or stir it with a spoon or spatula until the vegetables are coated with the dressing.

Sprinkle the bacon bits on top.

Sprinkle the sunflower nutmeats on top of that.

Hannah's 1st Note: You can make this salad several hours before serving. It's even better that way because the flavors blend. Just toss the vegetables and raisins with the dressing, cover the bowl with plastic wrap, and refrigerate it until your company arrives. Then all you have to do is sprinkle on the bacon bits and the sunflower seeds, and serve.

Yield: 12 to 16 servings.

Hannah's 2nd Note: I made this for a 6-person dinner party once, and I ended up with about half of the salad left in the bowl. I refrigerated it to see what would happen, and it was every bit as good the next day!

SALMON CAKES WITH DILL SAUCE OR EASY CELERY SAUCE

1 small can salmon***
2 slices bread, crusts removed *(you can use any type of bread)*
1 beaten egg *(just whip it up in a glass with a fork)*
1 teaspoon Worcestershire sauce *(or hot sauce, or lemon juice)*
1/2 teaspoon dry mustard *(that's the powdered kind)*
1/4 teaspoon salt
1/4 teaspoon onion powder
2 Tablespoons butter

Open your can of salmon and drain it in a strainer. Remove any bones or dark skin. Flake it with a fork and put it in a small mixing bowl.

Cut the crusts from two standard-sized slices of bread and tear the middle part into small pieces. Add the pieces to the bowl with the salmon.

Add the egg and mix it all up with a fork.

***Check the weight on your can of salmon. It should weigh between 7 ounces and 8 ounces — red salmon is best, but pink will do.

Mix in the Worcestershire sauce *(or lemon juice, or hot sauce),* the dry mustard, salt, and onion powder.

Stir it all up until it resembles a thick batter with lumps.

Divide the batter into thirds. *(You don't have to be exact — nobody's going to measure them when you're through. They'll be too busy eating them.)*

Spread a sheet of wax paper on a plate and pick up one of the lumps of batter. Squeeze it together with your hands to form a firm ball. Place it on the wax paper and flatten it like a hamburger patty. The patty should be about a half-inch thick.

Hannah's 1st Note: If you flatten your Salmon Cakes too much and you'd like to make them thicker, just go ahead. All you have to do is gather the batter into a ball again and start over.

Shape the other two lumps of batter into balls and then patties. Let them sit on the wax paper for a minute or two to firm up even more.

Melt the two Tablespoons of butter in a frying pan over medium heat.

Place the Salmon Cakes in the pan and fry them over medium heat until they're golden brown on the bottom. *(That should take approximately 2 minutes.)* Flip the patties over and brown the other side. *(Total frying time will be approximately 4 to 5 minutes.)* Remember that all you're doing is frying the egg. Everything else has already been cooked.

Drain the Salmon Cakes on a paper towel and transfer to a serving platter. Serve with Dill Sauce or Edna's Easy Celery Sauce. They're also wonderful with creamed peas or creamed corn.

Hannah's 2nd Note: When I do these for the family, I use my electric griddle and triple the recipe so I have nine Salmon Cakes. If you don't have an electric griddle or you prefer to use a frying pan, you can fry them and then put them in a single layer in a pan in an oven set at the lowest temperature to keep them warm until you've fried them all. Make sure to refrigerate any leftovers. I've put leftover Salmon Cakes in the refrigerator overnight and heated them in the microwave the next day for lunch. They're not quite as good as freshly fried, but they're still very good. *(They're also good cold.)*

Hannah's 3rd Note: You can also make Tuna Cakes, Shrimp Cakes, Crab Cakes, Chicken Cakes and any other "cake" you can think of. All you need to do is substitute 6 to 8 ounces of the canned, or cooked and chopped main ingredient of your choice for the salmon. *(This is why I always keep a can of salad shrimp, a can of tuna, and a can of chopped chicken in my pantry.)*

Yield: Serves 3 if you team it up with a nice green salad and a slice of something yummy for dessert. *(If you serve it alone, as a total lunch, it'll work for one person with a big appetite, or one person with a little appetite and a cat.)*

DILL SAUCE

Hannah's Note: This sauce is best if you make it at least 4 hours in advance and refrigerate it in an airtight container. *(Overnight is even better.)*

2 Tablespoons heavy cream
1/2 cup mayonnaise
1 teaspoon crushed fresh baby dill *(if you can't find baby dill, you can make it with 1/2 teaspoon dried dill weed, but it won't be as good)*

Mix the cream with the mayonnaise until

79

it's smooth, and then stir in the dill. Put the sauce in a small bowl, cover it with plastic wrap, and refrigerate it for at least 4 hours.

EDNA'S EASY CELERY SAUCE

Hannah's 1st Note: If you make your Salmon Cakes at the drop of a hat, the way I occasionally do, you won't have time to make the Dill Sauce. All Edna's Easy Celery Sauce requires is a can of cream of celery soup and some milk or cream.

Hannah's 2nd Note: The can of cream of celery soup should be in your pantry as a staple, along with a can of cream of mushroom soup, a can of tomato soup, and a can of cream of chicken soup. They're a good base for any sauce you want to make on the fly.

one can of cream of celery soup, undiluted *(10 to 11 ounces depending on brand name — I used Campbell's)*
milk or cream to thin it

Open the can. Dump it in a small microwave-safe bowl. Heat it in the microwave until it's piping hot. ***(Try 30 seconds and see if it's hot enough. If not, heat at 15-second increments until it is.)*** Thin it with milk or cream to sauce consistency.

80

Drizzle the sauce over the Salmon Cakes, sprinkle on a little parsley or fresh dill if you happen to have it, and serve immediately.

Hannah's 3rd Note: Edna tells me that you can also use undiluted cream of chicken soup *(if you're using the chicken variation),* cream of mushroom soup, or cream of garlic soup. She also said something about cream of asparagus soup for Shrimp Cakes, but I haven't tried it.

WANMANSITA CASSEROLE

Preheat the oven to 325 degrees F., rack in the middle position.

2 pounds lean hamburger***
2 medium onions, sliced
1 cup diced celery *(that's about 3 stalks)*
1 green bell pepper, seeded and diced
1 large package of crinkle noodles *(I used egg noodles that were twisted in the middle)*
2 cans *(14.5 ounces each)* **of diced tomatoes with juice**
1 can *(5 ounces)* **sliced water chestnuts****** *(Sally uses chopped)*

***If you use regular hamburger instead of lean, you'd better buy 2 and 1/2 or 3 pounds, because there's a lot of fat that'll cook off. If you buy extra lean hamburger, it probably won't have enough fat and you'll have to add some.

****Don't worry about the ounces on the water chestnuts — anything from 4 ounces to 8 ounces will do.

1 can *(4 ounces)* mushroom pieces

2 teaspoons cumin

2 teaspoons chili powder

2 teaspoons salt

1 teaspoon pepper *(freshly ground is best, of course)*

2 cups grated cheddar cheese

Start by spraying a 9-inch by 13-inch cake pan, or a half-size disposable steam table pan with Pam or another nonstick cooking spray. If you choose to use a disposable pan, set it on a cookie sheet to support the bottom and make it easier to move it from the counter to the oven.

Pour 6 quarts of water into a big pot and put it on the stove to boil. You'll use this to cook the noodles. *(If you start heating the water now, it should be boiling by the time you're ready to cook the noodles. If it boils too early and you're not ready, just turn down the heat a little. If it's not ready when you are, crank up the heat and wait for the boil.)*

Crumble the hamburger and brown it over medium heat in a large frying pan, stirring it around with a metal spatula and breaking it up into pieces as it fries. This should take about 15 or 20 minutes.

When the hamburger is nice and brown, put a bowl under a colander so that you can save about 1/3 cup of fat to use with the onions. Dump the hamburger into the colander to drain it.

Put the drained hamburger into the prepared baking pan.

Pour the 1/3 cup of hamburger grease back into the frying pan.

Peel the onions and slice them into 1/8 inch thick slices. *(When you do this they may fall apart in rings and that's perfectly okay.)*

Place the onion slices in the frying pan, but don't turn on the heat quite yet.

Dice the celery. Add it to the onion slices in the frying pan.

Cut open the green bell pepper and take out the seeds, the stem, and the tough white membranes. Chop the remaining pepper into bite-sized pieces. Once that's done, add them to the onions and celery in your frying pan.

Cook the aromatic vegetables *(that's what they call them on the Food Channel)* over medium heat until they're tender when pierced with a fork.

84

Drain them in the same colander you used for the hamburger, and then mix them up with the hamburger in your baking pan.

Add some salt to your boiling water on the stove. Then dump in the noodles, stir them around, let the water come back to a boil, and then turn down the heat a bit so the pot doesn't boil over. Set your timer for whatever it says on the noodle package directions and cook the noodles, stirring every minute or so to make sure they don't stick together.

Drain the cooked noodles in the same colander you've been using all along, add them to your baking pan, and mix them up with everything else.

Add the diced tomatoes, juice and all, to your baking pan. Wait to stir. You don't want to mush your noodles by stirring too much.

Open and drain the cans of water chestnuts and mushroom pieces in the colander that's still sitting in the sink.

Dump the water chestnuts and mushrooms on top of the tomatoes in your baking pan.

Sprinkle the cumin over the top of your casserole.

Sprinkle the chili powder on top of the cumin. *(Gary says to tell you that if your chili powder has been sitting around for as long as theirs has, it's a good idea to buy fresh.)*

Sprinkle on the salt and grind the pepper on top of that.

Now is the time to mix it all up. This might not be easy if the baking pan's too full to stir with a spoon. If that's happened, just wash your hands thoroughly and dive in with your fingers to mix everything up. When you're through, pat the casserole so it's nice and even on top, and call it a day.

Wash your hands again, and then cover the baking pan with a single thickness of foil.

Bake at 325 degrees F. for 60 minutes, or until you peek under the foil and see that it's hot and bubbling.

Remove the pan from the oven. Remove the foil slowly and carefully to avoid burning yourself with the steam that may roll out. Set the foil on the counter to use again in a few minutes.

Sprinkle the 2 cups of shredded cheddar cheese over the top and return the baking pan to the oven. Bake it, uncovered, for another 10 minutes, or until the cheese melts.

Cover the pan again with that foil you saved, and let your casserole sit on a cold burner or rack to set up for at least 10 minutes, and then serve and enjoy!

Hannah's 1st Note: Sally says to tell you that she made 4 pans of this for a luncheon meeting. There were 25 people and she had one whole pan left over.

Hannah's 2nd Note: Gary says to tell you that they didn't serve seconds, though.

Yield: Judging from the above notes, I'd guess that one pan of Wanmansita Casserole would serve 8 to 10 people, especially if you served fresh buttered rolls and a nice mixed green salad on the side.

"This is really good chicken salad," Alice Vogel said as she helped herself to a little more. "You know I don't cook very often. I just don't have the time. But do you think I could make it?"

"You could make it easy with some short-cuts," Edna Ferguson, the woman Hannah secretly called the queen of shortcuts, replied. She turned to her right where Florence Evans was sitting. "Do you have cooked chicken down at the Red Owl?"

"I've got better than that. I've got *cubed* cooked chicken and it's frozen. It'll keep for three months in your freezer and the cubes are about the same size as the ones Hannah cut for her salad."

"So then all I have to do is hard-boil some eggs, fry some bacon and crumble it, grate a carrot, and chop parsley?"

Florence shook her head. "Not even that. I've got hardboiled eggs in the deli section and crumbled bacon in a little pouch. It's probably not quite as good as homemade, but by the time you mix all those things together, nobody'll ever know."

Hannah remained silent. She really preferred to make things from scratch, but in Alice's case, she simply didn't have the time. Alice worked twelve-hour days at Ali's Alley, Lake Eden's bowling alley, and she usually made do with sandwiches and soup when she got home.

"Are you planning to invite Digger for lunch?" Ellie Kuehne teased her. "The last time Bert and I went bowling, you two were pretty friendly."

Alice smiled, but Hannah noticed that she was beginning to blush. "That's what Digger and I are . . . friends. I might invite him for Hannah's Chicken Salad, but maybe I'll invite Will."

"Who's Will?" Lisa asked, setting another platter of Herb's Herb biscuits on the table.

Alice shrugged. "He's the gas man. He works for Lake Eden GasCo and he came by to fix a gas leak in my garage. He's a really nice guy and he told me a funny story about why natural gas smells so bad."

"Tell us," Andrea encouraged. "I've always wondered about that."

All eyes were on Alice as she took a sip

from her water glass and cleared her throat. "Will said that natural gas has no smell at all, and that makes it dangerous because people can't tell if they have a gas leak or not. So way back when, the gas company used to scent it with attar of roses."

"Attar of roses smells nice," Carrie said. "My mother used to dab it on the radiator and it made the whole house smell good."

Alice smiled. "That was the problem. Nobody reported any gas leaks, and the gas company knew there had to be some. They figured that people liked the gas leaks because they made their homes smell good. So the bigwigs at the gas company had a meeting, and they decided that they should scent the gas with something that didn't smell good. They asked for suggestions and somebody came up with the essence of rotten cabbage. That's an awful smell."

No one said anything, but there were several nods around the table. Rotten cabbage was definitely not a good smell.

"The gas company didn't mention they were doing it, but they switched from attar of roses to the rotten cabbage smell one morning, and Will said that they were so swamped with calls about gas leaks, they had to put on an emergency crew."

"I believe it," Delores said, reaching for

another biscuit. "These are really good. How do you make them?"

"The recipe's under Breads and Muffins," Hannah told her mother. "I included all the recipes from the luncheon."

"I'm going to bake these tonight," Andrea declared, flipping through the binder to find the recipe. She read it through, gave a little nod, and then she looked up to see that everyone was staring at her. "Oh, come on! It's really simple. I know I'm culinarily challenged, but I think even I can handle this!"

Breads & Muffins

BERNADETTE'S POPOVERS, WITH FANCY BUTTERS

Preheat oven to 450 degrees F., rack in the middle position.

Spray a 12-cup muffin pan with Pam or other nonstick cooking spray. You can also grease them with clarified butter, oil, or lard if you prefer.

Hannah's 1st Note: Before I got this recipe, my popovers always looked as if they'd been run over by Earl Flensburg's tow truck. Now they're high, light, golden brown, and gorgeous.

4 eggs***
2 cups milk
2 cups flour *(not sifted)*
1 teaspoon salt

Hannah's 2nd Note: You should mix this recipe by hand with a whisk. If you use an

---

***If you think your eggs might be too small or too large, you can easily check them by mixing them up in a measuring cup. Four eggs should measure approximately one cup. If yours don't, adjust by adding more egg or pouring some out.

electric mixer, it will add too much air to the eggs.

Whisk the eggs until they're a light, uniform color, but not yet fluffy. It should take no more than a minute or so.

Add the milk and whisk it in until it's incorporated.

Measure out the flour and dump it in the bowl all at once. Dump in the salt on top of it. Then stir for a moment or two with a wooden spoon until all the flour has been moistened and incorporated. You will still have lumps *(like brownie batter)*, but that's fine. In this recipe, you actually want lumps!

Transfer the batter to a container with a spout *(I used a measuring cup)*. Pour the batter into the muffin cups, filling them almost to the top.

Bake at 450 degrees F. for exactly 30 minutes. *(Don't peek while they're baking or they'll fall!)*

When 30 minutes have passed, remove the pan to a cold burner or a wire rack and pierce the top of each popover with a sharp knife to release the steam.

Let the popovers stand in the pan for a

minute or two, and then tip them out into a napkin-lined basket.

Serve with sweet butter, salted butter, fruit butters, jams, jellies, or cream cheese.

Yield: 12 large popovers that everyone will love.

Hannah's 3rd Note: These popovers are also good at room temperature. I haven't done this yet, but I'm going to try filling them with egg salad, tuna salad, or salmon salad. If it works, it'll be a great dish for a brunch.

FANCY BUTTERS FOR POPOVERS

Hannah's 1st Note: Make these fancy butters the day before you plan to serve them. Take them out of the refrigerator an hour before serving.

CASHEW BUTTER:

1/2 cup softened butter *(1 stick, 1/4 pound)*
2 Tablespoons *(1/8 cup)* finely chopped cashews *(measure AFTER chopping)*

Soften the butter and place it in a small mixing bowl.

Chop the cashews ***(salted or unsalted — it doesn't really matter)*** in a food processor with the steel blade until they're as close to a paste as you can get them. ***(If you don't have a food processor, you can grind them in a food mill, chop them by hand and then crush them with a mortar and pestle, or grind them in a blender.)***

Measure 2 Tablespoons of crushed or finely chopped cashews. Mix the cashews with the butter, scrape the mixture into a small serving bowl, cover with plastic wrap, and refrigerate. When you uncover the bowl, place one perfect cashew on top of the cashew butter so everyone will know what it is.

Honey Butter:

1/2 cup softened butter *(1 stick, 1/4 pound)*
1 Tablespoon honey

Soften the butter and place it in a small mixing bowl.

Add the honey and stir until well blended. Scrape the mixture into a small serving bowl, cover with plastic wrap, and refrigerate.

Hannah's 2nd Note: I usually make a double batch of honey butter because everyone loves it so much.

Almond Butter:

1/2 cup softened butter *(1 stick, 1/4 pound)*
1 Tablespoon finely chopped or crushed blanched almonds *(measure AFTER chopping or crushing)*
1/2 teaspoon almond extract

Chop the blanched almonds in a food processor with the steel blade until they're as close to a paste as you can make them. *(If you don't have a food processor, you can grind them in a food mill, chop them by hand and then crush them with a mortar and pestle, or grind them in a blender.)*

Measure 1 Tablespoon of crushed or finely chopped almonds. Mix the almonds with the butter.

Add the almond extract and mix well.

Scrape the mixture into a small serving bowl, cover with plastic wrap, and refrigerate. When you uncover the bowl, place one perfect almond on top of the almond butter so everyone will know what it is.

DATE BUTTER:

1/2 cup softened butter *(1 stick, 1/4 pound)*
8 pitted dates, finely chopped
1 teaspoon flour

Cut each date into three pieces and place them in the bowl of a food processor. Sprinkle them with flour and chop them with the steel blade until they're as finely chopped as you can make them. *(You can add a little more flour if they stick together too much.)* If you don't have a food processor, you can try this with a blender, or chop them with a sharp knife by hand.

Mix the chopped dates with the butter, scrape the mixture into a small serving bowl, cover with plastic wrap, and refrigerate. When you uncover the bowl, place one pitted date on top of the date butter so everyone will know what it is.

ORANGE BUTTER:

1/2 cup softened butter *(1 stick, 1/4 pound)*
1 Tablespoon frozen orange juice concentrate
1 teaspoon orange zest*** *(optional)*

Measure out one Tablespoon of frozen orange juice concentrate and let it come up to room temperature.

Mix the orange juice concentrate with the softened butter. Add the orange zest if you decided to use it. *(It adds a lot!)*

Scrape the mixture into a small serving bowl, cover with plastic wrap, and refrigerate.

LEMON BUTTER:

1/2 cup softened butter *(1 stick, 1/4 pound)*
1 Tablespoon frozen lemonade concentrate
1 teaspoon lemon zest**** *(optional)*

***Orange zest is finely grated orange peel — only the orange part, not the white part.
****Lemon zest is finely grated lemon peel — only the yellow part, not the white part.

Measure out one Tablespoon of frozen lemonade concentrate and let it come up to room temperature.

Mix the lemonade concentrate with the softened butter. Add the lemon zest if you decided to use it. *(It adds a lot!)*

Scrape the mixture into a small serving bowl, cover with plastic wrap, and refrigerate.

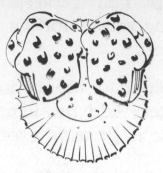

BLUE BLUEBERRY MUFFINS

Preheat oven to 375 degrees F., rack in the middle position.

THE BATTER:

3/4 cup melted butter *(1 and 1/2 sticks)*

1 cup sugar

2 beaten eggs *(just whip them up with a fork)*

2 teaspoons baking powder

1/2 teaspoon salt

1 cup fresh or frozen blueberries *(no need to thaw if they're frozen)*

2 cups plus one Tablespoon flour *(no need to sift)*

1/2 cup milk

1/2 cup blueberry pie filling

CRUMB TOPPING:

1/2 cup sugar

1/3 cup flour
1/4 cup softened butter *(1/2 stick)*

Grease the bottoms only of a 12-cup muffin pan *(or line the cups with double cupcake papers — that's what I do at The Cookie Jar)*. Melt the butter. Mix in the sugar. Add the beaten eggs, baking powder, and salt. Mix it all up thoroughly.

Put one Tablespoon of flour in a baggie with your cup of fresh or frozen blueberries. Shake it gently to coat the blueberries and leave them in the bag for now.

Add half of the remaining two cups of flour to your bowl and mix it in with half of the milk. Then add the rest of the flour and the milk, and mix thoroughly.

Here comes the fun part: Add 1/2 cup of blueberry pie filling to your bowl and mix it in. *(Your dough will turn a shade of blue, but don't let that stop you — once the muffins are baked, they'll look just fine.)* When your dough is thoroughly mixed, fold in the flour-coated fresh or frozen blueberries.

Fill the muffin tins three-quarters full and set them aside. If you have dough left over, grease the bottom of a small loaf pan and fill it with your remaining dough.

The crumb topping: Mix the sugar and the flour in a small bowl. Add the softened butter and cut it in until it's crumbly. *(You can also do this in a food processor with chilled butter and the steel blade.)*

Fill the remaining space in the muffin cups with the crumb topping. Then bake the muffins in a 375 F. degree oven for 25 to 30 minutes. *(The tea-bread should bake about 10 minutes longer than the muffins.)*

While your muffins are baking, divide the rest of your blueberry pie filling into half-cup portions and pop it in the freezer. I use paper cups to hold it and freeze them inside a freezer bag. All you have to do is thaw a cup the next time you want to make a batch of Blue Blueberry Muffins.

When your muffins are baked, set the muffin pan on a wire rack to cool for at least 30 minutes. *(The muffins need to cool in the pan for easy removal.)* Then just tip them out of the cups and enjoy.

These are wonderful when they're slightly warm, but the blueberry flavor will intensify if you store them in a covered container overnight.

Hannah's Note: Grandma Ingrid's muffin pans were large enough to hold all the dough from this recipe. My muffin tins are smaller and I always make a small loaf of Blue Blueberry bread with the leftover dough. If I make it for Mother, I leave off the crumb topping. She loves to eat it sliced, toasted, and buttered for breakfast.

*Herb's Herb Biscuits

Preheat oven to 425 degrees F., rack in the middle position.

1/4 cup salted butter *(1/2 stick, 2 ounces, 1/8 pound)*

1 Tablespoon dried fine herbs *(I used Morton & Bassett Herbs from Provence)****

10-ounce to 12-ounce tube of refrigerated, unbaked biscuits *(I used Pillsbury Simply Buttermilk biscuits)*

1/4 cup grated Parmesan cheese

If you want to mix your own dried herbs, use 2 teaspoons dried parsley, 1 teaspoon dried sage, 1/2 teaspoon ground rosemary, 1/2 teaspoon dried oregano, and 1/2 teaspoon ground thyme.

Melt the salted butter in the bottom of a 9-inch by 13-inch baking dish. You can do this by putting it into the oven until the

***Marge says that when she makes these biscuits for Herb, she uses fresh herbs from her kitchen window herb garden. If you want to do it Marge's way, use 2 Tablespoons finely minced fresh parsley, 1 Tablespoon finely minced fresh sage, 1 Tablespoon finely minced fresh thyme, and 1 teaspoon minced fresh basil.

butter melts or by melting the butter in the microwave and pouring it in the bottom of the dish.

If the herbs are not mixed, stir them together in a small bowl. Then sprinkle them over the melted butter as evenly as you can.

Open the tube of biscuits. Separate them and cut each biscuit into fourths with a knife. Roll each piece in the herbs and butter, and arrange them in the pan.

Bake the biscuits at 425 degrees F. for 12 minutes, or until they are golden brown.

Take the pan out of the oven and let it sit on a cold stove burner or a wire rack until all the butter in the bottom of the dish is absorbed. This shouldn't take longer than 5 minutes.

Serve the biscuits right in the pan.

Yield: Four times the number of biscuits in your tube.

MANGO BREAD

Preheat oven to 350 degrees F., rack in the middle position.

3/4 cup softened butter *(1 and 1/2 sticks)*

1 package *(8 ounces)* softened cream cheese *(the brick kind, not the whipped kind)*

2 cups white sugar *(granulated)*

2 beaten eggs *(just whip them up in a glass with a fork)*

1/2 teaspoon vanilla extract

1 and 1/2 cups mashed mangos *(you can use fresh and peel and seed your own, or you can buy them already prepared in the ready-to-eat section at your produce counter)*

3 cups flour *(don't sift — pack it down in the cup when you measure)*

1/2 teaspoon baking powder

1/2 teaspoon baking soda

1/2 teaspoon salt

1 cup chopped walnuts or pecans *(optional)*

Hannah's 1st Note: This is a lot easier with an electric mixer.

Beat the butter, cream cheese and sugar together until they're nice and fluffy. Add the beaten eggs and the vanilla, and mix them in.

Peel, seed, and slice the mangos *(or drain them and pat them dry if you've used prepared mangos)*. Mash them in a food processor with the steel blade, or puree them in a blender, or squash them with a potato masher until they're pureed. Measure out 1 and 1/2 cups of mashed mangos and add it to your mixing bowl. Stir well.

In another bowl, measure out the flour, baking powder, baking soda and salt. Mix them together.

Gradually add the flour mixture to the mango mixture, beating at low speed until everything is incorporated.

Mix in the walnuts or pecans by hand.

Coat the inside of two loaf pans *(the type you'd use for bread)* with nonstick cooking spray. Spoon in the mango bread batter.

Bake at 350 degrees F. for approximately one hour, or until a long toothpick or skewer inserted in the center comes out clean. If the top browns a bit too fast, tent a piece of foil over the top of the loaves.

You can also bake this in 6 smaller loaf pans, filling them about half full. If you use the smaller pans, they'll need to bake approximately 45 minutes.

Cool for 20 minutes in the pans. Then loosen the edges and turn the loaves out onto the wire rack.

Yield: Makes 2 bread-sized loaves, or 6 small loaves.

Hannah's 2nd Note: This bread is also good toasted. Lisa took it home from the contest and tried it the next morning for breakfast. She said she liked hers plain, but Herb wanted butter on his.

PEACH BREAD

Preheat oven to 350 degrees F., rack in the middle position.

3/4 cup softened butter *(1 and 1/2 sticks)*
1 package *(8 ounces)* **softened cream cheese** *(the brick kind, not the whipped kind)*
2 cups white sugar *(granulated)*
2 beaten eggs *(just whip them up in a glass with a fork)*
1/2 teaspoon almond extract
1 and 1/2 cups mashed peaches***
3 cups flour *(don't sift — pack it down in the cup when you measure)*
1/2 teaspoon baking powder
1/2 teaspoon baking soda
1/2 teaspoon salt
1 cup chopped blanched almonds

Hannah's 1st Note: This is a lot easier with an electric mixer.

Beat the butter, cream cheese and sugar together until they're nice and fluffy. Add

***You can use fresh and peel and slice your own, or you can buy them already sliced and prepared in the ready-to-eat section at your produce counter, or you can use canned peaches.

the beaten eggs and the almond extract, and mix them in.

Peel and slice the peaches *(or drain them and pat them dry if you've used prepared peaches or canned peaches)*. Mash them in a food processor with the steel blade, or puree them in a blender, or squash them with a potato masher until they're pureed. Measure out 1 and 1/2 cups of mashed peaches and add it to your mixing bowl. Stir well.

In another bowl, measure out the flour, baking powder, baking soda and salt. Mix them together.

Gradually add the flour mixture to the peach mixture, beating at low speed until everything is incorporated.

Mix in the almonds by hand.

Coat the inside of two loaf pans *(the type you'd use for bread)* with nonstick cooking spray. Spoon in the peach bread batter.

Bake at 350 degrees F. for approximately one hour, or until a long toothpick or skewer inserted in the center comes out clean. If the top browns a bit too fast, tent a piece of foil over the top of the loaves.

You can also bake this in 6 smaller loaf pans, filling them about half full. If you use the smaller pans, they'll need to bake approximately 45 minutes.

Cool for 20 minutes on a wire rack in the pans. Then loosen the edges and turn the loaves out onto the wire rack.

Yield: Makes 2 bread-sized loaves, or 6 small loaves.

Hannah's 2nd Note: This bread is also good toasted. Mother loves it toasted with honey butter on top.

If you want to make these as muffins, pour the batter into greased (or cupcake papered) muffin tins and bake at 375 degrees F. for 25 minutes or until golden on top. (Mini muffins should bake for 15 to 20 minutes or until slightly golden on top.)

Andrea realized that everyone was still staring at her and she gave a little shrug. "I've learned some things about cooking."

Hannah had all she could do to hold her tongue. The last time she'd gone to lunch at Andrea's house, several months before her sister had hired Grandma McCann to help her with the children and the meals, Andrea had served peanut butter sandwiches with mint jelly.

"Well, I have," Andrea insisted when no one said a word. "I know a lot more than I did when I tried to follow the recipe for Hannah's Lemon Meringue Pie."

There was total silence for a long, uncomfortable moment. Andrea finally broke the silence by laughing. "All right. Maybe I'll never be a good cook." She turned to look at Hannah. "And I release you from your promise. You can tell them what I did when I made the pie."

"I'll tell them over dessert," Hannah said,

motioning to Lisa to carry out the dessert tray.

"Is that a lemon pie?" Andrea asked, spotting the meringue on the top of the pies Lisa was carrying.

"No, it's a new recipe I'm testing for Peanut Butter and Jelly Pie."

"PBJ Pie?" Andrea looked intrigued.

"Yes. You can use any jam or jelly." Hannah paused and tried to be tactful. "But I really wouldn't try it with mint jelly. I don't think it would be very good. I used grape jelly in one pie, and peach jam in the other."

"There's a cake there, too," Delores pointed out. "What kind is that?"

"Something new that Lisa and I just baked. It's a Tapioca Cheesecake."

"Two desserts?" Claire Rodgers Knudson asked. "Is that . . . allowed?"

Grandma Knudson laughed and patted Claire's hand. "Of course it is, dear. Eating two desserts is never a sin as long as you take small bites."

LEMON MERINGUE PIE

Preheat oven to 350 degrees F., rack in the middle position.

1 nine-inch baked pie shell

THE FILLING:

3 whole eggs
4 egg yolks *(save the whites in a mixing bowl and let them come up to room temperature — you'll need them for the meringue)*
1/2 cup water
1/8 cup lime juice
1/3 cup lemon juice
1 cup white *(granulated)* **sugar**
1/4 cup cornstarch
1 to 2 teaspoons grated lemon zest
1 Tablespoon butter

Hannah's 1st Note: Using a double boiler makes this recipe foolproof, but if you're very careful and stir constantly so it doesn't scorch, you can make the lemon filling in a heavy saucepan directly on the stove over medium heat.

Put some tap water in the bottom of a double boiler and heat it until it simmers. *(Make sure you don't use too much water — it shouldn't touch the bottom of the pan on top.)* Off the heat, beat the egg yolks with the whole eggs in the top of the double boiler. Add the 1/2 cup water, lime juice, and lemon juice. Combine the sugar and cornstarch in a small bowl and stir until completely blended. Add this to the egg mixture in the top of the double boiler and blend thoroughly.

Place the top of the double boiler over the simmering water and cook, stirring frequently, until the lemon pie filling thickens *(5 minutes or so)*. Lift the top saucepan of the double boiler, the one containing the lemon filling you just made, and place it on a cold burner. Add the lemon zest and the butter to the filling, and stir thoroughly. Let the filling cool while you make the meringue.

THE MERINGUE:

Hannah's Note: This is a whole lot easier with an electric mixer!

4 egg whites
1/2 teaspoon cream of tartar
1/8 teaspoon salt
1/4 cup white *(granulated)* sugar

Add the cream of tartar and salt to the egg whites and mix them in. Beat the egg whites on high until they form soft peaks. Continue beating as you sprinkle in the sugar. When the egg whites form firm peaks, stop mixing and tip the bowl to test the meringue. If the egg whites don't slide down the side, they're ready.

Put the filling into the baked pie shell, smoothing it with a rubber spatula. Clean and dry your spatula. Spread the meringue over the filling with the clean spatula, sealing it to the edges of the crust. When the pie is completely covered with meringue, "dot" the pie with the flat side of the spatula to make points in the meringue. *(The meringue will shrink back when it bakes if you don't seal it to the edges of the crust.)*

Bake the pie at 350 degrees F. for no more than 10 minutes.

Remove the pie from the oven, let it cool to room temperature on a wire rack, and then refrigerate it if you wish. This pie can be served at room temperature, but it will slice more easily if it's chilled.

Hannah's 2nd Note: To keep your knife from sticking to the meringue when you cut the pie, dip it in cold water.

KEY LIME PIE

Preheat your oven to 325 degrees F., rack in the middle position.

THE CRUST:

Make your favorite graham cracker or cookie crumb crust in an 8-inch or 9-inch pie pan *(or buy one pre-made at the grocery store — I used a shortbread crust)*.

THE FILLING:

5 eggs
14-ounce can sweetened condensed milk
1/2 teaspoon lemon zest *(optional)****
1/2 cup sour cream
1/2 cup key lime juice****
1/4 cup white *(granulated)* **sugar**

Crack one whole egg into a medium-sized mixing bowl. Separate the remaining 4 eggs, placing the 4 yolks into the bowl with the

***If you don't have lemon zest, DO NOT substitute lime zest, especially from regular limes — it can be very bitter, and the little flecks of green aren't very appetizing.
****Key limes are difficult to find. If your store doesn't have them, look for frozen key lime juice. If you can't find that, just buy regular limes and juice those.

whole egg and the 4 whites into another mixing bowl. Leave the bowl with the 4 whites on your counter. They need to warm a bit for the meringue you'll make later.

Whisk the whole egg and the egg yolks until they're a uniform color. Stir in the can of sweetened condensed milk. Add the lemon zest, if you decided to use it, and the sour cream. Stir it all up and set the bowl aside.

Juice the limes and measure out 1/2 cup of juice in a small bowl.

Hannah's 1st Note: Key limes aren't easy to juice. They're very small, and a regular lime juicer won't work very well. I just roll them on my counter, pressing them down with my palm, until they're a little soft. Then I cut them in half on a plate *(so that I can save any juice that runs out)*, hold each half over a measuring cup, and squeeze them with my fingers. It's a little messy, but it works.

Add the 1/4 cup sugar to the key lime juice and stir until the sugar has dissolved. Now add the sugared lime juice to the bowl with your egg mixture and whisk it in.

Pour the filling you just made into the graham cracker or cookie crust.

Bake the pie at 325 degrees F. for 20 minutes. Take it out of the oven and set it on a rack to wait for its meringue.

DON'T TURN OFF THE OVEN! Instead, increase the oven temperature to 350 degrees F. to bake the meringue.

THE MERINGUE:

Hannah's Note: This is a whole lot easier with an electric mixer.

4 egg whites *(the ones you saved)*
1/2 teaspoon cream of tartar
a pinch of salt
1/3 cup white *(granulated)* sugar

Add the cream of tartar and salt to the bowl with your egg whites and mix them in. Beat the egg whites on HIGH until they form soft peaks.

Continue to beat at high speed as you sprinkle in the sugar. When the egg whites form firm peaks, stop mixing and tip the bowl to test the meringue. If the egg whites don't slide down the side, they're ready.

Spread the meringue over the filling with a clean spatula, sealing it to the edges of the crust. When the pie is covered with meringue, either "dot" it with the flat side of the spatula to make points in the meringue, OR smooth it out into a dome and make circular grooves with the tip of your spatula from the outside rim to the center, to create a flower-like design.

Bake the pie at 350 degrees F. for an additional 12 minutes.

Remove the pie from the oven, let it cool to room temperature on a wire rack, and then refrigerate it if you wish. This pie can be served at room temperature or chilled. It will be easier to cut and serve if it's chilled.

To keep your knife from sticking to the meringue when you cut the pie, dip the blade in cold water.

Hannah's 2nd Note: Key lime juice is a very pale green color, midway between green and yellow. The eggs and egg yolks added to the filling will color it more yellow than green. If you see a key lime pie that's green inside, the baker added green food coloring.

MOCK APPLE PIE

Preheat oven to 450 degrees F., rack in the center position. Yes, that's four hundred and fifty degrees F. and not a misprint.

Use your favorite piecrust recipe to make enough pastry for an eight-inch double crust pie.***

Assemble the following ingredients:

20 salted soda crackers
1/4 to 1/2 cup softened butter
1 and 1/2 cups cold water
1 and 1/2 cups white *(granulated)* sugar
3 Tablespoons lemon juice *(freshly squeezed is best)*
1 teaspoon cinnamon
1/2 teaspoon nutmeg
1 and 1/2 teaspoons cream of tartar

Butter the soda crackers. *(I ended up using just a bit over a quarter-cup of butter to do this.)* Put the buttered crackers in the saucepan, and break them up into fairly large pieces with a wooden spoon.

***If you're in a hurry, you can use two frozen pie shells — just thaw them and use one for the bottom and one for the top.

Add the water, sugar, lemon juice, cinnamon, nutmeg, and cream of tartar. Give everything a good stir with your spoon and bring the mixture to a boil over medium to high heat on the stovetop.

Once the boil has been reached, turn down the heat and simmer for exactly two minutes.

Set the saucepan aside on a cold burner.

Divide your piecrust dough in half. Roll out the bottom crust large enough to line an 8-inch pie plate.

Pour the soda cracker mixture into the lined pie plate and cover it with the top crust. Crimp the edges together. Cut a couple of slits in the top crust to let out the steam while the pie bakes.

Bake the pie at 450 degrees F., for 15 to 20 minutes, or until the top crust is nicely browned.

Cool and serve.

Hannah's Note: This pie has fooled everyone every single time I've served it!

Lisa says she likes this pie best with vanilla ice cream. Herb prefers it with cinnamon ice cream. Lisa's dad likes to accompany it with a slice of sharp cheddar. Herb's mom likes hers with sweetened whipped cream.

*Peanut Butter & Jelly Pie

DO NOT preheat your oven yet — you must make the crust first.

For The Crust:

2 cups vanilla wafer cookie crumbs (mea-sure AFTER crushing)
1/4 cup creamy peanut butter
1/4 cup white (granulated) sugar
2 Tablespoons (1/8 cup) cold water

In a medium-sized bowl with a fork, whisk together the crushed vanilla wafers, the peanut butter, and the white sugar until the resulting mixture is crumbly and well combined.

Add ONE **(only one, not both)** Tablespoon of water and attempt to form the mixture into a ball with your impeccably clean hands. Use the second Tablespoon of water if the first Tablespoon isn't enough to squeeze the mixture into a ball.

Once the ball is formed, spray a 9-inch pie pan with Pam or another nonstick cooking spray.

Set the ball of crust in the bottom of the pan, flatten it out with your hands, and press it up the sides. DON'T WASH

THE BOWL YOU USED FOR THE PIE CRUST — YOU CAN USE IT AGAIN FOR THE NEXT STEP.

Slip the pie plate in your freezer and set the timer for 30 minutes. Your peanut butter pie crust must freeze that long before you use it.

For The Peanut Butter Filling:

1 cup powdered *(confectioner's)* sugar
1/2 cup creamy peanut butter

Mix the powdered sugar with the peanut butter. You want to be able to spread it in the bottom of your pie crust, so you may need to heat the bowl a bit in the microwave once your peanut butter pie crust comes out of the freezer.

When your crust has chilled for 30 minutes, remove it from the freezer and set it on the counter.

Preheat your oven to 325 degrees F., rack in the middle position.

Spread the peanut butter filling on the bottom of the peanut butter crust. Set it on top of a drip pan *(I use an old cookie sheet with sides)* and leave it on the counter to wait for the "jelly" filling.

Don't wash the bowl you just used for the peanut butter filling. Simply wipe it out with a paper towel, and you can use it again for the "jelly" filling. *(Can you tell I hate to wash dishes?)*

FOR THE "JELLY" FILLING:

5 eggs
14-ounce can sweetened condensed milk
1/2 cup plain yogurt *(try to find whole milk yogurt — it's better)*
1/2 cup frozen grape juice concentrate*
1 Tablespoon grape jelly
1/2 teaspoon lemon zest *(optional)*****

Crack one whole egg into that same medium-sized mixing bowl. Separate the remaining 4 eggs, placing the 4 yolks into the bowl with the whole egg and the 4 whites into another mixing bowl. Leave the bowl

***You can use any flavor of frozen juice concentrate and jelly that you wish. You are only limited by the frozen juice concentrates and jelly or jam that your store carries. My small grocery store stocks frozen grape, frozen peach, frozen pineapple, frozen orange, frozen lemonade, frozen limeade, frozen pink grapefruit, and frozen apple.
****The lemon zest adds a little zing to your pie.

with the 4 whites on your counter. They need to warm a bit for the meringue you'll make later.

Whisk the whole egg and the egg yolks until they're a uniform color. Then stir in the can of sweetened condensed milk.

Add the yogurt and the grape juice concentrate. Stir it together until it's a uniform color and the frozen concentrate has melted.

Heat the Tablespoon of jelly until it melts and then stir it into the mixture.

Add the lemon zest, if you decided to use it, and stir well.

Pour the filling you just made on top of the peanut butter filling in your crust.

Bake the pie at 325 degrees F. for 20 minutes. Take it out of the oven and set it on a cool stovetop or a rack to wait for its meringue.

Hannah's 1st Note: The contents of your pie will be "jiggly". That's okay. It'll firm up later.

DON'T TURN OFF THE OVEN! Instead, increase the oven temperature to 350 degrees F. to bake the meringue.

4 egg whites *(the ones you saved in that bowl on the counter)*
1/2 teaspoon cream of tartar
a pinch of salt
1/3 cup white *(granulated)* **sugar**

Hannah's 2nd Note: This is a whole lot easier with an electric mixer!

Add the cream of tartar and the salt to the bowl with your egg whites and mix them in.

Beat the egg whites on HIGH until they form soft peaks.

Continue to beat at HIGH speed as you sprinkle in the sugar. When the egg whites form firm peaks, stop mixing and tip the bowl to test the meringue. If the egg whites don't slide down the side of the bowl, they're ready.

Spread the meringue over the filling with a clean rubber spatula, sealing it to the edges of the crust. When the pie is covered with meringue, either "dot" it with the flat side of the spatula to make points in the meringue, OR smooth it out into a dome and make circular grooves with the tip of your spatula from the outside rim to the center, to create a flower-like design.

Bake your Peanut Butter & Jelly Pie at 350 degrees F. for an additional 12 minutes.

Remove your pie from the oven and let it cool by setting the drip pan and the pie pan on a wire rack.

When the pie has cooled to room temperature, refrigerate it at least 3 hours before serving.

Yield: 6 large or 8 medium slices of incredibly delicious pie. I can almost guarantee you've never had anything like it before!

CHERRY CHEESECAKE

Preheat oven to 350 degrees F., rack in the middle position.

FOR THE CRUST:

2 cups vanilla wafer cookie crumbs (*mea-sure AFTER crushing*)
3/4 stick melted butter (*6 Tablespoons*)
1 teaspoon almond extract

Pour the melted butter and almond extract over the cookie crumbs. Mix with a fork until they're evenly moistened.

Cut a circle of parchment paper **(*or wax paper*)** to fit inside the bottom of a 9-inch Springform pan. Spray the pan with Pam or other nonstick cooking spray, set the paper circle in place, and spray with Pam again.

Dump the moistened cookie crumbs in

the pan and press them down over the paper circle and one inch up the sides. Stick the pan in the freezer for 15 to 30 minutes while you prepare the rest of the cheesecake.

FOR THE TOPPING:

2 cups sour cream
1/2 cup sugar
1 teaspoon vanilla

21-ounce can cherry pie filling*** *(I used Comstock Dark Sweet Cherry)*

Mix the sour cream, sugar, and vanilla together in a small bowl. Cover and refrigerate. Set the unopened can of cherry pie filling in the refrigerator for later.

FOR THE CHEESECAKE BATTER:

1 cup white *(granulated)* sugar
3 eight-ounce packages cream cheese at room temperature *(total 24 ounces)*
1 cup mayonnaise
4 eggs
2 cups white chocolate chips *(I used Ghirardelli 11-ounce bag)*

***If you don't like canned pie filling, make your own with canned or frozen cherries, sugar, and cornstarch.

2 teaspoons vanilla

Place the sugar in the bowl of an electric mixer. Add the blocks of cream cheese and the mayonnaise, and whip it up at medium speed until it's smooth. Add the eggs, one at a time, beating after each addition.

Melt the white chocolate chips in a microwave-safe bowl for 2 minutes. *(Chips may retain their shape, so stir to see if they're melted — if not, microwave in 15-second increments until you can stir them smooth.)* Cool the melted white chocolate for a minute or two and then mix it into the batter gradually at slow speed. Scrape down the bowl and add the vanilla, mixing it in thoroughly.

Pour the batter on top of the chilled crust, set the pan on a cookie sheet to catch any drips, and bake it at 350 degrees F. for 55 to 60 minutes. Remove the pan from the oven, but DON'T SHUT OFF THE OVEN.

Starting in the center, spoon the sour cream topping over the top of the cheesecake, spreading it out to within a half-inch of the rim. Return the pan to the oven and bake for an additional 5 minutes.

Cool the cheesecake in the pan on a wire rack. When the pan is cool enough to pick up with your bare hands, place it in the refrigerator and chill it, uncovered, for at least 8 hours.

To serve, run a knife around the inside rim of the pan, release the springform catch, and lift off the rim. Place a piece of waxed paper on a flat plate and tip it upside down over the top of your cheesecake. Invert the cheesecake so that it rests on the paper.

Carefully pry off the bottom of the Springform pan and remove the paper from the bottom crust.

Invert a serving platter over the bottom crust of your cheesecake. Flip the cheesecake right side up, take off the top plate, and remove the waxed paper.

Spread the cherry pie filling over the sour cream topping on your cheesecake. You can drizzle a little down the sides if you wish.

CHOCOLATE PEANUT BUTTER CAKE

Preheat oven to 350 degrees F., rack in the middle position.

WARNING: THERE ARE PEANUTS IN THIS RECIPE. MAKE SURE YOU ASK IF ANYONE IS ALLERGIC TO PEANUTS BEFORE YOU BAKE AND SERVE THIS CAKE !!!

Hannah's 1st Note: Lisa says she got the idea for this cake by watching Marge make her Cocoa Fudge Cake. Since Herb is crazy about Reese's Peanut Butter Cups, Lisa's cake combines peanut butter and chocolate.

Butter and flour a 9-inch by 13-inch sheet cake pan. *(You can also spray it with Pam or another nonstick cooking spray and then just lightly dust it with flour. You can also do what Lisa did and spray it with a product that mixes nonstick cooking spray with flour.)*

Hannah's 2nd Note: I was really leery of the nonstick cooking spray mixed with flour, but Lisa says it works just fine.

2 cups white *(granulated)* sugar
2 cups flour *(don't sift — just level it off

with a knife)

------

1 cup butter *(2 sticks, 1/2 pound, 8 ounces)*
1 cup peanut butter *(Lisa used Skippy creamy peanut butter)*
1 cup water

1/2 cup cream *(or evaporated milk, if you're all out of cream)*
1 teaspoon vanilla extract
1 teaspoon baking soda
2 eggs, beaten *(just whip them up in a glass with a fork)*

Hannah's 3rd Note: Lisa used the mixer down at The Cookie Jar to make this cake. She says you can also do it by hand if you don't have an electric mixer.

Mix the sugar and the flour together at low speed.

Put the butter, peanut butter, and water into a medium-sized saucepan. Turn the burner on medium heat and bring the mixture ALMOST to a boil. *(When it sends up little whiffs of steam and bubbles start to form around the edges, take it off the heat.)*

Pour the peanut butter mixture over the sugar and flour, and mix it all up together.

Rinse out the saucepan, but don't bother to wash it thoroughly. You'll be making a frosting, and you can use it again before you thoroughly wash it.

Whisk the cream, vanilla extract, baking soda, and eggs together in a small bowl.

SLOWLY, add this mixture to the large mixer bowl and combine it at medium speed. *(You have to go slowly with this step because you have the hot peanut butter mixture in your bowl and you're adding an egg mixture. This cake wouldn't be wonderful if you ended up with peanut butter flavored scrambled eggs!)*

Scrape down the mixing bowl with a rubber spatula, remove it from the mixer, and give it a final stir by hand.

Pour the batter into the 9-inch by 13-inch greased and floured cake pan.

Bake at 350 degrees F. for 30 to 35 minutes. When the cake begins to shrink away from the sides of the pan and a long toothpick inserted in the center of the cake comes out clean, it's done.

Hannah's 4th Note: Lisa uses my Never-fail Fudge Frosting on this cake. It's given as an alternative frosting at the end of Marge's Cocoa Fudge Cake recipe, but I'll write it down again here.

NEVERFAIL FUDGE FROSTING:

1/2 cup *(1 stick, 1/4 pound, 4 ounces)* salted butter
1 cup white *(granulated)* sugar
1/3 cup cream
1/2 cup chocolate chips
1 teaspoon vanilla extract
1/2 cup chopped salted peanuts *(optional)*

Place the butter, sugar, and cream into a medium-sized saucepan *(**You can use the one from the cake that you didn't wash.**)* Bring the mixture to a boil, stirring constantly. Turn down the heat to medium and cook for two minutes.

Add the half-cup chocolate chips, stir them in until they're melted, and remove the saucepan from the heat.

Stir in the vanilla.

Pour the frosting on the cake and spread it out quickly with a spatula. Whether you're pouring it on a warm cake or a cold cake, just grab the pan and tip it so the frosting covers the whole top.

Sprinkle the chopped salted peanuts *(if you decided to use them)* over the top of the frosting.

If you want this frosting to cool in a big hurry so that you can cut the cake, just slip it in the refrigerator, uncovered, for a half-hour or so.

Hannah's 5th Note: Lisa says to tell you that this cake is absolutely yummy if you serve it slightly warm. It's also wonderful at room temperature. If you keep it in the refrigerator, take it out 45 minutes or so before you plan to serve it.

COCOA FUDGE CAKE

Preheat oven to 350 degrees F., rack in the middle position.

Hannah's 1st Note: Marge says to tell you that she got this recipe from two girls she met on the bus to Fargo, Sandy and Patricia. They used margarine, but since Marge is from a dairy state and she knows that there's no acceptable substitute for butter, she uses regular salted butter in her cake. She says she made a couple of other changes too, but it's been so long she doesn't remember what they are.

Before you start, grease and flour a 9-inch by 13-inch cake pan. *(You can also spray with Pam or another nonstick cooking spray and then dust it lightly with flour.)*

2 cups white *(granulated)* **sugar**
2 cups flour *(don't sift — just level it off with a knife)*

---

1 cup butter *(2 sticks, 1/2 pound)*
1 cup water
3 Tablespoons unsweetened cocoa powder *(I used Hershey's)*

1/2 cup milk
1 teaspoon vanilla extract

1 teaspoon baking soda
2 eggs, beaten *(just whip them up in a glass with a fork)*

In a large bowl, stir the sugar and the flour together. Set it aside on the counter.

Put the butter, water, and cocoa powder into a saucepan and bring it to a boil over medium heat.

Pour the cocoa mixture over the sugar and flour, and mix it all up together. *(You can do this on medium speed with an electric mixer if you wish.)*

Hannah's 2nd Note: Marge says you shouldn't be a neatnik and wash your saucepan. If you make the frosting, you'll use it again.

Whisk the milk, vanilla extract, baking soda, and eggs together in a small bowl. *(I used a 2-cup Pyrex measuring cup.)*

Add the egg mixture to the large bowl. Stir it until it's thoroughly incorporated.

Pour the batter into a 9-inch by 13-inch greased and floured cake pan.

Bake at 350 degrees F. for 30 to 35 minutes. When the cake begins to shrink away from the sides of the pan, it's done.

Hannah's 3rd Note: This cake is delicious without frosting, or just lightly dusted with powdered sugar. If you want a frosting, try the one below. Start making it 5 minutes before the cake is due to come out of the oven and the frosting and the cake will be ready at the same time.

CHOCOLATE FROSTING

1/2 cup *(1 stick)* butter
3 Tablespoons unsweetened cocoa powder *(I used Hershey's)*
1/3 cup milk
1 teaspoon vanilla extract
one-pound box of powdered *(confectioner's)* sugar

Place the butter, cocoa powder, and milk in a medium-sized saucepan *(The one from before that you didn't wash.)* Bring them to a boil, stirring constantly.

Remove the pan from the heat and add the vanilla. Stir in the powdered sugar, a half-cup at a time, until the frosting is thickened but still "pourable." *(If that's not a word, it should be.)*

Pour the frosting on the hot cake, and

spread it out quickly with a spatula.

Hannah's 4th Note: Interruptions happen and it's not always possible to finish the frosting at the same time you take the hot cake from the oven. For that reason, I've come up with an alternative fudge frosting, one that can be poured over a piping hot cake, a warm cake, or a stone cold cake. Here it is:

NEVERFAIL FUDGE FROSTING

1/2 cup (1 stick, 1/4 pound, 4 ounces) salted butter
1 cup white (granulated) sugar
1/3 cup cream
1/2 cup chocolate chips
1 teaspoon vanilla extract
1/2 cup chopped pecans (optional)

Place the butter, sugar, and cream into a medium-sized saucepan **(You can use the one from the cake that you didn't wash.)** Bring the mixture to a boil, stirring constantly. Turn down the heat to medium and cook for two minutes.

Add the half-cup chocolate chips, stir them in, and remove the saucepan from the heat.

Stir in the vanilla and the chopped pecans,

if you decided to use them.

Pour the frosting on the cake and spread it out quickly with a spatula. Whether you're pouring it on a warm cake or a cold cake, just grab the pan and tip it so the frosting covers the whole top.

If you want this frosting to cool in a big hurry so that you can cut the cake, just slip it in the refrigerator, uncovered, for a half-hour or so.

Hannah's 5th Note: Marge says that this cake smells so good, you might have to keep it under lock and key until it's cool enough to cut.

FUDGE CUPCAKES

Preheat oven to 350 degrees F., rack in the middle position.

4 squares unsweetened baking chocolate *(1 ounce each)*
1/2 cup raspberry syrup *(for pancakes — I used Knott's red raspberry)****
1/4 cup white *(granulated)* **sugar**
1 and 2/3 cups flour *(don't sift)*
1 and 1/2 teaspoons baking powder
1/2 teaspoon salt
1/2 cup butter, room temperature *(1 stick, 1/4 pound)*
1 and 1/2 cups white sugar *(not a misprint — you'll use 1 and 3/4 cups sugar in all)*
3 eggs
1/3 cup milk

Line a 12-cup muffin pan with double cupcake papers. Since this recipe makes 18 cupcakes, you can use an additional 6-cup muffin pan lined with double papers, or you can butter and flour an 8-inch square cake pan or the equivalent.

***If you can't find raspberry syrup, mix 1/4 cup seedless raspberry jam with 1/4 cup light Karo syrup and use that.

145

Microwave the chocolate, raspberry syrup and 1/4 cup sugar in a microwave-safe bowl on HIGH for 1 minute. Stir. Microwave again for another minute. At this point, the chocolate will be almost melted, but it will maintain its shape. Stir the mixture until smooth and let cool to lukewarm. *(You can also do this in a double boiler on the stove.)*

Measure the flour, mix in the baking powder and salt, and set it aside. With an electric mixer *(or with a VERY strong arm)*, beat the butter and 1 and 1/2 cups sugar until light and fluffy. *(About 3 minutes with a mixer — an additional 2 minutes if you're doing it by hand.)* Add the eggs, one at a time, beating after each addition to make sure they're thoroughly incorporated. Add approximately a third of the flour mixture and a third of the milk. *(You don't have to be exact — adding the flour and milk in increments makes the batter smoother.)* When that's all mixed in, add another third of the flour and another third of the milk. And when that's incorporated, add the remainder of the flour and the remainder of the milk. Mix thoroughly.

Test your chocolate mixture to make sure it's cool enough to add. *(You don't want to cook the eggs!)* If it's fairly warm to the touch but not so hot you have to pull your hand away, you can add it at this point. Stir thoroughly and you're done.

Let the batter rest for five minutes. Then stir it again by hand, and fill each cupcake paper three-quarters full. If you decided to use the 8-inch cake pan instead of the 6-cup muffin tin, fill it with the remaining batter.

Bake the cupcakes in a 350 degree F. oven for 20 to 25 minutes. The 8-inch cake should bake an additional 5 minutes.

FUDGE FROSTING:

**2 cups semi-sweet *(regular)* chocolate chips *(a 12-ounce package)*
14-ounce can sweetened condensed milk**

18 cupcakes, or 12 cupcakes and 1 small cake, cooled to room temperature and ready to frost.

If you use a double boiler for this frosting, it's foolproof. You can also make it in a heavy saucepan over low to medium heat on the stovetop, but you'll have to stir it constantly with a wooden spoon or a heat-resistant spatula to keep it from scorching.

Fill the bottom part of the double boiler with water. Make sure the water doesn't touch the underside of the top.

Put the chocolate chips in the top of the double boiler, set it over the bottom, and place the double boiler on the stovetop at medium heat. Stir occasionally until the chocolate chips are melted.

Stir in the can of sweetened condensed milk and cook approximately 2 minutes, stirring constantly, until the frosting is shiny and of spreading consistency.

Spread it on the cupcakes, making sure to fill in the indentation on top of the cupcake with frosting.

Give the frosting pan to your favorite person to scrape.

These cupcakes are even better if you cool them, cover them, and let them sit for several hours *(or even overnight)* before frosting them.

Hannah's Note: If you want to make these in mini-cupcake tins, fill the cups 2/3 full and bake them at 350 degrees F. for 15 minutes.

HANNAH'S SPECIAL CARROT CAKE

Preheat oven to 350 degrees F., rack in the middle position.

2 cups white *(granulated)* **sugar**
3 eggs
3/4 cup vegetable oil *(not canola, or olive, or anything but veggie oil)*
1 teaspoon vanilla extract
3/4 cup sour cream *(or unflavored yogurt)*
2 teaspoons baking soda
2 teaspoons cinnamon *(or 1/2 teaspoon cardamom and the rest cinnamon)*
1 and 1/2 teaspoons salt
1 20-ounce can crushed pineapple, juice and all***
2 cups chopped walnuts *(or pecans)*

***That's about 1 and 1/2 cups of crushed pineapple and a scant cup of juice.

2 and 1/2 cups flour *(don't sift — pack it down when you measure)*
2 cups grated carrots *(also pack them down when you measure)*

Grease *(or spray with Pam or another nonstick cooking spray)* a 9-inch by 13-inch cake pan and set it aside.

Hannah's 1st Note: This is a lot easier with an electric mixer, but you can also make it by hand.

Beat the sugar, eggs, vegetable oil, and vanilla together in a large bowl. Mix in the sour cream *(or yogurt)*. Add the baking soda, cinnamon *(and cardamom if you used it)* and salt. Mix them in thoroughly.

Add the can of crushed pineapple *(including the liquid)* and the chopped nuts to your bowl. Mix them in thoroughly.

Add the flour by half-cup increments, mixing after each addition.

Grate the carrots. *(This is very easy with a food processor, but you can also do it with a hand grater.)* Measure out 2 cups of grated carrots. Pack them down in the cup when you measure them.

Mix in the carrots BY HAND. Grated carrots tend to get caught on the beaters of electric mixers.

Spread the batter in your prepared cake pan, and bake it at 350 degrees F. for 50 minutes, or until a cake tester *(I use a food pick that's a little longer than a toothpick)* inserted one inch from the center of the cake comes out clean.

Let the cake cool in the cake pan on a wire rack. When it's completely cool, frost with cream cheese frosting while it's still in the pan.

CREAM CHEESE FROSTING

1/2 cup softened butter
8-ounce package softened cream cheese
1 teaspoon vanilla extract
4 cups confectioner's *(powdered)* sugar
(no need to sift unless it's got big lumps)

Mix the softened butter with the softened cream cheese and the vanilla until the mixture is smooth.

Hannah's 2nd Note: Do this next step at room temperature. If you heated the cream cheese or the butter to soften it, make sure it's cooled down before you continue.

Add the confectioner's sugar in half-cup increments until the frosting is of proper spreading consistency. *(You'll use all, or almost all, of the sugar.)*

Hannah's 3rd Note: If you're good with the pastry bag, remove 1/3 cup of frosting and save it in a little bowl to pipe on frosting carrots and stems.

With a frosting knife *(or rubber spatula if you prefer)*, drop large dollops of frosting over the surface of your cooled cake. I usually end up with somewhere between 6 and 12 dollops. The dollops are like little stacks of frosting — you'll spread neighboring stacks together, working your way from one end to the other, until you've frosted the whole cake. *(This dollop method prevents uneven frosting thickness and "tearing" of the surface of your cake as you "pull" frosting from one end to the other.)*

If you decided to use the pastry bag to decorate your cake, mix most of the remaining frosting with one drop of yellow food coloring and one drop of red food coloring. Mix it thoroughly to make an orange frosting, and pipe little carrots on top to decorate your cake. You can save a bit of uncolored frosting to color green and dab green stems on the large end of the carrots.

HERB'S WEDDING COOKIE CAKE

This cake must be refrigerated to set up — make it the night BEFORE you plan to serve it.

4-quart bowl

2 pounds chocolate cookie wafers***

8 small packages of vanilla pudding mix****

10 cups *(2 and 1/2 quarts)* whole milk *(or half and half if you want to splurge)*

sweetened whipped cream for frosting and topping.

Line the inside of your bowl with long

***If you can't find chocolate cookie wafers in the cookie aisle of your grocery store, try the section where they keep ice cream toppings and ice cream cookies — that's where Florence Evans at the Red Owl in Lake Eden keeps them.

****The yield should be 2 cups per package if you make it according to the package directions. You can use sugar free instant, regular instant, or the kind you have to cook. All will work. *(You can also use 5 larger packages of pudding, each package yielding 3 cups of pudding — if you do this, use 2 cups of milk or half and half for each package — as you can see, this recipe is very flexible.)*

strips of plastic wrap, leaving enough wrap to fold back over the top when your cake is finished.

Cover the bottom of the bowl with chocolate cookie wafers, all the way out to the sides. You can break them in half or even in quarters if you want, but it's also okay just to overlap them. *(Unlike a jigsaw puzzle, it doesn't matter if some pieces don't fit together exactly.)*

Make the first two packages of pudding using 2 and 1/2 CUPS OF MILK, not the 4 cups called for in the directions on the box.

Pour approximately a third of the pudding over the layer of chocolate cookie wafers in your bowl. Gently spread it out with a rubber spatula. *(It doesn't have to be perfectly smooth, just not wildly uneven, that's all.)*

Put another layer of chocolate cookie wafers on top of the pudding in the bowl. *(Again, it doesn't have to be perfect — the pudding will soak into the cookie wafers and all will be forgiven.)*

Put half of the remaining pudding on top of the second layer of chocolate cookie wafers. Spread it out so it covers them.

Lay down another layer of chocolate cookie wafers and top it with the remaining pudding. Spread out the pudding and lay down another layer of chocolate cookie wafers. *(Don't bother to wash out the bowl or pan you used to make your pudding. You're just going to make another batch.)*

Using another 2 packages of pudding and another 2 and 1/2 cups of milk, make your second batch of pudding.

There are more chocolate cookie wafers to cover now, since the bowl is wider. Use half of the pudding to cover the cookies. Smooth the pudding with your rubber spatula, lay down another layer of chocolate cookie wafers, cover it with the remaining pudding, and top it with another layer of cookies. *(I'll bet you're already guessing what the rest of the cake will be like!)*

Make the third batch of pudding using 2 packages of mix and 2 and 1/2 cups of milk. Put half on top of the chocolate cookie wafers in your bowl, spread it out, and top it with more cookies. Now use the rest of the pudding and top it again with chocolate cookie wafers.

One more time! Make the final batch of

pudding using 2 packages of pudding mix and 2 and 1/2 cups of milk. Spread half the pudding over the chocolate cookie wafers, smooth it, and cover it with more cookies. Put on the rest of the pudding, smooth it, and this time cover it with a **DOUBLE LAYER OF CHOCOLATE COOKIE WAFERS.**

(Wasn't that easy? Even if you don't bake, you can make this cake.)

Fold in the edges of the plastic wrap to cover the contents of your bowl. Find a plate that will fit inside the bowl on top of the cake. Put it in right side up so that it'll push the cake down slightly. Set a weight on top of the plate. I use a can of fruit.

Refrigerate the cake until time to serve.

When you're ready to serve, remove the weight and the plate, peel back the plastic wrap, and center a serving platter, right side down, over the top of the bowl. Invert the bowl, lift it off, and peel off the plastic wrap.

Frost your cake with sweetened whipped cream. *(Hannah whips her own cream, but you can use the kind in the can if it's easier for you.)*

Slice the cake as you would a pie, in wedge-shaped pieces. Everyone will ooh and ahh when you do. Pass a dish of sweetened whipped cream for those who want more, and enjoy!

JANE'S MINI CHERRY CHEESECAKES

Preheat oven to 350 degrees F., rack in the center position.

24 cupcake liners *(48 if you're like me and you like to use double papers)*
24 vanilla wafer cookies
2 eight-ounce packages softened cream cheese *(room temperature)****
3/4 cup white *(granulated)* **sugar**
2 eggs
1 Tablespoon lemon juice
1 teaspoon vanilla
1 can cherry pie filling, chilled *(21 ounces net weight)*

Line two muffin pans *(the kind of pan that makes 12 muffins each)* with paper cupcake liners. Put one vanilla wafer cookie in the bottom of each cupcake paper, flat side down.

Chill the unopened can of cherry pie filling in the refrigerator while you make the mini cheesecakes.

***Use brick cream cheese, the kind that comes in a rectangular package. Don't use whipped cream cheese unless you want to experiment — whipped cream cheese, or low-fat, or Neufchatel might work, but I don't know that for sure.

You can do all of this by hand, but it's easier with an electric mixer on slow to medium speed:

Mix the softened cream cheese with the white sugar until it's thoroughly blended. Add the eggs one at a time, beating after each addition. Then mix in the lemon juice and vanilla, and beat until light and fluffy.

Spoon the cheesecake batter into the muffin tins, dividing it as equally as you can. When you're through, each cupcake paper should be between half and two-thirds full. *(They're going to look skimpy, but they'll be fine once they're baked and you put on the cherry topping.)*

Bake at 350 degrees F. for 15 to 20 minutes, or until top has set and has a satin finish. *(The center may sink a bit, but that's okay — the topping will cover that.)*

Cool the mini cheesecakes in the pans on wire racks.

When the cheesecakes are cool, open the can of cherry pie filling and place three cherries on top of every mini cheesecake. Divide the cherry juice equally among the 24 mini cheesecakes.

Refrigerate in the muffin tins for at least 4 hours before serving. *(Overnight is fine, too.)* Then take them out of the tins, carefully remove the cupcake papers, and place them on a silver platter for an elegant dessert at a finger food party.

Hannah's 1st Note: I made these with Comstock Dark Cherry Pie Filling and came up 4 cherries short. Lisa's can of regular cherry pie filling had 72 cherries, 3 for each of her Mini Cherry Cheesecakes.

Hannah's 2nd Note: If you prefer, you can use fresh fruit glazed with melted jelly instead of the canned cherry pie filling. You can also use any other pie filling you like.

KITTY'S ORANGE CAKE

Preheat oven to 350 degrees F., rack in the middle position.

- 1 box yellow cake mix *(1 pound, 2.25 ounces)*
- 1 package *(3 ounces)* orange Jell-O powder *(NOT sugar free)*
- 1 cup orange juice
- 1 teaspoon orange extract
- 1/2 cup vegetable oil
- 1 teaspoon orange zest *(optional — if you like it super orangey)*
- 4 eggs
- 1 cup semi-sweet mini chocolate morsels*** *(6-ounce package — I used Nestles)*

Grease and flour a Bundt pan. *(I sprayed mine with Pam and then floured it. You can also use baking spray, which already contains flour and eliminates one step.)*

***These are miniature chocolate chips. If you can't find them in your area, you can use regular size chocolate chips and cut them in halves or quarters. If you use them as is, they'll sink to the bottom and make your cake hard to remove from the pan. You can also shave chocolate and use that. It works even better than the mini chocolate chips.

Hannah's 1st Note: You can make this cake without an electric mixer if you have a strong arm and determination, but it's a lot easier if you use one.

Dump the dry yellow cake mix in a large mixing bowl. Mix in the orange Jell-O powder. Add the orange juice, orange extract, vegetable oil, and the orange zest **(if you decided to use it)**. Mix all the ingredients together until they are well blended.

Add the eggs one at a time, mixing after each addition.

Beat 2 minutes on medium speed with an electric mixer or 3 minutes by hand.

Fold in the mini chocolate morsels by hand.

Pour the cake batter into the Bundt pan.

Bake at 350 degrees F. for 45 to 55 minutes or until a cake tester inserted into the center of the cake comes out dry.

Cool on a rack for 20 to 25 minutes. Loosen the outside edges and the middle, and tip the cake out of the pan. Let the cake cool completely on the rack.

When the cake is cool, drizzle Orange-

Fudge Frosting over the crest and let it run down the sides. *(Or, if you don't feel like making a glaze, just let the cake cool completely and dust it with confectioner's sugar.)*

ORANGE-FUDGE FROSTING:

- 2 Tablespoons chilled butter *(1/4 stick, 1/8 cup)*
- 1 cup semi-sweet chocolate chips *(6-ounce bag)*
- 1 teaspoon orange extract
- 2 Tablespoons refrigerated orange juice

Place the butter in the bottom of a 2-cup microwave-safe bowl. *(I used a glass one-pint measuring cup.)* Add the chocolate chips. Heat on HIGH for 60 seconds.

Stir to see if the chips are melted. *(They tend to maintain their shape even when melted, so you can't tell by just looking.)* If they're not melted and can't be stirred smooth, heat them on HIGH at 15-second intervals until they are, stirring to check after each 15-second interval.

Add the orange extract and stir it in.

Add the orange juice Tablespoon by Tablespoon, stirring after each addition.

Pour the frosting over the ridge of the cake, letting it run partway down the sides. It will be thicker on top. That's fine. *(And if it's not, that's fine, too — you really can't go wrong with this cake.)*

Refrigerate the cake for at least 20 minutes without covering it. That "sets" the frosting. After that, the cake can be left out at room temperature if you wish.

Hannah's 2nd Note: When I bake this cake for Mother, I use both the orange extract and the orange zest. Mother adores the combination of orange and chocolate. Come to think of it, Mother adores ANY combination that includes chocolate.

LISA'S WEDDING COOKIE CAKE

This cake must be refrigerated to set up — make it the night BEFORE you plan to serve it.

4-quart bowl

2 one-pound packages of graham crackers

8 small packages of chocolate pudding mix***

10 cups *(2 and 1/2 quarts)* whole milk *(or half and half if you want to splurge)*

sweetened whipped cream for frosting and topping

Line the inside of your bowl with long strips of plastic wrap, leaving enough wrap to fold back over the top when your cake is finished.

***Read the yield on the pudding package — it should be 2 cups per package if you make it according to the package directions. You can use sugar free instant, regular instant, or the kind you have to cook. All will work. *(You can also use 5 larger packages of pudding, each package yielding 3 cups of pudding — if you do this, use 2 cups of milk or half and half for each package — as you can see, this recipe is very flexible.)*

Cover the bottom of the bowl with graham crackers, all the way out to the sides. You can break them in half or even in quarters if you want, but it's also okay just to overlap them. *(Unlike a jigsaw puzzle, it doesn't matter if some pieces don't fit together exactly.)*

Make the first two packages of pudding using 2 and 1/2 CUPS OF MILK, not the 4 cups called for in the directions on the box.

Pour approximately a third of the pudding over the layer of graham crackers in your bowl. Gently spread it out with a rubber spatula. *(It doesn't have to be perfectly smooth, just not wildly uneven, that's all.)*

Put another layer of graham crackers on top of the pudding in the bowl. *(Again, it doesn't have to be perfect — the pudding will soak into the graham crackers and all will be forgiven.)*

Put half of the remaining pudding on top of the second layer of graham crackers. Spread it out so it covers them.

Lay down another layer of graham crackers and top it with the remaining pudding. Spread out the pudding and lay down another layer of graham crackers. *(Don't bother to wash out the bowl or pan you used to make your pudding. You're just going to make another batch.)*

Using another 2 packages of pudding and another 2 and 1/2 cups of milk, make your second batch of pudding.

There are more graham crackers to cover now, since the bowl is wider. Use half of the pudding to cover the graham crackers. Smooth the pudding with your rubber spatula, lay down another layer of graham crackers, cover it with the remaining pudding, and top it with another layer of graham crackers. *(I'll bet you're already guessing what the rest of the cake will be like!)*

Make the third batch of pudding using 2 packages of mix and 2 and 1/2 cups of milk. Put half on top of the graham crackers in your bowl, spread it out, and top it with more graham crackers. Now use the rest of the pudding and top it again with graham crackers.

One more time! Make the final batch of pudding using 2 packages of pudding mix and 2 and 1/2 cups of milk. Spread half the pudding over the graham crackers, smooth it, and cover it with more graham crackers. Put on the rest of the pudding, smooth it and this time cover it with a **DOUBLE LAYER OF GRAHAM CRACKERS.**

(Wasn't that easy? Even if you don't bake, you can make this cake.)

Fold in the edges of the plastic wrap to cover the contents of your bowl. Find a plate that will fit inside the bowl on top of the cake. Put it in right side up so that it'll push the cake down when it settles. Set a weight on top of the plate. I use a can of fruit.

Refrigerate the cake until time to serve.

When you're ready to serve, remove the weight and the plate, peel back the plastic wrap, and center a serving platter, right side down, over the top of the bowl. Invert the bowl, lift it off, and peel off the plastic wrap.

Frost your cake with sweetened whipped cream. *(Hannah whips her own cream, but you can use the kind in the can if it's easier for you.)*

Slice the cake as you would a pie, in wedge-shaped pieces. Everyone will ooh and ahh when you do. Pass a dish of sweetened whipped cream for those who want more, and enjoy!

RHUBARB CUSTARD CAKE

Preheat oven to 350 degrees F., rack in the center position.

1 package *(1 lb., 2.25 oz.)* lemon cake mix
3 to 4 cups peeled, cut up rhubarb***
1 cup white *(granulated)* sugar
2 cups whipping cream or half and half *(I use half and half)*

sweetened whipped cream for a topping

Prepare the inside of a 9-inch by 13-inch cake pan by spraying the bottom and sides with nonstick cooking spray and then dusting it with flour. Shake off excess flour. *(You can also use baking spray, which has flour in it.)*

Mix the cake according to the package directions.

Pour the batter into the pan you prepared.

Spread out the rhubarb on top of the batter.

Sprinkle the top of the fruit with the sugar.

***You can use frozen rhubarb. Just thaw it and pat it dry with a paper towel.

Cover the sugar with the cream or half and half.

Bake at 350 degrees F. for 45 to 60 minutes. *(Mine took 50 minutes.)*

This cake won't "set up" exactly like a regular cake — the fruit and custard will sink to the bottom and will have the consistency of a thick pudding, or a trifle. The top half of the cake will be like a regular cake.

Cool the cake completely in the pan. Cut it into squares, put them in wide dessert bowls and top each serving with a generous dollop of sweetened whipped cream, or ice cream.

This pudding cake is good served warm, room temperature, or chilled.

SALLY'S FLOURLESS CHOCOLATE CAKE

Preheat oven to 375 degrees F., rack in the middle position.

Hannah's Note: This cake is going to fall in the center. There's just no way around it since there's no flour to hold it up. That really doesn't matter, because it's so delicious. Just be prepared to cover up the crater in the middle with plenty of whipped cream — Sally whips two cups of cream sweetened with 1/3 cup of powdered sugar, spreads it on the top, and shaves some bittersweet chocolate on top of that.

1 stick *(1/2 cup, 1/4 pound)* butter

8 ounces semi-sweet chocolate chips *(1 and 1/3 cups — I used Ghirardelli)*

4 egg yolks *(save the whites in a separate bowl for later)*

1/2 cup white *(granulated)* sugar

1/2 teaspoon rum extract *(or vanilla if you don't have rum)*

4 egg whites *(the ones you saved)*

1/4 cup white *(granulated)* sugar *(you'll use 3/4 cup in all)*

---

sweetened whipped cream to decorate top

shaved chocolate or chocolate curls to

decorate top *(optional)*
sliced or whole berries to decorate top
(optional)

Spray an 8-inch Springform pan with Pam or other nonstick cooking spray. *(An 8 1/2-inch Springform will also work, but a 9-inch is too big.)* Line the bottom of the pan with a circle of parchment paper *(wax paper will also work).* Spray the paper with Pam or other nonstick cooking spray.

In a small microwave-safe bowl, combine butter and semi-sweet chocolate chips. Melt for 1 minute on HIGH, stir, and heat for an additional 20 seconds if necessary. *(Some chocolate maintains its shape even when melted. Stir before you microwave for the additional time.)* Cover your bowl, or put it back in the microwave, to keep it warm.

In a medium bowl, beat 1/2 cup of granulated sugar with the egg yolks until they're light yellow in color. Mix in the rum extract. *(This is easy with an electric mixer, although you can do it by hand.)*

Stir a bit of the egg yolk mixture into the melted chocolate to temper it. Then add the chocolate to the egg yolk mixture and stir until it's well blended.

In a large bowl, using clean beaters, beat the egg whites until soft peaks form. Continue beating while sprinkling in the remaining 1/4 cup granulated sugar. Beat until stiff peaks form *(about 1/2 minute)*.

Stir just a bit of the egg white mixture into the bowl with the chocolate to temper it. Now add the chocolate to the bowl with the rest of the egg whites and gently fold it in with a rubber spatula. Continue folding until the mixture is a uniform chocolate color.

Pour the batter into the cake pan and smooth the top with a rubber spatula. Bake at 375 degrees F. for 35 minutes or until a wooden pick or cake tester inserted in the center comes out dry.

Cool in the pan on a wire rack for 15 minutes. Run a knife around the inside of the rim of the pan, invert the pan on a serving plate, and cool for another 10 minutes. Release the catch on the Springform pan and remove it. **DON'T PEEL OFF THE PARCHMENT PAPER UNTIL THE CAKE IS COMPLETELY COOL TO THE TOUCH.**

When you're ready to serve, fill in the crater in the center and frost the top of the cake with sweetened whipped cream. If you want it to look fancy, decorate it with chocolate shavings, chocolate curls, and/or a sprinkling of raspberries or strawberries. Slice it and serve it on dessert plates with plenty of excellent coffee.

Hannah's 2nd Note: This is really a type of chocolate soufflé and it's delicious!

SCANDINAVIAN ALMOND CAKE

Preheat oven to 350 degrees F., rack in the middle position.

Before you start to mix up this recipe, grease *(or spray with Pam or another non-stick cooking spray)* a 4-inch by 8-inch loaf pan. *(Mine was Pyrex and I measured the bottom.)*

Cut a strip of parchment paper *(or wax paper if you don't have parchment)* 8 inches wide and 16 inches long. Lay it in the pan so that the bottom is covered and the strip sticks out in little "ears" on the long sides of the pan. *(This makes for easy removal after your cake is baked.)* This will leave the two short sides of the pan uncovered, but that's okay. Press the paper down and then spray it again with Pam or another nonstick cooking spray.

1/4 cup sliced almonds *(optional — they make your cakes look pretty)*

1 stick *(1/2 cup, 1/4 pound, 4 ounces)* **salted butter**

1 and 1/4 cups white *(granulated)* **sugar**

1 egg *(I used an extra large egg)*

1/2 teaspoon baking powder

1 and 1/2 teaspoons almond extract

2/3 cup cream *(you can also use what*

Grandma Ingrid used to call "top milk" or what we now call half and half)
1 and 1/4 cups flour

If you decided to use the sliced almonds, sprinkle them in the very bottom of your paper-lined loaf pan. *(This cake is like a pineapple upside down cake — the bottom will be the top when you serve it.)*

Hannah's 1st Note: Now don't let this next step scare you. It's extremely easy, and it will keep your cakes from turning too brown around the edges.

Place the stick of butter in a one-cup Pyrex measuring cup or in a small microwave-safe bowl. Zap it for 40 seconds on HIGH, or until it's melted. *(You can also do this in a small saucepan on the stove.)* Now pour that melted butter through a fine-mesh strainer, the kind you'd use for tea *(or a larger mesh strainer lined with a double thickness of cheesecloth)*. After the melted butter has dripped through, dump the milk solids that have gathered in the strainer in the garbage *(or throw away the cheesecloth, if you've used that method)*. What you have left is clarified butter.

Set your clarified butter on the counter to

cool while you . . .

Mix the white sugar with the egg in a medium-sized bowl or in the bowl of an electric mixer. Beat them together until they're light and fluffy.

Add the baking powder and the almond extract. Mix well.

Cup your hands around the bowl with the clarified butter. If you can hold it comfortably and it's not so hot that it might cook the egg, add it to your bowl now and mix it in. If it's still too hot, wait until it's cooler and then mix it in.

Hannah's 2nd Note: In the following steps, you're going to add half of the cream and then half of the flour. You don't have to be precise and measure exactly half. Just dump in what you think is approximately half, and it'll be just fine.

Add half of the cream and mix it in.

Add half of the flour and mix it in.

Now add the rest of the cream and mix.

And then add the rest of the flour and mix thoroughly.

Pour the batter into the loaf pan you've prepared, and smooth the top with a spatula.

Bake the cake at 350 degrees F., for 50 to 60 minutes, or until a toothpick inserted in the center comes out clean.

Let the loaf pan sit on a wire rack or a cold burner for 15 minutes. Then loosen the cake from the short sides of the pan *(the sides without paper)* with a metal spatula or a knife.

Tip the cake out on a pretty platter, and remove the parchment paper. Let it cool, and then dust the top with powdered sugar if you wish.

Hannah's 3rd Note: Mother's friends, Joyce and Nancy, have special half-round loaf pans especially for baking Scandinavian Almond Cake. Joyce's cake bakes for the same length of time as mine does. Nancy's pan has a dark nonstick surface. It's heavier than Joyce's pan, and the dark surface makes it bake faster. Nancy bakes her cake for 35 to 40 minutes, or until a toothpick inserted in the center comes out clean.

STRAWBERRY SHORTCAKE SWENSEN

Serves 12 *(or 6 if they ask for second helpings)*

To make this dessert, you will need: Pound Plus Cake, three boxes of ripe strawberries, and a bowl of Hannah's Whipped Crème Fraiche. *(Pronounce it "Cremm Fresh" and everybody will think you speak French.)*

POUND PLUS CAKE

Preheat oven to 325 degrees F., rack in the middle position.

1 and 1/2 cups softened butter *(3 sticks, 12 ounces, 3/4 pound)*
2 cups white *(granulated)* sugar
4 eggs
1 cup sour cream *(you can substitute unflavored yogurt for a lighter cake)*
1/2 teaspoon baking powder

1 teaspoon vanilla

2 cups cake flour *(DO NOT SIFT — use it right out of the box)*

Hannah's Note: Pound Plus Cake must chill for 48 hours. Make it 2 days before you plan to serve it. You can also bake it, cool it, wrap it in plastic wrap and then in foil, and freeze it until you need it. This recipe makes 2 cakes. Each cake serves six people.

Generously butter and flour two 9-inch round cake pans. *(Don't use Pam or spray shortening — it won't work for this cake.)*

Cream softened butter and sugar in the bowl of an electric mixer. *(You can mix this cake by hand, but it takes some muscle.)* Add the eggs, one at a time, and beat until they're nice and fluffy. Then add the sour cream, baking powder and vanilla. Mix it all up and then add the flour, one cup at a time, and beat until the batter is smooth and has no lumps.

Pour the batter into the pans and bake at 325 degrees F. for 45 to 50 minutes. *(The cakes should be golden brown on top.)*

Cool in the pans on a rack for twenty minutes. Run a knife around the inside edges of the pans to loosen the cakes. Then turn them out on the rack.

After the cakes are completely cool, wrap each one in plastic wrap, sealing tightly. Wrap these packages in foil and store them in the refrigerator for 48 hours. Take them out an hour before you serve, but don't unwrap them until you're ready to assemble the dessert.

THE STRAWBERRIES

(Prepare these several hours before you serve.)

Wash 3 boxes of berries and remove stems. *(The easiest way to do this is to use a paring knife to cut off the top part of the berry.)* Slice all but a dozen or so, reserving the biggest and best berries to top each portion. Taste the berries and add sugar if they're too tart. Stir and refrigerate, covered tightly.

HANNAH'S WHIPPED CRÈME FRAICHE

(This will hold for several hours. Make it ahead of time and refrigerate it.)

2 cups heavy whipping cream
1/2 cup white *(granulated)* sugar
1/2 cup sour cream *(you can substitute unflavored yogurt, but it won't hold as*

well and you'll have to do it at the last minute)

1/2 cup brown sugar *(to sprinkle on top after you assemble the dessert)*

Whip the cream with the white sugar until it holds a firm peak. Test for this by shutting off the mixer, and "dotting" the surface with your spatula. Once you have firm peaks, gently fold in the sour cream. You can do this by hand or by using the slowest speed on the mixer.

ASSEMBLING STRAWBERRY SHORTCAKE SWENSEN

Cut each Pound Plus Cake into 6 pie-shaped wedges and place on dessert plates. Top with the sliced strawberries. Put several generous dollops of **Hannah's Whipped Crème Fraiche** on top and sprinkle with the brown sugar. Garnish with the whole berries you reserved. Serve and receive rave reviews.

Preheat oven to 350 degrees F., rack in the middle position.

For The Crust:

2 cups vanilla wafer cookie crumbs *(measure AFTER crushing)****
3/4 stick melted butter *(6 Tablespoons)*
1 teaspoon vanilla extract

Pour melted butter and vanilla extract over cookie crumbs. Mix with a fork until they're evenly moistened.

Cut a circle of parchment paper *(or wax paper)* to fit inside the bottom of a 9-inch Springform pan. Spray the pan with Pam or another nonstick cooking spray, set the paper circle in place, and spray with Pam again.

Place the moistened cookie crumbs in the bottom of the pan and press them down over the paper circle. Continue to press them until they reach one inch up the sides of the pan. Put the Springform pan in the freezer

***If you want a change from vanilla wafers, you can make a shortbread crust using Lorna Doone shortbread cookies. That's good, too!

for 30 minutes while you prepare the rest of the cheesecake.

FOR THE TAPIOCA:

1 can *(13.5 ounces)* coconut milk *(I used Dole)*****
2 large eggs
1/2 cup white *(granulated)* sugar
1/4 cup quick-cooking tapioca *(I used Kraft Minute Tapioca)******

In a medium-sized saucepan, off the heat, whisk the coconut milk and eggs together until they're a uniform color.

Add the sugar and the dry tapioca. Mix it all up and leave it on a cold burner for 5 minutes. You'll prepare the cheesecake topping while you wait.

FOR THE TOPPING:

2 cups sour cream
1/2 cup sugar

****You don't absolutely positively have to use coconut milk. You can substitute half and half or heavy cream if you can't find it in your store.
*****If you can't find the quick-cooking tapioca, you can still make this cheesecake. Just follow the directions on the box of regular tapioca to cook it.

1 teaspoon vanilla

Mix the sour cream, sugar, and vanilla together in a small bowl. Cover and refrigerate.

Preheat the oven to 350 degrees F., rack in the middle position. It'll have plenty of time to come up to temperature while you cook the tapioca and make the cheesecake batter.

Cook the tapioca mixture over MEDIUM-HIGH heat, stirring CONSTANTLY. *(Be careful — it's easy to burn.)* Bring it up to the boil and then pull it off the heat, give it a couple more stirs until it's no longer boiling, and let it cool while you make the cheesecake batter.

FOR THE CHEESECAKE BATTER:

1 and 1/2 cups white *(granulated)* sugar
3 eight-ounce packages cream cheese at room temperature *(total 24 ounces)*
4 eggs
1 teaspoon vanilla
1 teaspoon coconut extract******

******If you don't have coconut extract, you can substitute vanilla extract, bringing the total up to 2 teaspoons.

Place the sugar in the bowl of an electric mixer. Add the blocks of softened cream cheese and whip it up at medium speed until it's smooth.

Add the tapioca mixture a spoonful at a time, mixing it all into the batter.

Feel the sides of the mixing bowl. If the contents aren't so hot they'll cook the eggs, add them now, one at a time, beating thoroughly after each addition.

Shut the mixer off, scrape down the bowl, and then turn it back on again to add the vanilla and the coconut extracts.

All this should have taken you 30 minutes. Even if you're faster than I am, take your crust out of the freezer now; 10 minutes more or less won't make a difference.

Pour the batter you just made on top of the chilled crust, set the pan on a cookie sheet to catch any drips *(I use a cookie sheet with sides)*, and bake it at 350 degrees F. for 70 minutes. Remove the pan from the oven, but DON'T SHUT OFF THE OVEN.

Starting in the center, spoon the sour cream topping over the top of the cheesecake, spreading it out to within a half-inch of the rim. Return the pan to the oven and bake for an additional 15 minutes.

Cool the cheesecake in the pan on a wire rack. When the pan is cool enough to pick up with your bare hands, place it in the refrigerator and chill it, uncovered, for at least 8 hours.

To serve, run a knife around the inside rim of the pan, release the Springform catch, and lift off the rim. Place a piece of waxed paper on a flat plate and tip it upside down over the top of your cheesecake. Invert the cheesecake so that it rests on the paper.

Carefully pry off the bottom of the Springform pan and remove the paper from the bottom crust.

Invert a serving platter over the bottom crust of your cheesecake. Flip the cheesecake right side up, take off the top plate, and remove the waxed paper.

If you'd like to decorate your cheesecake, you can sprinkle on toasted coconut, place slices of fresh fruit around the edge, dot the top with berries in season, or sprinkle it with white chocolate or semi-sweet chocolate shavings. You could also melt either white chocolate or semi-sweet chocolate chips and

drizzle them in threads across the top. Or
. . . if you're like Lisa and handy with a pastry bag, you could decorate the top of your cheesecake with whipped cream rosettes in a white-on-white design. Your choices are limited only by your own imagination.

"I'm dying to hear about Andrea's lemon pie experience," Claire said once she'd flipped through the pie, cake, and frosting recipes.

"You said she followed your recipe?" Edna asked.

"That's right."

"The same recipe we have in here?" Grandma Knudson asked.

"Exactly the same."

"But that's the recipe you gave me to use down at the cafe," Rose said, looking confused. "And everybody loves your Lemon Meringue Pie."

Andrea gave a little groan. "Well, some of us can cook and some of us can't. And I'm in the group that can't. I thought I was following Hannah's directions exactly, but I goofed. Tell them, Hannah. It's okay."

Hannah began to smile. "It was a simple mistake for someone just learning how to cook. Andrea took everything literally.

When the list of ingredients called for four whole eggs, she set four whole eggs out on the kitchen counter. And when the recipe read, *Beat the egg yolks with the whole eggs in the top of the double boiler,* Andrea did exactly that."

"But . . . what's wrong with that?" Ellie asked.

Andrea started to laugh. "It's like Hannah said, I took everything literally. I put the egg yolks in the top of the double boiler and then I added the four whole eggs."

"Oh, no!" Claire said, covering her face with her hands. "You didn't!"

"She did," Hannah took up the story. "It was heartbreaking. Andrea was so proud of herself for baking a pie. It was Bill's birthday and lemon meringue pie is his favorite. We all got together for dinner at my place and I served Andrea's pie for dessert. I was impressed when I saw it. The meringue was absolutely perfect."

"If I'd known then what I know now, we would have just eaten the meringue and dumped the rest of the pie," Andrea commented.

"But we didn't," Hannah continued, "and Andrea did a beautiful job of slicing it and putting it on the antique dessert plates Mother gave me."

Andrea chuckled. "And then they tasted it. And Mother asked me if I'd added some chopped nuts to the recipe."

"And Andrea said no, she'd followed my recipe exactly. But everyone agreed that there was something crunchy in the lemon filling."

"Then I said, *No, that was probably the eggshells,*" Andrea confessed, *"And maybe I should have broken them up before I stirred the whole eggs into the lemon filling."*

There was silence for a moment, and then everyone started to laugh. Andrea laughed the hardest of all, and Hannah was glad she was no longer embarrassed about her baking mistake.

"I've got one, too. It's the reason I haven't tackled a cookie recipe again," Claire announced.

"What happened?" Lisa asked her.

"It was the first cookie recipe Grandma Knudson ever gave me," Claire told them, glancing over to smile at her new husband's grandmother. "Bob was taking Grandma to the doctor and I promised them that I was going to bake cookies while they were gone.

"I read through the recipe, got out all the ingredients, and got ready to do the first step. It said, *Cream the butter with the sugars,* and that stopped me cold."

"But why?" Alice asked the question.

"Because it didn't say how much cream to use!" Claire said.

Hannah started to laugh. She couldn't help it. It was true that some baking terminology could be confusing.

"Did Grandma bake your cookies for today?" Carrie asked sympathetically.

Claire shook her head. "My friend Leigh sent me a recipe that's so easy even I can make it. They're called Lime Balls, and they're really good."

"How about you, Andrea?" Carrie asked. "Did Hannah bake yours?"

"No, I did," Andrea looked proud. "You told me you really liked the lemon cookies I brought last year, the ones made from the cake mix, so I changed the recipe and experimented a little, and they're called Double Chocolate Puffs."

As the ladies began to discuss the cookies they'd brought for the cookie exchange, Hannah poured more coffee while Lisa sliced the cheesecake and served it. It was really too bad their youngest sister, Michelle, wasn't here. She was crazy about cheesecake, and she baked like a dream. She'd told Hannah she would try to make it now that Macalester College was in recess for the holidays, but obviously something had come up and she hadn't caught the early morning bus from Minneapolis.

Hannah turned around at the sound of footsteps on the stairs. "Michelle!" she called out. "You're just in time for Tapioca Cheesecake."

"Great! I could use a gallon of hot coffee, too. The bus got stuck just outside of Elk River and we had to wait for a replacement bus." Michelle held up a large tote bag. "I'm lucky my cookies got here at all. We were still waiting for the second bus at lunchtime and I thought they'd suffer the same fate as some of the Donner party."

"Michelle!" Delores chided her, but she was having trouble holding back a smile.

"Anyway . . . I need about a gallon of hot coffee and I'd love a piece of that cheese-cake. And then I want to know what kind of cookies everyone brought."

Cookie Exchange List of New Cookies & Bar Cookies

*Almond Fudge Cookies —
Rose McDermott

*Bourbon Brownies — *Bertie Straub*

*Cranberry Pineapple Drop Cookies —
Lisa Beeseman

*Chocolate Date Drops —
Edna Ferguson

*Double Chocolate Puffs (Chocolate
Whippersnappers) — *Andrea Todd*

*Heavenly Eggnog Cookies
— *Alice Vogel*

*Kiss My Grits Cookies
— *Hannah Swensen*

*Leigh's Lime Balls — *Claire Rodgers
Knudson*

*Lemon Softies
— *Carrie Rhodes Flensburg*

*Mincemeat Cookies
— *Grandma Knudson*

*Minty Marvels — *Florence Evans*

*Norwegian Chocolate Pizza
— *Ellie Kuehne*

*Raspberry Vanilla Swirls
— *Michelle Swensen*

ALL-NIGHTER COOKIES

Preheat oven to 350 degrees F., rack in the middle position.

Hannah's Note: Florence didn't have any bananas and I ended up taking one of Edna's shortcuts in this recipe. If you don't like shortcuts and want to do this the original way, use 2/3 cup very ripe, almost all black on the outside, pureed bananas instead of the baby food bananas and banana pudding mix. The other change you have to make is to use 4 cups flour instead of 3 and 1/2. The dough will be stickier and you'll have to chill it for at least 4 hours in order to make the dough balls. I made these cookies both ways, and Mother was the only one who could tell the difference. *(I still think it was a lucky guess.)*

1 and 1/2 cups melted butter *(3 sticks, 12 ounces, 3/4 pound)*

1 cup white *(granulated)* sugar

1 cup firmly packed brown sugar

2 beaten eggs *(just whip them up with a fork)*

1 teaspoon baking soda

1/2 teaspoon salt

1/2 cup baby food mashed bananas *(I used Gerber)*

5.1 ounce package banana cream pudding mix *(NOT sugar free) (I used Jell-O, 6-serving package)*

3 and 1/2 cups flour *(no sifting — pack it down in the cup when you measure)*

1 cup chopped nuts *(I used salted peanuts)*

2 cups peanut butter chips *(one 10-ounce package will do just fine)*

1/2 cup white *(granulated)* sugar for later

Melt the butter in large microwave bowl. Stir in the sugars, beaten eggs, baking soda, and salt.

Measure out a half-cup of baby food bananas and add them, along with the package of dry pudding mix. *(Make sure your baby food bananas don't have anything else, like cereal, added to them!)*

Mix in the flour by one-cup increments. Add the nuts and then the peanut butter chips. Stir until everything is incorporated.

Roll the dough into walnut-sized balls with your hands. *(If it's too sticky, chill it for 30 minutes or so, and try again.)*

Put 1/2 cup white sugar in a small bowl and roll the balls in it. Place the dough balls on a greased cookie sheet, 12 to a standard-sized sheet. Press them down with the heel of your hand, or with a metal spatula sprayed with Pam or other nonstick cooking spray.

Bake the cookies for 10 to 12 minutes at 350 degrees F., or until they're lightly golden in color. Let them cool for 2 minutes on the cookie sheet and then move them to a wire rack to finish cooling.

These cookies freeze well. Roll them up in foil, and place the rolls in a freezer bag.

Michelle asked for this recipe after Lonnie Murphy tasted them at The Cookie Jar. She says she's going to freeze some so he'll have them when he visits her, but she's going to mark the package "Raw Fish Patties" so her roommates won't get into them.

Yield: Approximately 8 to 10 dozen, depending on cookie size.

*ALMOND FUDGE COOKIES

Preheat oven to 325 degrees F., rack in the middle position.

2 cups melted butter *(4 sticks, 16 ounces, one pound)*

4 one-ounce squares semi-sweet chocolate *(I used Baker's)*

2 cups powdered sugar *(not sifted)*

1 cup white *(granulated)* sugar

2 eggs

1 teaspoon almond extract

1 teaspoon vanilla

1 teaspoon baking soda

1 teaspoon salt

4 and 1/4 cups flour *(not sifted — pack it down when you measure it)*

1/2 cup white sugar in a small bowl *(for later)*

7 to 8 dozen blanched almonds *(one to decorate each cookie)*

Melt the butter and chocolate squares in a saucepan over low heat, stirring constantly, or in the microwave. *(I melted mine in a quart measuring cup in the microwave on HIGH for 3 minutes.)* Once the butter and chocolate are melted, stir them smooth, transfer them to a large mixing bowl, and add the powdered and white sugars. Stir thoroughly and set the mixture aside to cool.

When the mixture is cool enough so it won't cook the eggs, add the eggs, one at a time, stirring after each addition. *(You can use an electric mixer at this point if you like.)* Then add in the almond and vanilla extracts, baking soda, and salt. Mix it all up thoroughly.

Add the flour in half-cup increments, mixing after each addition. You don't have to be precise — just divide your flour into roughly 4 parts. *(One very important reason for adding flour in increments is so that the whole mountain of flour won't sit there on top of your bowl and spill out all over the place when you try to stir it in.)*

Once the dough has been thoroughly mixed, roll one-inch dough balls with your fingers. *(You can also use a 2-teaspoon scooper to form the dough balls.)* Dip the balls in the bowl of white sugar and roll them around until they're coated.

Place the dough balls on a greased cookie sheet *(I usually spray mine with Pam or another nonstick cooking spray),* 12 dough balls to a standard-sized sheet. Flatten the dough balls a bit with your impeccably clean palm so that they won't roll off the cookie sheet on the way to the oven. *(Oh, yes. That's happened to me!)* Press one almond into the center of each cookie.

Bake the Almond Fudge Cookies at 325 degrees for 10 to 15 minutes. *(Mine took 12 minutes.)* Cool them on the cookie sheet for 2 minutes, and then remove the cookies to a wire rack to finish cooling.

Yield: Approximately 7 to 8 dozen mouth-watering cookies.

ALMOND KISSES

Preheat oven to 350 degrees F., rack in the middle position.

1 and 1/2 cups melted butter *(3 sticks)*
2 cups white sugar
1 teaspoon vanilla extract
1 teaspoon almond extract
1/8 cup molasses *(2 Tablespoons)*
1 and 1/2 teaspoons baking soda
1 teaspoon baking powder
1 teaspoon salt *(if you use salted almonds, cut the salt to 1/2 teaspoon)*
1 and 1/2 cups finely ground almonds *(grind them up in your food processor with the steel blade — they don't have to be blanched)*
2 beaten eggs *(just whip them up with a fork)*
4 cups flour *(no need to sift)*
13-ounce bag Hershey's Kisses *(or small squares of milk chocolate)*

Microwave the butter in your mixing bowl to melt it. Add the sugar, vanilla and almond extracts, and molasses. Stir until it's blended, then add the baking soda, baking powder and salt. Mix well.

Grind up the almonds in your food processor. Measure AFTER grinding. Add them to the bowl and mix. Pour in the beaten eggs and stir. Then add the flour and mix until all the ingredients are thoroughly blended.

Let the dough firm up for a few minutes. Then form it into walnut-sized balls and arrange them on a greased cookie sheet, 12 to a standard sheet.

Cut the Hershey's Kisses in half *(from the top down, so that each half has a point and a base)*. Press the halves into the middle of your cookie balls, cut side down. They'll look pretty on top as a yummy decoration. If you want to splurge a little, press a whole Hershey's Kiss into the center of the dough ball, base down and point sticking up. *(If you do splurge, you'll need double the amount of Hershey's Kisses or squares of chocolate. If your kids help you unwrap the Kisses, you should probably triple the amount!)*

Bake at 350 degrees F. for 10 minutes, or until the edges are just beginning to turn golden. *(Don't worry — The Hershey's Kisses won't melt.)* Cool on the cookie sheet for 2 minutes and then remove to a wire rack to finish cooling.

Yield: Makes 10 to 12 dozen cookies — if

that's too many, just cut the whole recipe in half. And if you have any Kisses left over, the baker deserves a treat!

ANGEL KISSES

Preheat oven to 275 degrees F., rack in the middle position.

(That's two hundred seventy-five degrees F., not a misprint.)

3 egg whites *(save the yolks in the refrigerator to add to scrambled eggs)*
1/4 teaspoon cream of tartar
1/2 teaspoon vanilla extract
1/4 teaspoon salt
1 cup white *(granulated)* **sugar**
2 Tablespoons flour *(that's 1/8 cup)*

---

approximately 30 Hershey's Kisses, unwrapped *(or any other small chocolate candy)*

Separate the egg whites and let them come up to room temperature. This will give you more volume when you beat them.

Prepare your cookie sheets by lining them with parchment paper *(works best)* or brown parcel-wrapping paper. Spray the paper with Pam or other nonstick cooking spray and dust it lightly with flour.

Hannah's Note: These are a lot easier to make with an electric mixer, but you can also do them by hand with a copper bowl and a whisk.

Beat the egg whites with the cream of tartar, vanilla, and salt until they are stiff enough to hold a soft peak. Add the cup of sugar gradually, sprinkling it in by quarter cups and beating hard for ten seconds or so after each sprinkling. Sprinkle in the flour and mix it in at low speed, or fold in with an angel food cake whisk.

Drop little mounds of dough on your paper-lined cookie sheet. If you place four mounds in a row and you have four rows, you'll end up with 16 cookies per standard-sized sheet.

Place one Hershey's Kiss, point up, in the center of each mound. Push the candies down, but not all the way to the bottom. *(You don't want the chocolate to actually touch the parchment paper.)* Drop another little mound of meringue on top of the candy to cover it up.

Bake at 275 degrees F. for approximately 40 minutes, or until the meringue part of the cookie is slightly golden and dry to the touch.

Cool on the paper-lined cookie sheet by setting it on a wire rack. When the cookies are completely cool, peel them carefully from the paper and store them in an airtight container in a dry place. *(A cupboard shelf is fine, just NOT the refrigerator!)*

Yield: 3 to 4 dozen cookies with a nice chocolate surprise in the center.

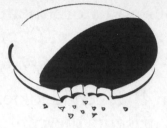

BLACK AND WHITES

DO NOT preheat oven, dough must chill before baking.

- **2 cups chocolate chips** *(12-ounce package)*
- **3/4 cup butter** *(1 and 1/2 sticks)*
- **2 cups brown sugar** *(or white sugar with a scant 2 Tablespoons molasses mixed in)*
- **4 eggs**
- **2 teaspoons vanilla extract**
- **2 teaspoons baking powder**
- **1 teaspoon salt**
- **2 cups flour** *(not sifted — pack it down in the cup when you measure it)*
- **1/2 cup powdered** *(confectioner's)* **sugar in a small bowl for later**

Melt the chocolate chips with the butter. *(Microwave on high power for 2 minutes, then stir until smooth.)*

Mix in the sugar and let the mixture cool.

Add the eggs, one at the time, mixing well after each addition.

Mix in the vanilla extract, baking powder, and salt.

Add the flour, one cup at a time, mixing after each addition.

Cover the bowl with plastic wrap and chill the dough for at least 4 hours. *(Overnight is even better.)*

When you're ready to bake, preheat the oven to 350 degrees F., rack in the middle position.

Roll walnut-sized dough balls with your hands. *(Messy — wear plastic gloves if you wish.)* Drop the dough balls into a bowl with the powdered sugar and roll them around until they're coated. *(If the dough gets too warm, stick it back in the refrigerator until you can handle it again.)*

Place the dough balls on a greased cookie sheet, 12 to a standard sheet. *(They will flatten when they bake.)*

Bake the cookies at 350 degrees F. for 12 to 14 minutes. Cool on the cookie sheet for

2 minutes, then remove to wire rack to cool completely.

Yield: Approximately 5 to 6 dozen, depending on cookie size.

BOGGLES

Preheat oven to 350 degrees F., rack in the middle position.

2 cups butter *(4 sticks, 16 ounces, 1 pound)*

2 cups brown sugar

2 cups white *(granulated)* sugar

1 teaspoon baking powder

1 teaspoon baking soda

1 teaspoon salt

4 eggs, beaten *(just whip them up in a glass with a fork)*

2 teaspoons vanilla extract

1/2 teaspoon cinnamon

1/4 teaspoon nutmeg *(freshly ground is best)*

4 cups flour *(pack it down in the cup when you measure it)*

3 cups sweetened dried cranberries *(Craisins or another brand)****

3 cups rolled oats *(uncooked oatmeal — I used Quaker Quick 1-Minute)*

Preheat oven to 350 degrees. Melt butter in large microwave-safe bowl. Add sugars

***If you can't find the cranberries where you live you can substitute any chopped dried fruit such as dates, apricots, peaches, etc.

and let cool a bit. Add the baking powder, baking soda, salt, eggs, vanilla, and spices. Add flour and mix. Then add the cranberries and oats, and mix everything up. The dough will be quite stiff.

Drop by teaspoon onto a greased cookie sheet, 12 cookies to a sheet.

Bake at 350 degrees F. for 12 to 15 minutes. Cool on the cookie sheet for 2 minutes. Remove to rack until cool.

Yield: 10 to 12 dozen, depending on cookie size.

These freeze well if you roll them in foil and put them in a freezer bag.

BUTTER-SCOTCHIES

Preheat oven to 350 degrees F., rack in the middle position.

1 cup butter *(2 sticks, 1/2 pound — melted)*
1 cup brown sugar
1 cup white *(granulated)* sugar
2 eggs — beaten *(just whip them up in a glass with a fork)*
1 teaspoon baking powder
1/2 teaspoon baking soda
1/2 teaspoon salt
1 teaspoon vanilla extract
2 cups flour *(don't sift — pack it down in the cup when you measure it)*
2 cups butterscotch chips *(an 11-ounce package will do just fine)*
1 and 1/2 cups rolled oats *(uncooked oatmeal — I used Quaker Quick 1-Minute rolled oats)*

Melt the butter in a large microwave-safe bowl. *(About 90 seconds on HIGH.)*

Add the sugars and let it cool a bit. Then add the beaten eggs, baking powder, baking soda, salt, and vanilla extract.

Mix in the flour and then the butterscotch chips. Add the rolled oats and mix it in thoroughly.

Let the dough rest, uncovered, for 10 minutes to allow the butter to solidify.

You can either drop this dough by rounded teaspoons onto a greased cookie sheet, 12 cookies to a sheet, or roll the dough in balls with your hands and place them on the cookie sheet, pushing them down just a bit so they won't roll off on their way to the oven. *(I prefer rolling the dough balls — the cookies turn out nice and round.)*

Bake at 350 degrees F. for 12 to 15 minutes. Cool on the cookie sheet for 2 minutes and then remove the cookies to a wire rack to cool completely.

These cookies freeze really well if you roll them in foil and put them in a freezer bag.

Yield: This recipe makes approximately 8 to 9 dozen cookies, depending on cookie size.

Hannah's Note: Mother's friend Carrie just loves these when I use one cup of butterscotch chips and one cup of milk chocolate chips.

CANDY CANE COOKIES

Preheat oven to 375 degrees F., rack in the middle position.

THE TOPPING:

1/2 cup hard peppermint candy, crushed***
1/2 cup white *(granulated)* sugar

THE COOKIE DOUGH:

1 cup softened butter *(2 sticks, 8 ounces, 1/2 pound)*
1 cup powdered *(confectioner's)* sugar
1 beaten egg *(just mix it up in a cup with a fork)*
1/4 teaspoon salt
1 and 1/2 teaspoons almond extract
1 teaspoon vanilla extract
2 and 1/2 cups flour *(pack it down in the cup when you measure it)*
1/2 teaspoon red food coloring

***You can use round red-and-white peppermint candies that look like buttons, regular candy canes, or any other peppermint candy that you can crush into small separate pieces. You could even use pastel mints, the tiny little "pillows" you'll find in a pretty bowl right next to the mixed nuts at almost every Lake Eden wedding reception.

Hannah's 1st Note: Lisa and I prefer to use the big round peppermint candies that practically melt in your mouth because they're a lot easier to crush.

To make the topping, place the peppermint candies in a sturdy plastic bag and crush them with a rolling pin or a mallet. You'll need 1/2 cup to top your cookies.

In a small bowl, mix the half-cup crushed peppermint candies with the half-cup white sugar. Set the bowl aside for now.

To make the dough, you'll need two bowls, a small and a medium-sized.

In the medium-sized bowl, combine the softened butter, powdered sugar, beaten egg, salt, and extracts. Stir until they're well combined. Then add the flour in half-cup increments, stirring after each addition.

Round up the dough and divide it in half. Put one half in the small bowl and cover it with plastic wrap so it won't dry out. This will be the white part of your Candy Cane Cookies.

Blend the red food coloring into the other half ***(the dough in the medium-sized bowl)***. Mix it until it's a uniform color. This will be the red part of your Candy Cane Cookies.

Lightly flour a breadboard or rectangular cutting board and place it on your counter. You'll use this surface to roll the dough.

Remove a teaspoon of white dough from the small bowl and roll it into a four-inch long roll by pushing it back and forth with the palms of your impeccably clean hands.

Remove a teaspoon of red dough from the bowl and form a similar four-inch long roll.

Place the two rolls side by side on the board, hold them together, and twist them like a rope so that the resulting cookie resembles a candy cane. Pinch the ends together slightly so they won't separate.

Place the cookie on an **UNGREASED** standard-sized cookie sheet and bend down the top to make a crook. You should be able to get four Candy Cane Cookies in a row and three rows to a cookie sheet.

Hannah's 2nd Note: The first time we made these, we rolled out a dozen white parts first and then we rolled out a dozen red parts. Our dough got too dry sitting on the board and the red and white twists we formed came apart. Now we shape these cookies one at a time and keep the dough bowls covered with plastic wrap when we're not rolling. I'd really recommend forming these cookies one at a time.

Once you've completed twelve cookies, cover your bowls of dough with plastic wrap. You don't want them to dry out between batches.

Before you put your first pan of cookies in the oven to bake, spread out a length of foil and place a wire rack on top of it. This will hold your hot cookies when you decorate them with the peppermint candy and sugar topping. Once the cookies are completely cool, they can be transferred to a foil-lined box or a platter and you can round up any topping that's fallen through the rack to use again.

Bake your cookies at 375 degrees F. for 9 minutes. *(They should be just beginning to turn golden when you remove them from the oven.)*

Immediately remove the cookies from the baking sheet and place them on the wire rack. Sprinkle them with the mixture of candy and sugar while they are still very hot.

Continue to roll, shape, bake, and top your cookies until you run out of dough.

Yield: Approximately 4 dozen cookies, depending on cookie size.

CAPPUCCINO ROYALES

Preheat oven to 350 degrees F., rack in the middle position.

2 cups melted butter *(4 sticks, 16 ounces, 1 pound)*

1/4 cup instant coffee powder *(I used Folger's)*

2 teaspoons vanilla extract

2 teaspoons brandy or rum extract***

3 cups white *(granulated)* **sugar******

3 beaten eggs *(just whip them up in a glass with a fork)*

2 teaspoons baking soda

1 teaspoon baking powder

3 cups milk chocolate chips

5 and 1/2 cups flour *(don't sift — pack it down in the measuring cup)*

Melt the butter in a large microwave-safe bowl at 3 minutes on HIGH. Or melt it in a saucepan over LOW heat on the stovetop, and then transfer it to a mixing bowl.

***If you can't find rum or brandy extract at your store, you can substitute vanilla — that will give you a total of 4 teaspoons of vanilla extract.

****If you prefer a sweeter cookie, roll the dough balls in extra granulated sugar and flatten before baking.

Mix in the instant coffee powder, vanilla extract, and rum or brandy extract. Stir until the coffee powder has dissolved.

Add the sugar, beaten eggs, baking soda, and baking powder. Mix well.

Stir in the milk chocolate chips. Mix until they're evenly distributed.

Add the flour in roughly one cup increments, stirring after each addition. Mix until the flour is thoroughly incorporated.

Form walnut-sized dough balls with your fingers. Roll them in a small bowl with granulated sugar if you decided you wanted them sweeter.

Place the dough balls on a greased cookie sheet, 12 cookies to a standard-sized sheet. *(I used Pam to grease my cookie sheet, but any nonstick cooking spray will do.)*

Flatten the dough balls with the back of a metal spatula or with the palm of your impeccably clean hand.

Bake the cookies at 350 degrees F. for 9 to 11 minutes. Let them cool on the cookie sheet for 2 minutes, and then transfer the cookies to a wire rack to complete cooling.

Yield: 12 to 14 dozen cookies *(depending on cookie size)*.

Hannah's Note: These cookies freeze well if you have any left over.

CASHEW CRISPS

Preheat oven to 350 degrees F., rack in the middle position.

- **1 and 1/2 cups melted butter** *(3 sticks, 12 ounces, 3/4 pound)*
- **2 cups white** *(granulated)* **sugar**
- **2 teaspoons vanilla extract**
- **1/8 cup molasses** *(2 Tablespoons)*
- **1 and 1/2 teaspoons baking soda**
- **1 teaspoon baking powder**
- **1/2 teaspoon salt**
- **1 and 1/2 cups finely ground salted cashews** *(grind them up in your food processor with the steel blade — measure AFTER grinding)*
- **2 beaten eggs** *(just whip them up with a fork)*
- **3 cups flour** *(no need to sift — pack it down in the cup when you measure it)*

Microwave the butter in your mixing bowl to melt it. Add the sugar, the vanilla extract, and the molasses. Stir until it's blended, then add the baking soda, baking powder and salt. Mix well.

Grind up the cashews in your food processor. Measure AFTER grinding. Add them to the bowl and mix. Pour in the beaten eggs and stir. Then add the flour in one-cup increments, stirring after each addition. Mix until all the ingredients are thoroughly blended.

Let the dough sit for a few minutes to firm up. Then use your fingers to form the dough into small walnut-sized balls. Arrange the dough balls on a greased cookie sheet, 12 to a standard sheet. *(These dough balls spread out so make them fairly small. If the dough is too sticky to form into balls, chill it for twenty or thirty minutes in the refrigerator and then try again. Chilling it overnight is fine, too.)*

Flatten the balls slightly with a spatula or the palm of your impeccably clean hand, just enough so that they won't roll off when you put them in the oven. *(Don't laugh — it's happened!)*

Bake at 350 degrees F. for 10 to 12 minutes, or until the edges turn golden brown. Cool on the cookie sheet for 2 minutes, then remove the cookies to a wire rack to finish cooling.

These cookies freeze well if you roll them up in foil and place them in a freezer bag.

Yield: Approximately 10 dozen delicious cookies, depending on cookie size.

CHERRY WINKS

Preheat oven to 375 degrees F., rack in the middle position.

1 cup melted butter *(2 sticks, 8 ounces, 1/2 pound)*
1 cup white *(granulated)* sugar
2 beaten eggs *(just whip them up in a glass with a fork)*
1 teaspoon vanilla extract
3 Tablespoons cherry juice *(from the maraschino cherries called for below)*
1 teaspoon baking powder
1/2 teaspoon baking soda
1/2 teaspoon salt
1 and 1/2 cups chopped pecans *(measure AFTER chopping)*
2 cups all-purpose flour *(not sifted — pack it down in the cup when you measure it)*

---

4 cups corn flakes
1 small jar of maraschino cherries for a garnish

Melt the butter and add the white sugar. Stir well.

Mix in the eggs, vanilla extract, cherry juice, baking powder, baking soda, and salt.

Stir in the chopped pecans.

Add the flour in one-cup increments, mixing after each addition.

Crush the corn flakes and put them in a small bowl. Four cups of corn flakes will yield approximately 2 cups of crushed corn flakes. *(I put them in a plastic bag, seal it, and then crush them with my fingers.)*

Form walnut-sized dough balls with your impeccably clean hands. *(If the dough is too sticky, chill it for a half hour or so and then try it again.)* Roll the dough balls in the crushed corn flakes and place them on a greased cookie sheet, 12 to a standard sheet. Smush them down a bit so they won't roll off on their way to the oven.

Cut the cherries into quarters and place one on the top of each cookie. Press the cherry down with the tip of your finger.

Bake at 375 degrees F. for 10 to 12 minutes, or until nicely browned. Cool on the cookie sheet for 2 minutes, and then transfer the cookies to a wire rack to finish cooling.

Yield: 6 to 7 dozen pretty and delicious cookies, depending on cookie size.

Hannah's Note: These cookies freeze well. They also hold up well for packaging and shipping.

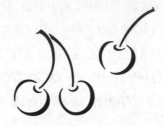

CHIPPERS

Preheat oven to 350 degrees F., rack in the middle position.

1 and 1/2 cups softened butter *(3 sticks, 3/4 pound, 12 ounces)*
1 and 1/2 cups white *(granulated)* **sugar**
2 egg yolks
1/2 teaspoon salt
2 teaspoons vanilla extract
2 and 1/2 cups all-purpose flour *(no need to sift — pack it down in the cup when you measure it)*
1 and 1/2 cups finely crushed plain salted potato chips *(measure AFTER crushing)*
1 and 1/2 cups finely chopped pecans *(measure AFTER chopping)*
1/2 teaspoon finely grated lemon zest *(optional) (zest is just the colored part of the peel, not the white)*

1/3 cup white *(granulated)* **sugar for a topping**
approximately 5 dozen pecan halves for decoration

Hannah's 1st Note: Use regular potato chips, the thin salty ones. Don't use baked chips, or rippled chips, or chips with the peels on, or kettle fried, or flavored, or anything that's supposed to be better for you than those wonderfully greasy, salty old-fashioned potato chips.

In a large mixing bowl, beat the butter, sugar, egg yolks, salt, and vanilla until they're light and fluffy. *(You can do this by hand, but it's a lot easier with an electric mixer.)*

Add the flour, one cup or so at a time, mixing after each addition.

Mix in the crushed potato chips, chopped pecans, and lemon zest *(if you decided to use it)*. Mix thoroughly.

Form one-inch dough balls with your impeccably clean hands and place the dough balls on an UNGREASED cookie sheet, 12 to a standard-sized sheet.

Place the 1/3 cup of sugar in a small bowl. Spray the bottom of a glass with Pam or another nonstick cooking spray, dip it in the sugar, and use it to flatten each dough ball. *(Dip the glass in the sugar for each ball.)* Place a pecan half in the center of each cookie and press it down slightly.

Bake at 350 degrees F., for 10 to 12 minutes, or until the cookies are starting to turn golden at the edges. Let them cool on the cookie sheet for 2 minutes and then remove them to a wire rack to cool completely.

Yield: Approximately 5 dozen yummy, crunchy cookies, depending on cookie size.

Hannah's 2nd Note: Mother loves these when I use orange zest instead of lemon zest. Since the orange flavor isn't as strong as the lemon, I use one whole teaspoon of orange zest when I bake Chippers for her. I also substitute one teaspoon orange extract for the vanilla.

CHOCOLATE ALMOND TOAST

Preheat oven to 350 degrees F., rack in the middle position.

1 and 1/2 cups melted butter *(3 sticks, 12 ounces, 3/4 pound)*

1 cup cocoa powder *(unsweetened)*

2 and 1/2 cups brown sugar

5 large eggs, beaten *(just whip them up in a glass with a fork)*

4 teaspoons baking soda

1 teaspoon salt

2 teaspoons vanilla extract

6 cups flour *(not sifted — pack it down in the cup when you measure it)*

1 cup slivered almonds

Melt the butter and mix in the cocoa until it's thoroughly blended. Stir in the brown sugar. Let it cool slightly and then mix in the beaten eggs. Add the soda, salt, and vanilla. Stir until well blended. Add the flour and slivered almonds, and mix thoroughly.

Pat the dough into free form loaves, one inch high, 5 or 6 inches long, and 3 inches wide. Place them on a greased cookie sheet and bake them at 350 degrees F. for 40 minutes.

Cool the loaves on the cookie sheets for approximately 5 minutes and then slice them *(just like bread)* into one-inch-thick pieces with a sharp knife. *(The end pieces don't need more baking — save them to dunk in your coffee while the rest are baking.)* Place them on their cut sides on the greased cookie sheets. Bake the slices an additional 5 minutes, flip them over to expose the other cut side, and bake them for an additional 10 minutes. Let them cool on the cookie sheets for 2 minutes and then remove them to a wire rack to complete cooling.

These are great dunking cookies. If you want to make them look like frosted biscotti, just dip the tops in melted chips (*I used milk chocolate)*, set them on a piece of wax paper, and refrigerate them to set the chocolate.

Yield: Approximately 3 dozen, depending on cookie size.

CHOCOLATE CHIP CRUNCH COOKIES

Preheat oven to 350 degrees F., rack in the middle position.

1 cup salted butter *(2 sticks, 1/2 pound — melted)*

1 cup white *(granulated)* **sugar**

1 cup brown sugar *(pack it down in the cup)*

2 teaspoons baking soda

1 teaspoon salt

2 teaspoons vanilla

2 beaten eggs *(you can just beat them up in a cup with a fork)*

2 and 1/2 cups flour *(not sifted — pack it down in the measuring cup)*

2 cups corn flakes

1 to 2 cups chocolate chips

Melt the butter, add the sugars, and stir them all together in a large mixing bowl. Add the soda, salt, vanilla, and beaten eggs. Mix well. Then add the flour and stir it in. Measure out the corn flakes and crush them with your hands. Then add them to your bowl, along with the chocolate chips. Mix everything up thoroughly.

Let the dough sit on the counter for a minute or two to rest. *(It doesn't really need to rest, but you probably do.)*

Form the dough into walnut-sized balls with your fingers and place them on a greased cookie sheet, 12 to a standard sheet. *(I used Pam to grease my cookie sheets.)* Press the dough balls down just a bit with your impeccably clean hand so they won't roll off on the way to the oven.

Bake at 350 degrees F. for 10 to 12 minutes. Cool on the cookie sheet for 2 minutes, then remove the cookies to a wire rack until they're completely cool. *(The rack is important — it makes them crisp.)*

Yield: Approximately 6 to 8 dozen, depending on cookie size.

Hannah's Note: If your cookies spread out too much in the oven, either chill the dough in the refrigerator before baking, or turn the dough out on a floured board and knead in approximately 1/3 cup more flour.

CHOCOLATE COVERED CHERRY DELIGHTS

Preheat oven to 350 degrees F., rack in the middle position.

- 1 cup melted butter *(2 sticks, 8 ounces, 1/2 pound)*
- 2 cups white *(granulated)* sugar
- 2 eggs, beaten *(just whip them up in a glass with a fork)*
- 1/2 teaspoon baking powder
- 1/2 teaspoon baking soda
- 1/2 teaspoon salt
- 2 teaspoons vanilla extract
- 1 cup cocoa powder *(unsweetened — for baking)*
- 3 cups flour *(not sifted — pack it down in the cup when you measure it)*
- 2 small, 10-oz. jars of maraschino cherries***

- 1 pkg. chocolate chips *(12-oz. pkg. — 2 cups)*
- 1/2 cup sweetened condensed milk *(that's sweetened condensed, NOT evaporated)*

Melt the butter and mix in the white sugar.

***When you drain the cherries, reserve the juice to use in the frosting.

Set it aside on the counter to cool.

When the mixture has cooled to a temperature that won't cook the eggs, stir in the eggs and mix thoroughly.

Add the baking powder, baking soda, salt, vanilla extract, and cocoa, stirring after each addition.

Add the flour in one-cup increments, mixing after each addition. *(The dough will be stiff and a bit crumbly.)*

Drain the maraschino cherries into a strainer over a bowl to reserve the juice. Remove the cherry stems.

Pat the dough into walnut-sized balls with your fingers. Place the dough balls on a greased cookie sheet, 12 to a standard-sized sheet. Press them down in center with your impeccably clean thumb to make a deep indentation. *(If the health board's around, use the bowl of a small spoon.)* Place one cherry in each indentation.

Combine the chocolate chips and the sweetened condensed milk in a microwave-safe bowl. Heat them on HIGH for 1 minute. Stir. If the chips are not melted, process on HIGH in 1-minute increments until they can be stirred smooth. *(You may have to keep zapping this to keep it from hardening as you bake the cookies.)*

Add approximately 1/8 cup *(2 Tablespoons)* of the reserved cherry juice to the melted chocolate mixture you made. Stir it into a thick frosting. If the frosting is too thick, add more juice in small increments. *(Test it with a teaspoon. If it doesn't glob off, it's too thick.)*

Spoon the frosting over the center of each cookie, just enough to cover each cherry. Make sure it doesn't drip down the sides.

Bake at 350 degrees F. for 10 to 12 minutes. Let the cookies cool on cookie sheet for 2 minutes, then remove to a wire rack to finish cooling.

Hannah's Note: For those who don't like cherries, substitute well-drained pineapple tidbits, using the juice to thin the frosting. You can also use pecan halves or macadamia nuts and thin the frosting with cold coffee or water. If you don't have anything to go on top, just glob the chocolate mixture into the indentations. That's good too.

Yield: 8 to 10 dozen, depending on cookie size.

A plate of these should be in every psychiatrist's office — two Chocolate Covered Cherry Delights will lift anyone out of a depression.

*Chocolate Date Drops

Preheat oven to 350 degrees F., rack in the middle position.

1 and 1/2 cups chopped dates *(You can buy them chopped in the store or chop pitted dates yourself)*

1 and 1/2 cups orange juice *(if you've chopped the dates yourself, use only 1 cup of orange juice)*

___

4 and 1/2 cups all purpose flour *(don't sift — just scoop it out and level it off with a knife)*

1 teaspoon salt

1 teaspoon baking powder

1 teaspoon baking soda

___

1 cup softened butter *(2 sticks, 8 ounces, 1/2 pound)*

1 and 1/2 cups white *(granulated)* **sugar**

3 eggs, beaten *(just whip them up in a glass with a fork)*

___

1 cup semi-sweet chocolate chips

___

Approximately 1/2 cup white *(granulated)* **sugar for later**

___

Walnut halves to decorate the cookies

Hannah's 1st Note: Hank, the bartender down at the Lake Eden Municipal Liquor Store, suggested that you could use 1/4 cup of orange liqueur mixed with 1 and 1/4 cups of orange juice to plump the chopped dates. (It was snowing and I didn't have orange liqueur when I tested these, so I used straight orange juice.)

Put the dates and the orange juice in an uncovered saucepan on the stovetop. Heat on MEDIUM HIGH until the liquid just barely begins to boil. Quickly turn the heat down to SIMMER. Simmer the mixture on the stovetop for 20 minutes. Then pull the saucepan off the heat, turn off the burner, and let the mixture cool for another 20 to 30 minutes.

Hannah's 2nd Note: If you're in a hurry, you can speed up this cooling process by sticking the pan in the refrigerator until the mixture is approximately room temperature.

In a medium-sized mixing bowl, combine the flour, salt, baking powder, and baking soda. *(I stir mine gently with a whisk so that everything's mixed together.)* Set the bowl aside.

Hannah's 3rd Note: I used an electric mixer for this part of the recipe. You can do it by hand, but it takes some muscle.

Mix the softened butter and sugar together until they're light and fluffy.

Add the eggs, one at a time, and beat until the mixture is a uniform color.

Check the date mixture to see if it's cool enough so that it won't cook the eggs. If it is, you can work with it now. If it's not, have a cup of coffee and let it cool a little more.

Take your bowl out of the mixer and blend in the date mixture by hand.

Fold in half of the flour mixture carefully. The object is to keep the dough fluffy.

Fold in the chocolate chips.

Fold in the remainder of the flour mixture.

Put approximately 1/2 cup sugar into a small bowl. Drop the dough from a tea-spoon ***(or Tablespoon if you want larger cookies)*** into the bowl of sugar. Form the drops into balls with your fingers and move them to a lightly greased cookie sheet ***(I lined my cookie sheet with parchment paper and sprayed it lightly with Pam)***, 12 cookie dough drops to a standard-sized sheet.

Place a walnut half on top of each cookie, pressing it down slightly.

Bake the Chocolate Date Drops at 350 degrees F. for 9 to 10 minutes, or until just lightly browned. *(Larger cookies will take a bit longer to bake.)*

Yield: 5 to 6 dozen deliciously soft cookies.

CHOCOLATE MINT SOFTIES

Preheat oven to 350 degrees F., rack in the middle position.

2 one-ounce squares unsweetened baking chocolate

1/2 cup *(1 stick, 4 ounces, 1/4 pound)* butter at room temperature

2/3 cup brown sugar, firmly packed

1/3 cup white *(granulated)* sugar

1/2 teaspoon baking soda

1/2 teaspoon salt

1 large egg

1 teaspoon peppermint extract

1/2 teaspoon chocolate extract *(if you can't find it, just use vanilla)*

2 cups flour *(pack it down in the cup when you measure it)*

3/4 cup sour cream

3/4 cup very coarsely chopped pecan pieces *(you'll want some big pieces)*

Line your cookie sheets with foil. Leave little "ears" of foil sticking up on the side, large enough to grab later. *(This is so you can slide the cookies and the foil right off the sheet when they're baked.)*

Unwrap the squares of chocolate and break them apart. Put them in a small microwave-safe bowl. *(I use a 16-ounce measuring cup.)* Melt them for 90 seconds on HIGH. Stir them until they're smooth and set them aside to cool while you mix up your cookie dough.

Hannah's 1st Note: Mixing this dough is a lot easier with an electric mixer. You can do it by hand, but it'll take some muscle.

Combine the butter and sugars in the bowl of an electric mixer. Beat them on medium speed until they're smooth. This should take less than a minute.

Add the baking soda and salt, and resume beating on medium again for another minute, or until they're incorporated.

Add the egg and beat on medium until the batter is smooth *(an additional minute should do it)*. Add the peppermint and chocolate extracts, and mix for about 30 seconds.

Shut off the mixer and scrape down the bowl. Then add the melted chocolate and mix again for another minute on medium speed.

Shut off the mixer and scrape down the bowl again. At low speed, mix in half of the flour. When that's incorporated, mix in the sour cream.

Scrape down the bowl again and add the rest of the flour. Beat until it's fully incorporated.

Remove the bowl from the mixer and give it a stir with a spoon. Mix in the pecan pieces by hand. *(A firm rubber spatula works nicely.)*

Use a teaspoon to spoon the dough onto the foil-lined cookie sheets, 12 cookies to a standard-sized sheet. *(If the dough is too sticky for you to work with, chill it for a half-hour or so, and try again.)* Bake the cookies at 350 degrees F., for 10 to 12 minutes, or until they rise and become firm.

Slide the foil from the cookie sheet and onto a wire rack. Let the cookies cool on the rack while the next sheet of cookies is baking. When the next sheet of cookies is ready, pull the cooled cookies onto the counter or table and slide the foil with the hot cookies on the rack. Keep alternating until all the dough has been baked.

When all the cookies are cool, set them out on wax paper for frosting.

CHOCOLATE BUTTER FROSTING:

   2 one-ounce squares unsweetened baking chocolate, melted

1/3 cup butter, room temperature
2 cups powdered *(confectioner's)* **sugar**
1 and 1/2 teaspoons vanilla extract
approximately 2 Tablespoons cream *(or milk)*

Unwrap the squares of chocolate and break them apart. Put them in a small microwave-safe bowl. *(I use a 16-ounce measuring cup.)* Melt them for 90 seconds on HIGH. Stir until smooth and set aside to cool.

When the chocolate is cool, mix in the butter. Then stir in the powdered sugar. *(There's no need to sift unless it has big lumps.)*

Mix in the vanilla extract and the cream. Beat the frosting until it's of spreading consistency.

Hannah's 2nd Note: This frosting is the no-fail type. If it's too thick, add a bit more cream. If it's too thin, add a bit more powdered sugar.

Frost your cookies and leave them on the waxed paper until the frosting has hardened. *(If you're like me, you'll sneak one while the frosting is still soft, just to test it, of course.)*

When the frosting has hardened, arrange

the cookies on a pretty platter and enjoy. They store well in a covered container if you separate the layers with wax paper.

Hannah's 3rd Note: Lisa says that when she's in a hurry and doesn't have time to make a frosting, she just sprinkles the cookies with a little powdered sugar while they're still warm. She does a second sprinkling when they're cool and calls it a day.

Yield: Approximately 6 dozen cookies.

CINNAMON CRISPS

Preheat oven to 325 degrees F., rack in the middle position.

- **2 cups melted butter** *(4 sticks, 16 ounces, 1 pound)*
- **1 cup white sugar**
- **2 cups brown sugar** *(loosely packed)*
- **2 beaten eggs** *(just whip them up with a fork)*
- **2 teaspoons vanilla extract**
- **1 teaspoon cinnamon**
- **1 teaspoon baking soda**
- **1 teaspoon cream of tartar** *(critical!)*
- **1 teaspoon salt**
- **4 and 1/4 cups white flour** *(not sifted — pack it down in the cup when you measure it)*

Dough ball rolling mixture:
1/2 cup white sugar
1 teaspoon cinnamon

Melt the butter. Add the white sugar and brown sugar, and mix well. Let the mixture sit on the counter and cool to room temperature.

When the sugar and butter mixture is cool, stir in the eggs. Mix well.

Add the vanilla extract, cinnamon, baking soda, cream of tartar, and salt. Mix thoroughly.

Add flour in one-cup increments, mixing after each addition.

Use your impeccably clean hands to roll the dough into walnut-sized balls. *(If the dough is too sticky, chill for an hour before trying it again.)*

Preheat the oven to 325 degrees F. Combine the sugar and cinnamon in a small bowl to make the dough ball rolling mixture. *(Mixing it with a fork works nicely.)*

Roll the dough balls in the mixture and then place them on a greased *(or sprayed with Pam or another nonstick cooking spray)* cookie sheet, 12 to a standard-sized sheet. Flatten the dough balls with a greased metal spatula or the palm of your impeccably clean hand.

Bake at 325 degrees F. for 10 to 15 minutes. *(The cookies should have a touch of gold around the edges.)* Cool the Cinnamon Crisps on the cookie sheet for 2 minutes, then remove them to a wire rack to complete cooling.

Yield: Approximately 8 dozen, depending on cookie size.

COCALATTAS

Preheat oven to 350 degrees F., rack in the middle position.

- 1 cup melted butter *(2 sticks, 8 ounces, 1/2 pound)*
- 3/4 cup white *(granulated)* sugar
- 3/4 cup brown sugar, firmly packed
- 1 teaspoon baking soda
- 2 teaspoons coconut extract***
- 1/2 teaspoon salt
- 2 beaten eggs *(whip them up in a glass with a fork)*
- 1 cup finely chopped coconut *(from approximately 2 cups coconut flakes)*
- 2 and 1/4 cups flour *(don't sift — pack it down in your measuring cup)*
- 1 cup chocolate chips *(that's a 6-ounce package)*

Melt the butter. *(Microwave it for one and a half minutes on HIGH in a microwave-safe container, or melt it in a pan on the stove over LOW heat.)* Mix in the white sugar and

***It's not absolutely positively necessary that you use coconut extract, but the cookies will be much more delicious if you do. If you can't find it, or you're making these in the middle of a blizzard and you can't get to the store, just use vanilla extract.

the brown sugar. Add the baking soda, co-conut extract, and salt. Mix thoroughly.

Add the beaten eggs and stir them in.

Chop the coconut flakes in a food processor with the steel blade. *(Most people like the coconut chopped because then it doesn't stick between their teeth, but you don't have to go out and buy a food processor to make these cookies. Just find the finest, smallest flakes you can in the store, spread them out on a cutting board and chop them up a little finer with a knife.)* Measure the coconut AFTER it's chopped. Pack it down when you measure it, add it to your bowl, and stir thoroughly.

Add half of the flour and all of the chocolate chips. Stir well to incorporate. Finish by mixing in the rest of the flour.

Let the dough "rest" for ten minutes on the counter, uncovered. Use a teaspoon *(one from your silverware drawer, not a measuring spoon)* to drop mounds of dough onto **UNGREASED** cookie sheets, 12 cookies to a standard-sized sheet. If the dough is too sticky to handle, chill it for 20 to 30 minutes and try again.

Bake at 350 degrees F. for 9 to 11 minutes

or until golden brown around the edges.

Let cool for 3 minutes, then remove the cookies from the baking sheet and transfer them to a wire rack to finish cooling.

Yield: Approximately 6 dozen, depending on cookie size.

Lisa's Note: Herb's great-grandmother's recipe calls for chipped chocolate, so I used chocolate chips. Hannah says that if chocolate chips had been available when Herb's great-grandmother was alive, she probably would have used them.

These are Herb's new favorite cookies. He says they taste like a crunchy Mounds bar. The Pineapple Right Side Up Cookie Bars that Hannah makes especially for him are still his favorite bar cookie.

COCOA SNAPS

DO NOT preheat oven yet — dough must chill before baking.

- **1 and 1/2 cups melted butter** *(3 sticks, 12 ounces, 3/4 pound)*
- **2 cups cocoa powder** *(unsweetened)*
- **2 cups brown sugar** *(pack it down when you measure it)*
- **3 large eggs, beaten** *(just whip them up in a glass with a fork)*
- **4 teaspoons baking soda**
- **1 teaspoon salt**
- **2 teaspoons vanilla extract**
- **3 cups flour** *(not sifted — pack it down in the cup when you measure it)*

1/2 cup white *(granulated)* sugar in a small bowl for coating dough balls

Melt butter and mix in cocoa until it's thoroughly blended. Add brown sugar. Let it cool slightly and then mix in beaten eggs. Add soda, salt, and vanilla extract, and stir.

Add the flour in one-cup increments, mixing after each addition.

Cover the dough with plastic wrap and chill it in the refrigerator for at least 1 hour. *(Overnight is fine, too.)*

When you're ready to bake, preheat the oven to 350 degrees F., rack in the middle position.

Roll the dough into walnut-sized balls with your impeccably clean hands. This dough may be sticky, so roll only enough for the cookies you plan to bake immediately. Then cover the dough again and return it to the refrigerator.

Roll the dough balls in the bowl of white sugar to coat them. Place them on a greased *(or sprayed with Pam or another nonstick cooking spray)* cookie sheet, 12 to a standard-sized sheet. Flatten them with a spatula *(or the heel of your impeccably clean hand if the health board's not around)*.

Bake at 350 degrees F. for 10 minutes. Cool on the cookie sheets for 2 minutes, and then remove the cookies to a wire rack to finish cooling. *(If you leave them on the cookie sheets for too long, they'll stick.)*

Tracey says these taste like her favorite chocolate animal crackers, except better because she doesn't have to pick them out from all the vanilla ones in the box.

CORN COOKIES

Preheat oven to 375 degrees F., rack in the middle position.

1 cup butter *(2 sticks, 8 ounces, 1/2 pound)*
2 cups white *(granulated)* **sugar**
1 large egg, beaten
1 15-ounce *(by weight)* **can mashed pumpkin** *(I used Libby's)*
1 cup chopped walnuts
1 cup golden raisins
1 teaspoon cinnamon
1/2 teaspoon cardamom
1 teaspoon salt
2 teaspoons vanilla extract
2 teaspoons baking powder
2 teaspoons baking soda
4 cups flour *(no need to sift — pack it down in the cup when you measure it)*

---

1 package of candy corn

Melt the butter in a microwave-safe bowl for 90 seconds on HIGH.

Add the sugar to the melted sugar and mix well. Set the bowl on the counter and let the mixture cool to room temperature.

When the butter and sugar mixture has cooled, add the egg and stir it in until it's thoroughly incorporated. Then add the mashed pumpkin, chopped walnuts, raisins, cinnamon, cardamom, salt, vanilla extract, baking powder, and baking soda. Mix thoroughly.

Add the flour in one-cup increments, mixing after each addition. Let the cookie dough sit for 5 minutes to "rest."

Drop by spoonfuls on a greased cookie sheet, 12 cookies per standard-sized sheet. Flatten the cookies with a greased spatula. *(If the dough is too sticky, refrigerate it for 20 to 30 minutes and then try it again.)*

Bake the Corn Cookies at 375 degrees F. for 8 to 10 minutes.

When the cookies come out of the oven, leave them on the cookie sheets and immediately press pieces of candy corn on top as a design. Do this right away so that the candy will stick after the cookies have cooled.★★★

Let the cookies cool on the sheets for 2

★★★If you fail to put on the candy corn when the cookies are still hot from the oven, you can put it on later using a little dab of powdered sugar frosting (powdered sugar with a tiny bit of milk) as "glue."

minutes and then transfer them to a wire rack to cool completely.

Yield: 6 to 7 dozen, depending on cookie size.

Tracey's friends really loved these cookies and they all offered to help me decorate them next year.

*CRANBERRY PINEAPPLE DROP COOKIES

DO NOT preheat your oven — this cookie dough must chill overnight before baking.

- 2 cans *(8 ounces net weight for each can)* crushed pineapple *(I used Dole)*
- 1 cup *(2 sticks, 8 ounces, 1/2 pound)* salted butter, softened
- 2 cups white *(granulated)* sugar
- 8 ounces sour cream *(that's one cup)*
- 1/2 teaspoon pineapple extract *(if you can't find it, substitute vanilla extract)*
- 1 and 1/2 teaspoons vanilla extract
- 1 teaspoon salt
- 3 teaspoons baking powder *(that's 1 Tablespoon)*
- 1 teaspoon baking soda
- 3 large eggs
- 3 cups sweetened dried cranberries***
- 5 cups flour *(pack it down in the cup when you measure it)*
- 2 cups chopped pecans *(or any other nut you like)*

- 1 cup white *(granulated)* sugar in a small

***Lisa and I use cherry-flavored Craisins down at The Cookie Jar.

bowl for rolling dough balls**

Hannah's 1st Note: Mixing up these cookies takes no time at all if you use an electric mixer.

Open the can of crushed pineapple and dump it in a strainer. It needs to drain while you start the cookie dough.

In a large bowl, mix the softened butter with the sugar until they're light and fluffy.

Add the sour cream and mix well.

Mix in the pineapple extract, vanilla extract, salt, baking powder, and baking soda.

Add the eggs, one at a time, mixing after each addition.

Pat the drained, crushed pineapple

****Lisa likes to roll her dough balls in decorator sugar with large crystals. This is usually available in colors at grocery stores during the holiday season. If you can't find it there, you can try a cake decorating store. Lisa uses this sugar because it gives the cookies a nice crunch on the outside that contrasts nicely with the soft inside. She says you can also use regular white table sugar. The crunch will be less, but the cookies will taste the same.

down in the strainer to get out all the juice. You can even pat it dry with a paper towel. When it's as juice-free as you can get it, add it to your cookie dough and mix it in.

Mix in the sweetened dried cranberries.

Add the flour in one-cup increments, mixing after each addition.

Mix in the chopped pecans *(or other chopped nuts)* and mix well.

Cover your cookie dough with plastic wrap, pressing it down on top of the dough in your bowl. Refrigerate it overnight.

When you're ready to bake the next morning, preheat your oven to 350 degrees F., rack in the middle position.

Use a teaspoon *(one from your silverware drawer, not a measuring spoon)* to scoop out enough dough to make a ball that's 1 inch in diameter. Drop the dough ball into the sugar in the bowl and roll it around with your fingers until it's coated. Then place it on a greased *(or sprayed with Pam or another nonstick cooking spray)* cookie sheet, 12 cookies to a standard-sized sheet. *(You can also cover your cookie sheets with parchment paper or baking paper.)*

Use the flat blade of a metal spatula to flatten the cookies on the cookie sheet.

Bake the Cranberry Pineapple Drop Cookies at 350 degrees F. for 15 to 18 minutes or until nicely golden on top. *(Mine took 16 minutes.)*

Let the cookies cool for two minutes on the cookie sheet and then remove them to a wire rack to cool completely.

Yield: Approximately 6 dozen delicious cookies.

Hannah's 2nd Note: When we bake these down at The Cookie Jar, Lisa and I usually top half of the cookies with red sugar and the other half with green sugar.

Lisa's Note: Pineapple is Herb's favorite fruit. Last Christmas I had to bake 4 batches of these cookies. Every time I baked a batch and put them in the freezer, Herb found them and ate them before I could serve them to company. I guess I should have wrapped them in freezer paper and labeled them Lutefisk, the way Hannah suggested. By the way,

Cranberry Pineapple Drop Cookies freeze beautifully.

DESPERATION COOKIES

Preheat oven to 350 degrees F., rack in the middle position.

2 cups melted butter *(4 sticks, 16 ounces, 1 pound)*
3 cups white *(granulated)* **sugar**
1 and 1/2 cups brown sugar
4 teaspoons vanilla extract
4 teaspoons baking soda
2 teaspoons salt
4 beaten eggs *(just whip them up in a glass with a fork)*
5 cups flour *(no need to sift — pack it down when you measure it)*
3 cups chips***
4 cups chopped nuts****

Melt the butter. *(Microwave it for 3 min-*

***Use any combination of regular chocolate chips, butterscotch chips, white chocolate chips, milk chocolate chips, vanilla chips, cherry chips, strawberry chips, peanut butter chips, or any other flavors you think will go together.
****Use any nuts you like including walnuts, pecans, cashews, almonds, even peanuts. If you don't have enough nuts to make 4 cups, fill in with crushed corn flakes, Rice Krispies, coconut, raisins, or any dried fruit.

utes on HIGH in a microwave-safe container, or melt it in a pan on the stove.)

Mix the white sugar and the brown sugar into the bowl with the butter. Let it cool down to room temperature.

When the mixture is cool, add the vanilla extract, baking soda, and salt. Mix thoroughly.

Add the beaten eggs and stir it all up. Then add half of the flour, all of the chips, and the chopped nuts. Stir well to incorporate.

Finish by adding the rest of the flour and mixing it in thoroughly.

Drop by teaspoons onto greased *(or sprayed with Pam or another nonstick baking spray)* cookie sheets, 12 cookies to a standard-sized sheet. If the dough is too sticky to handle, chill it 20 to 30 minutes and then try it again.

Bake the Desperation Cookies at 350 degrees F. for 10 to 12 minutes or until nicely browned.

Let the cookies cool for 2 minutes, then remove them from the baking sheet and transfer them to a wire rack to finish cooling.

Yield: Approximately 10 dozen delicious cookies.

DOLL FACE COOKIES

Preheat oven to 375 degrees F., rack in the middle position.

(THIS IS NOT AN OMISSION — THESE COOKIES HAVE NO EGGS)

1/2 cup melted butter *(1 stick, 4 ounces, 1/4 pound)*
1 cup brown sugar, tightly packed
1/2 cup molasses***
1 teaspoon baking soda
1/2 teaspoon salt
1/2 teaspoon cinnamon
1 teaspoon lemon juice
2 and 1/2 cups flour *(no need to sift — pack it down in the cup when you measure it)*
1/2 cup milk

---

1 cup *(approximately)* **golden raisins, regular raisins, or currants to decorate**

Melt the butter in a large microwave-safe bowl on **HIGH** for 50 seconds. Set the bowl aside on the counter to cool to room tem-

***Measuring molasses will be easier if you spray your measuring cup with nonstick cooking spray before pouring it in.

perature.

When the butter has cooled, stir in the brown sugar and molasses. Add the baking soda, salt, and cinnamon. Mix thoroughly. Then mix in the teaspoon of lemon juice.

Add half of the flour to your bowl and mix it up. Slowly pour in the milk, a little at a time, and mix as you go. Add the rest of the flour and stir until it's thoroughly incorporated.

Drop the dough by rounded teaspoons onto UNGREASED cookie sheets, 12 cookies to a standard-sized sheet. Put three raisins on top of each cookie. Use two for the eyes and one for the mouth.

Bake for 10 to 12 minutes at 375 degrees F. Let the cookies cool on the sheet for 2 minutes and then transfer them to a wire rack to cool completely.

Yield: 4 to 5 dozen, depending on cookie size.

Immelda Giese, Father Coultas's house-keeper, ordered three dozen Doll Face Cookies for Father's altar boys. When she came in to pick up the order, one of the cookies looked just like Sister Theresa. (She thought it did, not me!) The last I heard, Im-melda was trying to talk Father Coultas into displaying the cookie in a glass case at the church.

*DOUBLE CHOCOLATE PUFFS
(CHOCOLATE WHIPPERSNAPPERS)

DO NOT preheat your oven quite yet — this cookie dough needs to chill before baking.

- 1 large beaten egg *(just whip it up in a glass with a fork)*
- 2 cups Cool Whip *(measure this — Andrea said her tub of Cool Whip contained a little over 3 cups)*
- 1 cup mini chocolate chips *(Andrea used a 6-ounce package of Nestles Mini Morsels)*
- 1 package *(approximately 18 ounces)* chocolate cake mix, the size you can bake in a 9-inch by 13-inch cake pan *(Andrea used Betty Crocker Chocolate Fudge)*

1/2 cup powdered *(confectioner's)* sugar in a separate small bowl *(you don't have to sift it unless it's got big lumps)*

First of all, chill 2 teaspoons from your silverware drawer by sticking them in the freezer. You want them really ice cold. This will make it a lot easier to form the cookies after the dough is mixed.

Pour the beaten egg into a large bowl.

271

Stir in the Cool Whip.

Stir in the mini chocolate chips.

Sprinkle the cake mix over the top and fold it in, stirring only until everything is combined. The object here is to keep as much air in the batter as possible.

Hannah's Note: Andrea said this dough is very sticky. It's much easier to work with if you chill it. Just cover the bowl and stick it in the refrigerator for an hour.

When your cookie dough has chilled for an hour, preheat your oven to 350 degrees F., rack in the middle position.

Take your dough out of the refrigerator, your spoons out of the freezer, and scoop the dough one teaspoon at a time into the bowl of powdered sugar. Roll the dough around with your fingers to form powdered sugar–coated cookie dough balls.

Place the sugar-coated cookie balls on a greased cookie sheet. ***(Andrea used parchment paper sprayed with nonstick cooking spray on top of a cookie sheet.)*** Place 12 cookies on each cookie sheet.

Bake the cookies at 350 degrees F., for 10 minutes. Let them cool on the cookie sheet for no more than 2 minutes, and then move them to a wire rack to cool completely. *(This is easy if you line your cookie sheets with parchment paper — then all you have to do is grab the corner and pull it onto the wire rack.)*

Yield: 3 to 4 dozen yummy cookies, depending on cookie size.

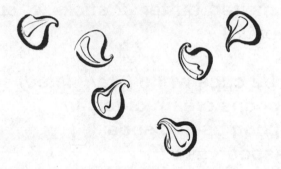

DOUBLE FLAKE COOKIES

DO NOT preheat oven — dough must chill before baking.

This recipe is from Lisa's cousin, Betty Harnar. Betty's cookies are slightly different than the ones we make at The Cookie Jar, so if you don't like them blame us. If you love them the way the folks in Lake Eden do, please give Betty all the credit.

1 **cup melted butter** *(2 sticks, 8 ounces, 1/2 pound)*

3 **eggs**

1 **and 1/2 cups white** *(granulated)* **sugar**

2 **teaspoons cream of tartar**

1 **teaspoon baking soda**

1/2 **teaspoon salt**

1 **teaspoon coconut extract** *(if you don't have it, you can use vanilla extract)*

1 **and 1/2 cups flour** *(no need to sift — pack it down in the cup when you measure it)*

2 **cups instant mashed potato flakes**

1 **cup coconut flakes, firmly packed**

3/4 **cup finely chopped pecans or walnuts** *(measure AFTER chopping)*

---

approximately 1/2 cup white sugar in a bowl for later

Melt the butter. Set it aside to let it cool a bit.

Crack the eggs into a mixing bowl and whip them up with a whisk for a minute. *(They don't have to be fluffy, just thoroughly mixed.)*

Pour the sugar into the eggs and stir it all up. Add the cream of tartar, baking soda, salt, and coconut extract. Mix well.

If the melted butter is not so hot it'll cook the eggs, stir it into the egg mixture.

Add the flour in one-cup increments, mixing after each addition.

Measure out two cups of mashed potato flakes and add them to the mixture. Then add the coconut flakes. *(If you're like me and you don't care for stringy coconut, chop it up in a food processor with the steel blade before you add it to your bowl.)* Once the coconut has been mixed in, stir in the chopped nuts and mix thoroughly.

Cover the dough tightly and refrigerate it for at least 4 hours. Overnight is even better.

When you're ready to bake, preheat the oven to 350 degrees F., rack in the center position.

Form balls of cookie dough, 1 inch in diameter, with your hands. Roll the balls in the bowl of granulated sugar and place them on a greased cookie sheet *(I used Pam — you can use any nonstick cooking spray)*, 12 sugared dough balls to a standard-sized sheet. Flatten the balls a bit with a metal spatula or the heel of your impeccably clean hand.

Bake at 350 degrees F. for 10 to 12 minutes, or until Double Flake Cookies are golden around the edges. Cool them on the cookie sheet for 2 minutes and then transfer the cookies to a wire rack to cool completely.

Yield: Approximately 8 dozen yummy, crunchy cookies, depending on cookie size.

Mother likes these best as sandwich cookies. I spread one cookie bottom with chocolate frosting and sandwich another cookie on top. *(The bottoms should be together, making the cookie sandwiches slightly convex.)* Bertie's customers down at the Cut n' Curl like them best if the sandwich filling is raspberry jam. I think that's because the chocolate melts if they eat them under the hair dryers.

Hannah's Note: You're really supposed

to chill this dough, but if you absolutely positively can't wait to bake them, you can. Just be prepared to wet your hands frequently as you roll the cookie balls so the dough won't stick to them.

FUDGE-AROONS

DO NOT preheat oven — this dough must chill before baking.

1 cup chocolate chips
1 cup butter *(2 sticks, 8 ounces, 1/2 pound)*
1/2 cup brown sugar
1 and 1/2 cups white *(granulated)* **sugar**
2 teaspoons vanilla extract
1/2 teaspoon salt
1 teaspoon baking soda
2 beaten eggs *(just whip them up with a fork)*
3 and 1/2 cups flour *(not sifted — pack it down when you measure it)*

Put the cup of chocolate chips and the cup of butter in a 4-cup measuring bowl and microwave on HIGH for 2 minutes. Stir until smooth, take it out and set it on the counter to let the mixture cool while you do the next step.

Combine the brown sugar and white sugar in a large mixing bowl. Add the vanilla, salt, and baking soda. Mix in the two beaten eggs.

Check the chocolate chip and butter mixture. If it's cool enough to touch, add it to the sugar mixture and stir thoroughly.

Add the flour in half-cup increments, stirring after each addition.

Cover your bowl and refrigerate it. This dough must chill for at least an hour. *(Overnight is fine, too.)*

The coconut *("aroon")* filling must also chill. Mix it up now.

Coconut Filling:

- 2 cups shredded coconut
- 1 cup white *(granulated)* sugar
- 1 cup flour *(not sifted — pack it down when you measure it)*
- 1/2 stick cold butter *(1/4 cup, 1/8 pound)*
- 2 large eggs

In a food processor with the steel blade, zoop up the coconut with the sugar and flour. Pulse it several times so that the coconut flakes are no longer than a quarter inch.

Cut the butter into 4 pieces and add them to your work bowl. Pulse again, until the mixture looks like coarse meal.

Crack the eggs into a small bowl or a cup, and whisk them up with a fork. Add them to your work bowl and pulse until they're incorporated into the mixture.

(If you don't have a food processor, you don't have to buy one to make this cookie — it's just a little messier when the coconut flakes are longer. To make this cookie without a food processor, just add all of the ingredients except the butter to a small bowl and stir them up. Then melt the butter and mix it in.)

Cover and chill the coconut mixture for at least an hour. *(Overnight is fine, too.)*

When you're ready to bake, preheat the oven to 350 degrees F., rack in the middle position.

Form balls of chocolate dough, 1 inch in diameter, with your impeccably clean hands. Place them on a greased cookie sheet, 12 to a standard-sized sheet. Press them down with the heel of your impeccably clean hand to flatten them.

Form balls of coconut just a bit smaller than the chocolate balls you made. Place them on top of each squashed chocolate ball. Squish those down. Now you have two balls, both squashed.

Make 12 more chocolate balls, the same size as the first ones, and put them on top of the squashed coconut balls. Press them down slightly to make little "sandwiches."

Bake at 350 degrees F. for 9 to 11 minutes. Let the cookies cool on the sheet for at least two minutes. When they're cool enough to remove, use a spatula to move them to a wire rack to complete cooling.

Yield: 5 to 6 dozen yummy cookies.

If you have any coconut mixture left over, form coconut balls, 12 to a baking sheet, put a milk chocolate chip on top of each ball and press it down slightly, and bake at 350 degrees F. for 10 minutes.

Norman wants me to make these cookies even chewier — he says it'll provide more revenue for his dental clinic. (He's kidding . . . I think.)

GERMAN CHOCOLATE CAKE COOKIES

DO NOT preheat oven yet — make the cookie dough first.

COOKIE DOUGH:

- 1 cup salted butter *(2 sticks, 8 ounces, 1/2 pound)*
- 1 cup milk chocolate chips *(6 ounce package)*
- 2 cups white *(granulated)* sugar
- 2 large eggs, beaten *(just whip them up in a glass with a fork)*
- 1/2 teaspoon baking powder
- 1/2 teaspoon baking soda
- 1/2 teaspoon salt
- 2 teaspoons vanilla extract
- 3 cups flour *(no need to sift — pack it down in the cup when you measure it)*

FROSTING:

- 1/2 cup firmly packed brown sugar
- 3/4 cup tightly packed coconut
- 1/2 cup chopped pecans
- 1/4 cup chilled salted butter *(1/2 stick, 2 ounces, 1/8 pound)*
- 2 egg yolks, beaten

In a microwave-safe bowl, melt the butter and chocolate chips on HIGH for 2 minutes. Stir until smooth.

In another mixing bowl, mix the sugar and the eggs. Add the baking powder, baking soda, salt, and vanilla extract.

Stir the melted chocolate mixture until it's fairly warm to the touch, but not so hot it'll cook the eggs. Add it to the mixing bowl and mix it in thoroughly.

Add the flour in one-cup increments, mixing after each addition. *(Dough will be stiff and a bit crumbly.)*

Cover the dough with plastic wrap and set it aside while you make the frosting.

Combine the sugar and coconut in a food processor. Mix with the steel blade until the coconut is in small pieces.

Add the chopped pecans. Cut the butter into four chunks and add them. Process with the steel blade until the butter is in small bits.

Separate the yolks, place them in a glass, and whip them up with a fork. Add them to your bowl and process until they are thoroughly incorporated.

Hannah's Note: If you don't have a food processor, you can make the frosting by hand using softened butter.

Preheat the oven to 350 degrees F., rack in the middle position.

Chill the frosting in your refrigerator while the oven's preheating. It'll make it easier to work with. This will be especially true if you've made the frosting by hand and haven't chopped the coconut into shorter shreds.

Pat the cookie dough into one-inch balls with your fingers. Place the balls on a greased cookie sheet *(or sprayed with Pam or another nonstick cooking spray)*, 12 to a standard sheet. Press down in the center of each ball with your thumb to make a deep indentation. *(If the health board's around, use the bowl of a small spoon.)*

Pat the frosting into half-inch balls with your fingers. Place them in each indentation.

Bake at 350 degrees F. for 10 to 12 minutes. Let the cookies cool on the cookie sheet for 2 minutes, then remove them to a wire rack to finish cooling.

Yield: 5 to 6 dozen, depending on cookie size.

HANNAH'S BANANAS

DO NOT preheat oven — this dough must chill before baking.

- **1 and 1/2 cups melted, salted butter** *(3 sticks, 12 ounces, 3/4 pound)*
- **2 cups white** *(granulated)* **sugar**
- **2 beaten eggs** *(just whip them up in a glass with a fork)*
- **3/4 cup mashed very ripe bananas** *(2 medium or 3 small)*
- **1 and 1/2 teaspoons baking soda*****
- **1 teaspoon salt**
- **4 cups flour** *(no need to sift — pack it down in the cup when you measure it)*
- **2 cups finely chopped walnuts or pecans** *(measure AFTER chopping)*

1/2 cup white *(granulated)* **sugar for later**

Melt the butter in a large microwave-safe bowl. Stir in the sugar, beaten eggs, baking soda, and salt. Choose bananas that have black freckles on the skin so that they're almost overripe. Mash them until they're smooth *(you can do this in a food processor or by hand)*. Add the banana puree to the

***If you don't like the taste of baking soda, you can substitute one teaspoon baking powder.

mixing bowl and combine thoroughly.

Mix in the flour, one cup at a time, mixing after each addition. Then cover your bowl with plastic wrap and refrigerate it for 4 hours *(overnight is fine, too)*.

When you're ready to bake, preheat the oven to 350 degrees F., rack in the middle position.

Roll the chilled dough into walnut-sized balls with your hands. *(This dough is quite sticky — you can wear plastic gloves if you like, or wet your hands slightly so the dough won't stick to them.)*

Put 1/2 cup white sugar in a small bowl and roll the balls in it. Place the dough balls on a greased cookie sheet, 12 to a sheet. Press them down just a little so they won't roll off on the floor when you put them in the oven. Then return your bowl to the refrigerator and let it chill until it's time to roll more.

Bake for 10 to 12 minutes at 350 degrees F., or until they're lightly golden in color. They'll flatten out, all by themselves. Let them cool for 2 minutes on the cookie sheet and then move them to a wire rack to finish cooling.

These cookies freeze well. Roll them up in foil, place the rolls in a freezer bag, and they'll be fine for 3 months or so, if they last that long.

Yield: Approximately 10 dozen, depending on cookie size.

Lisa's cousin Beth says these are great when they're dunked in hot chocolate.

Carrie Rhodes also loves these cookies. She says that middle-aged women should eat bananas every day because they need extra potassium. (I bit my tongue when she said "middle-aged" — Carrie's at least fifty-five and people don't usually live to be a hundred and ten!)

*Heavenly Eggnog Cookies

Preheat oven to 275 degrees F., rack in the middle position.

(Not a misprint — that's two hundred seventy-five degrees F.)

Hannah's 1st Note: Don't even THINK about making these if it's raining or humid. Meringue does best on very dry days. **(Winter in Minnesota is usually dry, so they're perfect for the holiday season.)**

3 egg whites *(save the yolks to add to scrambled eggs the next morning)*
1/4 teaspoon cream of tartar
1/2 teaspoon rum extract *(you can also use real rum)*
1/4 teaspoon freshly grated nutmeg *(if you use jarred ground nutmeg make sure it's fresh)*
1/4 teaspoon salt
1 cup white *(granulated)* **sugar**
2 Tablespoons flour *(that's 1/8 cup)*
1/2 cup finely chopped pecans *(chopped almonds or walnuts are also good)*

Separate the egg whites and let them come up to room temperature. This will give you more volume when you beat them.

Prepare your baking sheets by lining them with parchment paper *(works best)* or brand new brown parcel-wrapping paper. Spray the paper with Pam or other nonstick cooking spray and dust it lightly with flour. You can also use baking spray *(the kind with flour in it)* and eliminate the dusting-with-flour step.

Beat the egg whites with the cream of tartar, rum extract, nutmeg, and salt until they are stiff enough to hold a soft peak.

Hannah's 2nd Note: To test for soft peaks, just shut off your mixer and tap the egg white mixture with the flat side of your rubber spatula. If the mixture forms a little peak when you remove the spatula and the tip of the peak bends over like a blade of grass in the wind, it's ready and you can go on to the next step.

Add the cup of sugar gradually, sprinkling it in by quarter cupfuls and then turning the mixer on HIGH speed. Beat hard for ten seconds or so after each sprinkling.

Shut off the mixer and sprinkle in the flour. Turn on the mixer at LOW speed and mix it in. You can also remove the bowl from the mixer at this point and fold in the flour with a mixing spoon or rubber spatula.

By hand, with a mixing spoon or a rubber spatula, gently fold in the chopped pecans. The object here is not to lose the air you've beaten into the egg whites.

Drop little spoonfuls of dough on your paper-lined cookie sheet with a teaspoon. *(Lisa and I use a melon scooper at The Cookie Jar.)* If you place four mounds in a row and you have five rows, you'll end up with 20 cookies per sheet.

Bake at 275 degrees F. for 40 to 50 minutes, or until the meringue part of the cookie is firm to the touch and the cookies turn a nice golden color.

Cool the Heavenly Eggnog Cookies on the paper-lined cookie sheet by setting it on a wire rack. When the cookies are completely cool, peel them carefully from the paper and store them in an airtight container in a dry place.

Hannah's 3rd Note: Your refrigerator is NOT a dry place!

Yield: 3 to 4 dozen delicious cookies that have the eggnog taste even though they don't have any egg yolks inside.

*Kiss My Grits Cookies

Preheat oven to 350 degrees F., rack in the middle position.

1 cup white *(granulated)* sugar
1 cup *(2 sticks, 8 ounces, 1/2 pound)* salted butter, softened
2 large eggs
1/2 teaspoon salt
1 Tablespoon *(3 teaspoons)* vanilla extract
3/4 cup instant grits *(I used Quaker Instant Grits Original)*
2 cups all-purpose flour *(pack it down in the cup when you measure it)*
3/4 cup shredded coconut
approximately 60 Hershey's Kisses chocolate candy

Hannah's 1st Note: These are simple to make if you use an electric mixer.

Measure out one cup of white, granulated sugar and place it in the bottom of a large mixing bowl or in the bowl of your electric mixer.

Soften 1 cup of salted butter and add it to your mixing bowl.

Beat the sugar and the butter until the mixture is light and fluffy.

291

Add the eggs, one at a time, beating after each addition.

Add the salt and the Tablespoon of vanilla extract. Mix them in thoroughly.

Mix in 3/4 cup dry, instant grits.

Add 2 cups of all-purpose flour one cup at a time, beating after each addition.

Chop the coconut a little finer with the steel blade in your food processor or with a sharp knife on a cutting board. *(I've heard some people say that they like the taste of coconut, but don't like the way it sticks between their teeth. Chopping it finer solves that problem.)*

Prepare your cookie sheets by greasing them, spraying them with Pam or another nonstick cooking spray, or lining them with parchment paper. All three methods will work. *(I lined mine with parchment paper.)*

Drop the dough by teaspoonfuls onto the cookie sheets, 12 cookies to a standard-sized sheet.

Press a Hershey's Kiss chocolate candy into the top of each cookie, the point up. If there are any left over, the baker probably needs a dose of chocolate about now.

Bake your Kiss My Grits Cookies at 350 degrees F. for 12 to 15 minutes, or until they begin to turn slightly golden around the edges. *(Mine took 13 minutes.)*

Cool the cookies on the cookie sheets for 2 minutes and then remove them to a wire rack to cool completely. *(If you used parchment paper, just pull the paper over to the rack and leave the cookies on the paper until they're cool.)*

Yield: Makes 4 to 5 dozen scrumptious cookies everyone will like.

Hannah's 2nd Note: You might want to hold off telling the kids that they're eating grits until they take their third or fourth cookie.

DO NOT preheat your oven — these cookies require NO BAKING!

- **1/2 cup *(1 stick, 4 ounces, 1/4 pound)* salted butter, softened**
- **1-pound box *(approximately 3 and 3/4 cups)* powdered *(confectioner's)* sugar**
- **6-ounce tube frozen limeade concentrate *(You'll find this in the frozen juice section at your market — I used Minute Maid Limeade)***
- **1 Tablespoon key lime juice*****
- **2 drops green food coloring *(optional)***
- **1 box (14 ounces net weight) vanilla wafers *(I used Nabisco Nilla Wafers)***
- **1 cup shredded coconut *(I used Baker's Angel Flake Coconut)***

Prepare a cake pan by lining it with wax paper. You're going to use it to hold and refrigerate your lime balls once you've made them.

Hannah's 1st Note: You can use an electric mixer to make these little treats, or you

---

***If you can't find key lime juice, you can use regular lime juice. Of course it's best if you squeeze it yourself.

can do it by hand.

Hannah's 2nd Note: Let the tube of frozen limeade concentrate thaw on the counter while you start mixing the first few ingredients.

If you don't want to wait for your cold butter to warm to room temperature, you can soften it in the microwave. Here's how you do it:

Unwrap a stick of refrigerated butter. Put it on a paper plate. Heat it for 5 seconds on HIGH in your microwave. Roll it forward so the topside is now on the side. Heat it for another 5 seconds on HIGH. Roll it forward again and heat it for another 5 seconds on HIGH. Roll it forward for the 3rd time and heat for another 5 seconds. Take the plate out of the microwave and transfer the softened butter to your mixing bowl.

Hannah's 3rd Note: Check the powdered sugar to make sure it doesn't have lumps. If it does, you'll have to sift out the lumps by using a flour sifter or putting it through a fine wire-mesh strainer.

Sprinkle the powdered sugar on top of the softened butter in your bowl and mix it all up.

If the frozen limeade has thawed, add it to your mixing bowl. If it hasn't, spoon it out of the container, put it into a microwave-safe bowl, and heat it on HIGH for 20 seconds. Stir to see if it's melted. If it's not, heat it in 20-second increments, stirring after each increment, until it's melted. Add the melted limeade concentrate to your bowl and mix it in thoroughly.

Add the Tablespoon of lime juice and mix it in.

Add the green food coloring *(if you decided to use it)* and mix that in thoroughly.

Crush the vanilla wafers. You can do this easily with a food processor and the steel blade, or in a blender. You can also do it by putting the wafers in a two-gallon-size freezer bag, placing it on the counter, and crushing the wafers with a rolling pin. If you use the rolling pin method, crush half of the box of wafers at a time.

Add the crushed wafers to your bowl and mix them in.

Place the coconut in a medium-sized bowl. You'll be coating your lime balls with it. *(I like to put my coconut in the food processor and use the steel blade to chop it even finer. I've found that most people who say they don't like coconut are really not objecting to the way it tastes, but the tendency it has to stick between their teeth.)*

Use your impeccably clean hands to form little balls from the mixture. *(Lisa and I use a 2-teaspoon scooper at The Cookie Jar.)* The balls should be about 1 inch in diameter, approximately the size of bonbons.

When you finish forming each ball, roll it in the bowl of coconut to coat it, and then place it in the cake pan.

When you've finished forming and coating all your lime balls and placing them in the cake pan, cover them with another sheet of wax paper and refrigerate them for 2 to 3 hours before serving. If you're not serving them for several days, place a sheet of foil over the cake pan and secure it tightly. Keep the cake pan in the refrigerator until you're ready to serve.

If you're giving these as gifts, you can place them in pretty cookie tins. You can also put them in little paper mini muffin cups and place them in a candy box. Remember to tell your lucky recipients to keep them refrigerated.

*Lemon Softies

Preheat oven to 375 degrees F., rack in the middle position.

1 and 1/4 cups white *(granulated)* sugar

1 cup *(2 sticks, 8 ounces, 1/2 pound)* salted butter, softened

3 large eggs

1/2 teaspoon salt

1 teaspoon baking soda

1 and 1/2 cups lemon pie filling *(I used Comstock — my can was 15.5 ounces net weight, and it was exactly 1 and 1/2 cups)*

1 Tablespoon lemon juice

the zest of one lemon *(that's only the yellow part of the lemon rind, finely grated)*

3 and 1/4 cups all-purpose flour *(pack it down in the cup when you measure it)*

1 cup crushed corn flakes *(it takes about 2 cups corn flakes to make 1 cup of crushed corn flakes)*

30 red maraschino cherries OR 30 pecan

or walnut halves to garnish your cookies

Hannah's 1st Note: Unless you have a very strong stirring arm, use an electric mixer to make this cookie dough.

Place the sugar in the bowl of an electric mixer.

Place the butter, which must be softened to room temperature, on top of the sugar.

Turn the mixer to LOW and mix for one minute. Gradually increase the speed of the mixer, scraping down the sides of the bowl frequently and beating for one minute at each level, until you arrive at the highest speed.

Beat at the highest speed for at least 2 minutes or until the resulting mixture is very light and fluffy.

Turn the mixer down to LOW and add the eggs, one at a time, beating after each addition.

Continue to mix on LOW speed while you add the salt and the baking soda. Mix until they are thoroughly incorporated.

Measure out a cup and a half of lemon pie

filling. With the mixer on LOW speed, add the pie filling to your bowl and mix it in. Then add the lemon juice and lemon zest and mix that in.

Mix in the flour, one cup at a time, mixing after each addition. *(You don't have to be exact — just add the flour in 4 increments.)*

Shut off the mixer and scrape down the sides of the bowl. Then give the mixture a final stir by hand. The resulting cookie dough should be fluffy, but not at all stiff like sugar cookie or chocolate chip cookie dough. Let the bowl sit on the counter while you . . .

Line your cookie sheets with parchment paper. It's the easiest way to bake these cookies. If you don't have parchment paper and you really don't want to go out to get any, grease your cookie sheets heavily, or spray them thoroughly with Pam or another nonstick cooking spray.

If you haven't already done so, crush the corn flakes and measure out one cup. Place the finely crushed corn flakes in a shallow bowl. This is what you'll use to coat the outside of your Lemon Softie dough balls.

Using a teaspoon *(not the measuring kind,*

but one from your silverware drawer), drop a rounded teaspoon of cookie dough into the crushed corn flakes. Use your fingers and a light touch to form it into a ball. Lift the ball gently and place it on your baking sheet. Continue to form dough balls covered with crushed corn flakes, 12 to a standard-sized cookie sheet. Top each dough ball with a maraschino cherry half *(rounded side up)* or a walnut or pecan half, and press it down gently.

Bake your Lemon Softies at 375 degrees F., for 12 minutes. Take them out of the oven and slide the cookie-laden parchment paper onto a wire rack to cool. If you used greased cookie sheets, you're going to have to let the cookies sit on the cookie sheets for 2 minutes and then remove them to a wire rack with a metal spatula. Let the cookies cool completely before you attempt to remove them from the wire rack.

Yield: Approximately 4 to 5 dozen soft and moist cookies, depending on cookie size.

LISA'S WHITE CHOCOLATE SUPREMES

Preheat the oven to 350 degrees F., rack in the middle position.

- 1 cup melted butter *(2 sticks, 8 ounces, 1/2 pound)*
- 3/4 cup white (granulated) sugar
- 3/4 cup brown sugar *(pack it down in the cup when you measure it)*
- 2 teaspoons vanilla extract
- 1 and 1/2 teaspoons baking soda
- 1/2 teaspoon salt
- 2 eggs, beaten *(just whip them up in a glass with a fork)*
- 2 and 1/4 cups flour *(don't sift — pack it down in the cup when you measure it)*
- 2 cups white chocolate chips *(I used an 11-ounce package)*
- 1 and 1/2 cups chopped macadamia nuts *(measure BEFORE chopping)*

Melt the butter in a microwave-safe bowl or in a saucepan on the stovetop.

Mix in the white sugar and the brown sugar, beating until the resulting mixture reaches a smooth texture and is a uniform color.

Stir in the vanilla extract, baking soda, and salt. Mix well.

Feel the sides of the bowl. If it's not so hot it'll cook the eggs, add them now. Mix thoroughly.

Add the flour, one cup at a time, mixing after each cup.

Add the white chocolate chips and the macadamia nuts to your bowl and mix thoroughly.

Hannah's 1st Note: Macadamia nuts are expensive. Feel free to substitute pecans in this recipe.

Drop the dough by teaspoonfuls onto an UNGREASED cookie sheet, 12 cookies to a standard-sized sheet. *(You can also line your cookie sheets with parchment paper if you wish.)*

Bake at 350 F. for 10 to 12 minutes or until nicely browned.

Take the cookies out of the oven. Let them cool for 2 minutes, then remove them from the baking sheet and transfer them to a wire rack to finish cooling.

Hannah's 2nd Note: Lisa developed this recipe, and it's just like they say in the potato chip commercials — you can't eat just one.

LITTLE SNOWBALLS

Preheat oven to 350 degrees F., rack in the middle position.

1 and 1/2 cups melted butter *(3 sticks, 12 ounces, 3/4 pound)*
3/4 cup powdered sugar *(that's confectioner's sugar)*
1 and 1/2 teaspoons vanilla
1/2 teaspoon nutmeg *(freshly ground is best)*
1/2 teaspoon salt
3 and 1/2 cups flour *(no need to sift)*
1 cup finely chopped nuts***
more powdered sugar for coating cookies

Melt the butter in a microwave-safe bowl for 60 seconds on HIGH, or in a pan on the stovetop over MEDIUM heat.

***Mother likes these with chopped walnuts. Andrea prefers pecans. I think they're best with hazelnuts. Tracey adores these when I substitute a cup of flaked coconut for the nuts and form the dough balls around a small piece of a milk chocolate bar or a couple of milk chocolate chips.

In a large mixing bowl, mix the melted butter and the powdered sugar together.

Add the vanilla, nutmeg, and salt. Mix well.

Add the flour in one-cup increments, mixing after each addition.

Stir in the nuts. *(If you work quickly, while the butter is still warm, the dough will be softer and easier to mix.)*

Form the dough into one-inch balls *(just pat them into shape with your impeccably clean fingers)*, and place them on an ungreased cookie sheet, 12 to a standard-sized sheet.

Bake the Little Snowballs at 350 degrees F., for 10 minutes, or until they are "set" *(that means no longer squishy)* but not browned.

Let the cookies cool for two minutes and then roll them in powdered sugar. *(You must do this while they're still warm.)* Place them on a wire rack and let them cool thoroughly.

When the cookies are cool, roll them in powdered sugar a second time. Let them rest for several minutes on the rack and then store them in a cookie jar or a covered bowl.

MERRY BERRY COOKIES

DO NOT preheat the oven — this cookie dough has to chill before baking.

- 1 and 1/2 cups melted butter *(3 sticks, 12 ounces, 3/4 pound)*
- 2 cups white *(granulated)* sugar
- 1/2 cup melted raspberry, blackberry, strawberry, or any berry jam *(I used Knott's seedless raspberry)*
- 2 beaten eggs
- 1/2 teaspoon baking soda
- 1 teaspoon salt
- 4 cups flour *(pack it down in the cup when you measure — don't sift it)*

- 1/3 cup white *(granulated)* sugar for later
- 1/3 cup berry jam for later

Melt the butter in a large microwave-safe bowl. Add the white sugar and mix it in thoroughly. Let the bowl sit on the counter while you do the next step.

Melt the jam in the microwave or in a saucepan over low heat. Once it's the consistency of syrup, mix it in with the butter and sugar.

Add the eggs, one at a time, mixing after each addition.

307

Mix in the baking soda and salt. Stir until they're thoroughly incorporated.

Add the flour in one-cup increments, mixing after each addition. Give a final stir, cover the mixing bowl with plastic wrap, and refrigerate the dough for at least 2 hours. *(Overnight's even better.)*

When you're ready to bake, preheat the oven to 350 degrees F., rack in the middle position.

Place 1/3 cup sugar in a small bowl on the counter. You'll use it to coat your cookies.

Roll the chilled dough into walnut-sized balls with your impeccably clean hands. Roll the balls in the bowl with the sugar, and then place them on a greased standard-sized cookie sheet, 12 cookies to a sheet. *(Alternatively, you can spray your cookie sheets with Pam or another nonstick cooking spray instead of greasing them, or simply line them with parchment paper.)*

Flatten the dough balls with a greased spatula. Make a small indentation with your thumb or index finger in the center of each cookie. Fill the indentation with a small bit of jam *(about 1/8 teaspoon)*.

Bake the cookies for 10 to 12 minutes at 350 degrees F. Let them cool for 2 minutes on the cookie sheet, and then transfer them to a wire rack to finish cooling. *(If you used parchment paper, all you have to do is pull the cookie-laden paper onto the wire rack.)*

These cookies freeze well. Roll them up in foil, put them in a freezer bag. You may want to be sneaky about labeling the cookies or the kids will find them and eat them frozen. *(If you write "Pork Kidneys" on the freezer bag, the kids will probably leave them alone.)*

Yield: 8 to 10 dozen pretty and tasty cookies, depending on cookie size.

Preheat oven to 375 degrees F., rack in the middle position.

1 and 1/4 cups white *(granulated)* sugar

1 cup *(2 sticks, 8 ounces, 1/2 pound)* salted butter, softened

3 large eggs

1/2 teaspoon salt

1 teaspoon baking soda

1 and 1/2 cups mincemeat *(I used Crosse & Blackwell Mincemeat Filling & Topping)*

3 cups all-purpose flour *(pack it down in the cup when you measure it)*

---

4 to 5 dozen walnut halves

OR

3/4 cup vanilla cream glaze *(glaze recipe follows the cookie recipe)*

Hannah's 1st Note: If you decide to use the Vanilla Cream Glaze instead of the half walnuts on top of your cookies, make the glaze first. If you want to decorate your cookies with the half-walnuts instead of the glaze, read on . . .

Hannah's 2nd Note: Unless you have a very strong stirring arm, use an electric mixer to make this cookie dough.

Place the sugar in the bowl of an electric mixer.

Place the butter, which must be softened to room temperature, on top of the sugar.

Turn the mixer to LOW and mix for one minute. Gradually increase the speed of the mixer, scraping down the sides of the bowl frequently and beating for one minute at each level, until you arrive at the highest speed.

Beat at the highest speed for at least 2 minutes or until the resulting mixture is very light and fluffy.

Turn the mixer down to LOW and add the eggs, one at a time, mixing after each addition. Then add the salt. When that's mixed in, add the baking soda and mix until it's incorporated.

Measure out a cup and a half of mincemeat. Turn the mixer on LOW speed and add the mincemeat to your bowl.

Add the flour in one-cup increments, mixing after each addition. Shut off the mixer and scrape down the sides of the bowl. Give the mixture a final stir by hand. *(The resulting cookie dough should be fluffy, but not at all stiff like sugar cookie or chocolate chip cookie dough.)*

Line your cookie sheets with parchment paper. It's the easiest way to bake these cookies. If you don't have parchment paper and you really don't want to go out to get any, grease your cookie sheets heavily, or spray them thoroughly with Pam or another nonstick cooking spray.

Using a teaspoon *(not the measuring kind, but one from your silverware drawer)*, drop rounded teaspoons of cookie dough on your baking sheet, 12 to a standard-sized sheet. If you are NOT going to glaze these cookies with Vanilla Cream Glaze *(recipe follows below)*, top each cookie with a half-walnut, pressing it down slightly.

Bake your Mincemeat Cookies at 375 degrees F., for 12 minutes. Take the cookies out of the oven and slide the cookie-laden parchment paper onto a wire rack to cool. *(If you used greased cookie sheets, you're going to have to let the cookies sit on the cookie sheets for 2 minutes and then remove them to a wire rack with a metal spatula.)*

Yield: Approximately 4 to 5 dozen tasty

and attractive cookies.

*Vanilla Cream Glaze

1 Tablespoon vanilla extract
1/4 cup less 1 Tablespoon heavy *(whipping)* cream
3 cups powdered *(confectioner's)* sugar

Place 1 Tablespoon vanilla extract into a quarter-cup measuring cup.

Fill the quarter-cup measuring cup with heavy cream and set it on the counter.

Measure 3 cups powdered sugar and place them in a small bowl. Do not pack it down in the cup when you measure it, but do level the top off with a table knife.

Whisk the vanilla and cream into the bowl with the powered sugar until it's well blended.

Cover the glaze with plastic wrap and set it aside to wait for the cookies to be baked. Then brush the warm cookies with the glaze and let them cool completely.

Hannah's 3rd Note: If there's any glaze left over, add a little more powdered sugar and mix it until it's of frosting consistency. Let the kids spread it on graham crackers or soda crackers (salt side down) for a special treat.

Yield: Approximately 3/4 cup glaze.

*Minty Marvels

Preheat oven to 350 degrees F., rack in the middle position.

- 2 cups *(4 sticks, 16 ounces, 1 pound)* salted butter, softened
- 1 cup powdered *(confectioner's)* sugar *(pack it down in the cup when you measure it)*
- 1/2 teaspoon salt
- 1 teaspoon vanilla extract
- 1 egg, beaten *(just whip it up in a glass with a fork)*
- 1/2 cup finely chopped pecans *(chop them until they're almost powdery)*
- 4 cups all-purpose flour *(scoop it up in the measuring cup and then level off the top with a table knife)*
- 8 dozen Junior Mints *(approximately 6 small boxes)*

- 1 cup powdered *(confectioner's)* sugar *(don't pack it down this time around)*
- 1 Tablespoon red decorating sugar
- 1 Tablespoon green decorating sugar

Hannah's 1st Note: I used an electric mixer when I made these. The dough has to be very well mixed.

In the bowl of an electric mixer, combine

the softened butter, powdered sugar, salt, and vanilla extract. Mix it on MEDIUM speed until it's light and fluffy.

Turn the mixer down to LOW speed and add the egg and the pecans. Mix well.

When the pecans are incorporated, add the flour, one cup at a time, mixing after each addition. Shut off the mixer, scrape down the sides of the bowl with a rubber spatula, and mix a bit more.

Take the bowl out of the mixer, give it a final stir by hand, and set it aside on the counter.

With your fingers, shape a Tablespoonful of cookie dough into a ball around one Junior Mint.

Place the dough balls at least 1 inch apart on an ungreased or parchment-lined cookie sheet. Press them down slightly so that they won't roll off on the way to the oven.

Bake the dough balls at 350 degrees F. for 10 to 12 minutes, or until the cookies are "set" and the bottoms are just beginning to turn golden. *(To judge this, you'll have to open the oven and lift one cookie up just a bit to see.)*

While your cookies are baking, place the powdered sugar, red decorating sugar, and green decorating sugar in a small bowl. Mix it all up with a fork. You want the colored sugars to be as evenly distributed as possible.

Hannah's 2nd Note: If you'd like these cookies to really sparkle with color, use colored decorating sugar with large sugar crystals. It's available in grocery stores during the holiday season and you can also find it in some cake decorating stores.

Let your cookies cool on the cookie sheet for 2 minutes, and then move them to a wire rack. *(This is easy if you've used parchment paper — just pull it off the sheet and onto the rack.)*

While they're still hot, roll the cookies in the bowl of sugars, one at a time, and then place them back on the wire rack or back on the parchment paper if you've used it. Don't worry if the powdered sugar soaks into the cookie in some spots. You're going to roll them in the sugars again after they've cooled completely.

Once the Minty Marvels have cooled approximately 25 minutes, roll them in the sugar a second time.

Hannah's 3rd Note: These cookies freeze well. Just let them thaw at room temperature and then roll them in a bowl with the sugars again to refresh the pretty sugar coating.

Yield: Approximately 8 dozen cookies, depending on cookie size.

MOCK TURTLES

DO NOT preheat oven — dough must chill before baking.

1 and 1/2 sticks chilled butter *(3/4 cup, 6 ounces)*
2 cups flour *(pack it down in the cup when you measure it)*
3/4 cup powdered *(confectioner's)* sugar
1/2 teaspoon salt
1/2 cup chocolate chips *(I used Ghirardelli semi-sweet)*
1 egg
approximately 3 dozen Kraft Caramels *(the soft kind that are individually wrapped — they're about a half-inch square)*

Cut the butter into 12 pieces and place them in a work bowl. With two forks, mix in the flour, powdered sugar, and salt. Continue mixing until the dough is crumbly.

Hannah's 1st Note: You can also do this in a food processor with the steel blade, the same way you'd mix pie crust. It's a lot easier that way.

Melt the chocolate chips in a small microwave-safe bowl *(I use a glass measuring cup)* for 40 seconds on HIGH. Stir them to see if they're melted. *(Chocolate chips may maintain their shape until they're stirred.)* If they're not melted, microwave them in 20-second intervals until they are.

Add the melted chips to the dough mixture. Stir *(or process, if you've used a food processor)* until the chocolate is mixed in and the crumbly dough is a uniform color. Beat the egg in a small cup or bowl and add it to the work bowl. Mix it in *(or process with the steel blade)* until a soft, piecrust-type dough results.

Divide the dough into four equal parts. Tear off four pieces of wax paper about a foot and a half long. You'll use these to hold your dough when you roll it out. Turn a piece of wax paper so that the long side faces you and place one piece of dough in the center. Using your hands, roll the dough into a log that's approximately 12 inches long and 3/4 inch wide. Do the same for the three remaining pieces of dough.

Wrap the rolls in the wax paper you used to roll them and put them into a freezer bag. Freeze them for an hour or two until firm. *(Overnight is fine, too.)*

When you're ready to bake, take out the dough and let it warm up on the counter for fifteen minutes. Then preheat the oven to 325 degrees F., rack in the middle position.

Unwrap a roll of dough and cut it into 3/4 inch pieces with a sharp knife. Place the pieces cut side down on a greased or parchment-covered cookie sheet, 12 pieces to a standard-sized sheet.

Unwrap 6 caramels and cut them in half. I find this is easiest if you dip the blades of your kitchen scissors in water and then cut the caramels with the scissors. You can also spray the blades of your kitchen scissors with Pam and try it that way.

Press a half caramel into the center of each chocolate cookie. Be careful not to press it all the way to the bottom. *(If the dough is still too cold to press in the caramels, let it warm up a bit more and try again.)* Make sure your caramels are surrounded by cookie dough and won't melt over the sides of the cookies when they bake.

Bake each pan of cookies at 325 degrees F., for approximately 15 minutes, or until firm to the touch. Let the cookies cool for a minute or two on the pan and then remove them to a wire rack to complete cooling.

When all the cookies are baked and cooled, spread foil or waxed paper under the wire rack containing the cookies and prepare to glaze them. *(I use extra-wide foil because it's easy to crimp up the edges and make it into a disposable drip pan.)*

CHOCOLATE GLAZE:

1 and 1/3 cups milk chocolate chips *(I used Ghirardelli)*
1/3 cup water
1/3 cup light corn syrup *(I used Karo)*
1 cup white *(granulated)* sugar
approximately 6 dozen pecan halves

Measure out the chips and put them in a small bowl so they're ready to add when it's time.

In a saucepan, combine the water, corn syrup, and white sugar. Place the saucepan on high heat, and STIRRING CONSTANTLY, bring the contents to a boil. Boil for 15 seconds, still STIRRING CONSTANTLY, and pull it off the heat.

Dump in the chips, all at once, and poke them down until almost all of them are covered by the hot syrup mixture. Let the saucepan sit on a cold burner (or on a pad on the counter) for 2 and 1/2 minutes.

Gently stir the mixture with a whisk *(a fork will also work)* until it's almost completely smooth. Be careful not to whisk in air, or you'll get bubbles.

Set the glaze down on a potholder next to your cookies. Spoon a little over the top of each cookie and let it drizzle down the sides. *(You can also pour it over the cookies, but that's a little harder to do.)* When you're all through, top each cookie with a pecan half, making sure the nut sticks to the chocolate glaze.

Leave the cookies on the wire rack until the glaze has hardened. This will take approximately 30 minutes. Then eat and enjoy!

Lisa's Note: When I'm in a hurry and don't have time to glaze the cookies, I just sprinkle them with a little powdered sugar, serve them with chocolate ice cream, and call it a day.

Hannah's 2nd Note: Norman says to warn any friends with temporary fillings that the caramels in the center of these cookies are chewy.

Hannah's 3rd Note: You can store these cookies in a box lined with wax paper in the refrigerator, but take them out at least thirty minutes before you serve them so that the caramel in the center will soften and not break a tooth!

Yield: Approximately 6 dozen very tasty cookies.

MOLASSES CRACKLES

DO NOT pre-heat oven yet. Dough must chill before baking.

- 1 and 1/2 cups melted butter *(3 sticks, 12 ounces, 3/4 pound)*
- 2 cups white *(granulated)* sugar
- 1/2 cup molasses *(use Brier Rabbit green label or a very dark molasses)*
- 2 beaten eggs *(just whip them up in a glass with a fork)*
- 4 teaspoons baking soda
- 1 teaspoon salt
- 3 teaspoons cinnamon***
- 1 teaspoon nutmeg *(freshly ground is best)*
- 4 cups flour *(don't sift it — pack it down in the cup when you measure it)*

1/2 cup white sugar in a small bowl for rolling the dough balls

*** I use 2 and 1/2 teaspoons cinnamon and 1/2 teaspoon cardamom when I want a deeper, richer flavor.

Melt the butter in a large microwave bowl. Mix in the sugar and the molasses. Let it cool on the counter while you mix up the eggs.

When the mixture in the bowl is not so hot it'll cook the eggs, add them and stir them in thoroughly. Then add the baking soda, salt, cinnamon, and nutmeg, stirring after each addition.

Add flour in one-cup increments, mixing after each addition. The dough will be quite stiff at this point.

Cover the dough with plastic wrap and refrigerate it for at least two hours. *(Overnight is even better.)*

When you're ready to bake, preheat oven to 350 degrees F., rack in the middle position.

Roll the chilled dough into walnut-sized balls. Put some sugar in a small bowl and roll the balls in it to coat them. Place them on a greased cookie sheet *(12 to a standard-sized sheet)*. Press them down just a little so they won't roll off when you carry them to the oven.

Bake at 350 degrees F. for 10 to 12 minutes. The cookies will flatten out, all by themselves. Let them cool for 2 minutes on the cookie sheets and then move them to a wire rack to finish cooling.

Hannah's Note: Molasses cookies freeze well. Roll them up in foil, put them in a freezer bag, and they'll be fine for 3 months or so. *(You'd better lock your freezer if you want them to last that long.)*

Yield: 8 to 10 dozen, depending on cookie size.

MYSTERY COOKIES

Preheat oven to 350 degrees F., rack in the middle position.

1/2 cup melted butter *(1 stick, 4 ounces, 1/4 pound)*

3 and 1/2 cups white *(granulated)* **sugar**

2 beaten eggs *(just whip them up in a glass with a fork)*

1 can *(net weight 10 and 3/4 ounces)* **con-densed tomato soup** *(the regular plain kind, not "Cream of Tomato" or "Tomato with Basil" or anything else fancy — I use Campbells)*

2 teaspoons cinnamon

2 teaspoons nutmeg

2 teaspoons baking soda

2 teaspoons salt

2 cups raisins *(either golden or regular)*

2 cups chopped walnuts *(measure after you chop them)*

4 and 1/2 cups flour *(not sifted — pack it down when you measure it)*

Microwave the butter in a microwave-safe mixing bowl to melt it. Stir in the sugar and let it cool to almost room temperature.

When the mixture is not so hot it'll cook the eggs, mix them in.

Open the can of condensed tomato soup, add that to your bowl, and then mix it in thoroughly. Then add in the cinnamon, nutmeg, baking soda, and salt. Mix thoroughly.

Add the raisins and the walnuts, and stir them in.

Add the flour in one-cup increments, mixing after each addition.

Let the dough sit for ten minutes or so to rest. Drop the dough by teaspoons onto a cookie sheet you've greased or sprayed with Pam or another nonstick cooking spray. Place 12 cookies on a standard-sized cookie sheet. *(If the dough is too sticky to scoop, you can chill it for a few minutes, or dip your teaspoon into a glass of cold water.)*

Bake at 350 degrees F. for 10 to 12 minutes or until the cookies are golden brown on top. Remove from the oven and let them cool on the cookie sheet for 2 minutes *(no longer or they'll stick)*, and then transfer them to a wire rack to complete cooling.

A batch of Mystery Cookies yields about 10 dozen. *(I know that's a lot, but they'll be gone before you know it.)* They're soft and chewy and a real favorite. *(And if you don't tell the kids that they're getting a helping of tomatoes with their cookies, I guarantee they'll never guess.)*

*Norwegian Chocolate Pizza

Preheat oven to 350 degrees F., rack in the middle position.

Hannah's 1st Note: Ellie always brings these to Mother's cookie exchange in pizza boxes from her restaurant, Bertanelli's Pizza.

4 cups quick oatmeal *(I used Quaker Quick-1 Minute)*
1 cup *(2 sticks, 8 ounces, 1/2 pound)* **salted butter, softened**
3/4 cup brown sugar *(pack it down in the cup when you measure it)*

6-ounce package semi-sweet chocolate chips *(that's one cup of chips)*
3/4 cup creamy peanut butter***

---

shredded coconut
red candied cherries, chopped****
chopped nuts of your choice

***Some people have peanut allergies. If you plan to serve this to someone who does, substitute almond butter for the peanut butter. You could also substitute Nutella (a hazelnut chocolate butter) if you can find it in your area.

****If you can't find red candied cherries, you can use well-drained maraschino cherries.

Line a cookie sheet with parchment paper.

In a medium-sized bowl, mix the oatmeal, softened butter, and brown sugar together.

Round the mixture up in a large ball with your impeccably clean hands and place it in the center of the parchment-lined cookie sheet.

Pat the mixture into a circle about the size of a small pizza.

Push the outside edges up a bit so that they form what looks like a crust.

Bake the "pizza" at 350 degrees F. for approximately 15 minutes, or until it turns brown and bubbles a bit.

Take your "pizza" out of the oven and let it cool slightly while you make your toppings.

If you have a double boiler, use it to make the topping. If you don't, use a heavy saucepan and stir it to keep the contents from scorching.

Combine the chocolate chips and the peanut butter over LOW heat. Stir it until everything melts and blends together.

Remove the topping from the heat and

pour it over your "pizza" crust.

Decorate the top of your pizza with the coconut to simulate shredded cheese, the chopped cherries to simulate chopped to-matoes, and the chopped nuts to simulate sausage pieces.

Hannah's 2nd Note: Be creative with your "pizza" toppings. See if you can find some-thing to simulate pepperoni, or green pep-per, or any other real pizza topping you can think of. Remember, the toppings don't go in the oven so you can use any sweet treat you can find at the grocery store.

Refrigerate your pizza until it has hard-ened. To serve, you can either cut it in slices with a pizza cutter just like a real pizza, or break it into pieces like toffee or peanut brittle.

Yield: One small-size pizza that everyone will love.

OATMEAL RAISIN CRISPS

Preheat oven to 375 degrees F., rack in the middle position.

- **1 cup melted butter** *(2 sticks, 8 ounces, 1/2 pound)*
- **2 cups white sugar**
- **2 teaspoons vanilla extract**
- **1/2 teaspoon salt**
- **2 teaspoons baking soda**
- **2 large eggs, beaten** *(just whip them up with a fork)*
- **2 and 1/2 cups flour** *(no need to sift)*
- **1 cup raisins** *(either regular or golden, you choose)*
- **2 cups GROUND dry oatmeal** *(measure BEFORE grinding)*

Melt the butter in a large microwave-safe bowl. Add the sugar and mix it in. Then mix in the vanilla extract, salt, and baking soda.

When the mixture has cooled to room temperature, stir in the beaten eggs.

Add the flour in one-cup increments, mixing after each addition.

Mix in the raisins.

Prepare your oatmeal. *(I used Quaker Quick-1 Minute.)* Measure out two cups of oatmeal and put them in the food processor, chopping it with the steel blade until it's the consistency of coarse sand. Transfer it to your mixing bowl and mix it in. *(This dough will be fairly stiff.)*

Roll walnut-sized dough balls with your impeccably clean hands and place them on a greased cookie sheet, 12 to a standard sheet. *(If it's too sticky to roll, place the bowl in the refrigerator for thirty minutes and try again.)* Squish the dough balls down with a fork in a crisscross pattern *(like peanut butter cookies)*.

Bake at 375 degrees F. for 10 to 12 minutes. Remove the Oatmeal Raisin Crisps from the oven and cool them on the cookie sheet for 2 minutes. Then transfer the cookies to a wire rack to cool completely.

Yield: 6 to 7 dozen, depending on cookie size.

These cookies freeze well if you roll them up in foil and place them in a freezer bag. They also hold together well for shipping.

Andrea likes these and she's never liked raisins — go figure.

OLD FASHIONED SUGAR COOKIES

DO NOT preheat oven — dough must chill before baking.

- **2 cups melted butter** *(4 sticks, 16 ounces, 1 pound)*
- **2 cups powdered sugar** *(don't sift unless it's got big lumps and then you shouldn't use it anyway)*
- **1 cup white** *(granulated)* **sugar**
- **2 eggs**
- **2 teaspoons vanilla extract**
- **1 teaspoon lemon zest** *(optional)*
- **1 teaspoon baking soda**
- **1 teaspoon cream of tartar** *(critical!)*
- **1 teaspoon salt**
- **4 and 1/4 cups flour** *(don't sift — pack it down in the cup when you measure it)*

1/2 cup white sugar in a small bowl *(for coating dough balls)*

Melt the butter in a microwave-safe bowl or in a saucepan on the stovetop. Add the sugar and mix thoroughly. Let the mix cool to room temperature.

Mix in the eggs, one at a time, mixing after each egg is added. Then mix in the vanilla extract, lemon zest, baking soda, cream of tartar, and salt.

Add the flour in one-cup increments, mixing after each addition.

Chill the dough for at least one hour. *(Overnight is fine, too.)*

When you're ready to bake, preheat oven to 325 degrees F. with the rack in the middle position.

Use your impeccably clean hands to roll the dough in walnut-sized balls. Roll the dough balls in the bowl of white sugar to coat them.

Hannah's 1st Note: You can make Old-Fashioned Sugar Cookies special by mixing white sugar 2 to 1 with colored sugar for holidays. You could use orange for Halloween, red, white and blue for Independence Day, green for St. Pat's Day, red and green for Christmas, and multi-colored for birthdays.

Place the sugar-coated dough balls on a cookie sheet you've greased, sprayed with Pam or another nonstick cooking spray, or covered with parchment paper. Place 12 cookies on each standard-sized cookie sheet. Flatten the dough balls with the back of a metal spatula or the palm of your impeccably clean hand.

Bake at 325 degrees F. for 10 to 15 minutes. *(The cookies should have a tinge of gold on the top.)* Cool the cookies on cookie sheet for 2 minutes, then remove them to a rack to finish cooling.

Hannah's 2nd Note: These cookies can be decorated with frosting piped from a pastry bag for special occasions or left just as they are.

Yield: Approximately 10 dozen crunchy, buttery, sugary cookies.

ORANGE SNAPS

DO NOT preheat the oven — this dough needs to chill before baking.

- 1 and 1/2 cups melted butter *(3 sticks, 12 ounces, 3/4 pound)*
- 2 cups white *(granulated)* sugar
- 1/2 cup frozen orange juice concentrate *(I used Minute Maid)*
- 2 beaten eggs *(just whip them up in a glass with a fork)*
- 2 teaspoons baking soda
- 1 teaspoon salt
- 1/2 teaspoon orange zest***
- 4 cups flour *(don't sift — pack it down in*

***The orange zest adds a burst of flavor. Zest is finely grated orange peel, just the orange part, not the white. You can use a grater to grate the orange part of the peel, or a zester, which removes a thin layer of peel in strips. If you use a zester, you'll have to finely chop the strips of peel with a knife.

the cup when you measure it)

1/3 cup white *(granulated)* sugar in a small bowl for coating dough balls

Melt the butter in large microwave-safe bowl. Add the sugar and orange juice concentrate, and stir it all up. Let the mixture cool to room temperature.

Add the beaten eggs, baking soda, salt, and orange zest, stirring after each addition.

Add the flour in one-cup increments, mixing thoroughly after each increment.

Cover the bowl with plastic wrap and refrigerate the dough at least 2 hours *(overnight's even better)*.

When you're ready to bake, preheat your oven to 350 degrees F., rack in the middle position.

Roll the chilled dough into walnut-sized balls with your impeccably clean hands. Put 1/3 cup white sugar in a small bowl and roll the balls in it to coat them. Place them on a greased cookie sheet *(or a cookie sheet you've sprayed with Pam or another nonstick cooking spray)*, 12 dough balls to a standard-sized sheet. Press the dough balls down just a little so they won't roll off on the floor when you put them in the oven.

Bake for 10 to 12 minutes at 350 degrees F. The dough balls will flatten out, all by themselves. Let the cookies cool for 2 minutes on the cookie sheet and then move them to a wire rack to finish cooling.

Yield: Approximately 7 to 8 dozen cookies, depending on cookie size.

PARTY COOKIES

DO NOT preheat the oven — this cookie dough must chill before baking.

- **2 cups melted butter** *(4 sticks, 16 ounces, 1 pound)*
- **2 cups powdered sugar** *(not sifted — pack it down in the cup when you measure it)*
- **1 cup white** *(granulated)* **sugar**
- **2 eggs**
- **2 teaspoons vanilla extract** *(or any other flavoring you wish)*
- **1 teaspoon baking soda**
- **1 teaspoon cream of tartar** *(critical!)*
- **1 teaspoon salt**
- **4 and 1/4 cups flour** *(not sifted — pack it down in the cup when you measure it)*
- **food coloring** *(at least 3 different colors)*

1/2 cup white sugar in a bowl for coating the dough balls

Melt the butter in a microwave-safe bowl or in a saucepan on the stovetop. Add the sugars and mix well. Set the bowl on the counter and let the mixture cool to room temperature.

When the mixture is not so hot it'll cook the eggs, add them, one at a time, mixing after each egg. Then add the vanilla extract, baking soda, cream of tartar, and salt. Mix well.

Add the flour in half-cup increments, mixing after each addition.

Divide the cookie dough into fourths and place each fourth on a piece of wax paper. *(You'll work with one fourth at a time.)* Place one fourth in a bowl and stir in drops of food coloring until the dough is slightly darker than the color you want. *(The cookies will be a shade lighter after they're baked.)* Place the colored dough back on the waxed paper and color the other three parts. *(You can leave one part uncolored, if you like.)*

Let the dough firm up for a few moments. Then divide each different COLOR into four parts so you have sixteen lumps of dough in all. Place a sheet of plastic wrap on your counter and roll each lump into a dough rope with your hands *(just as if you were making bread sticks)*. The sixteen dough ropes should each be about 12 inches long.

To assemble, stack four dough ropes of different colors, two on the bottom, two on the top, near the edge of the plastic wrap.

Squeeze them together a bit and push in the ends so they're even. Flip the bottom edge of the plastic wrap over the top and roll them up together tightly in one multi-colored roll. Twist the ends of the plastic wrap, fold them over on top of the roll, and refrigerate the rolls as you make them. When you're all finished, you'll should have four rolls of multi-colored cookie dough, wrapped and chilling in your refrigerator.

Let the dough chill for at least an hour *(overnight is fine, too)*. When you're ready to bake, preheat the oven to 325 degrees F., rack in the middle position.

Grease *(or spray with Pam or another non-stick cooking spray)* a standard-sized cookie sheet. Place the bowl with the half cup white sugar next to your cookie sheets.

Take out one dough roll, unwrap it, and slice it into half inch thick rounds. *(Each dough roll should make about 24 cookies.)* Place each round into the bowl of sugar and flip it over so it coats both sides. Position the sugar-coated rounds on the baking sheet. Don't place more than 12 cookies on each sheet. Return the unused dough to the refrigerator until you're ready to slice more cookies.

Bake the cookies at 325 degrees F. for 12 to 15 minutes, just until they begin to turn slightly golden around the edges. Cool them on the cookie sheet for 2 minutes, and then transfer them to a wire rack to complete cooling.

These cookies freeze very well if you stack them in a roll, wrap them in foil, and place the foil rolls in a freezer bag that you put in the freezer. You can also freeze the multi-colored unbaked dough rolls by leaving them in the plastic wrap and placing them in a freezer bag in the freezer.

Yield: Approximately 8 dozen pretty party cookies.

PEANUT BUTTER & JAM COOKIES (PBJs)

Preheat oven to 350 degrees F., rack in the middle position.

1 cup melted butter *(2 sticks, 8 ounces, 1/2 pound)*
2 cups brown sugar *(firmly packed)*
1/2 cup white *(granulated)* sugar
1 teaspoon vanilla extract
1 teaspoon baking powder
1 and 1/2 teaspoons baking soda
1/2 teaspoon salt
1 cup peanut butter
2 beaten eggs *(just whip them up in a glass with a fork)*
1/2 cup chopped salted peanuts *(measure AFTER chopping)*
3 cups flour *(don't sift — pack it down when you measure it)*
approximately 1/2 cup fruit jam *(your choice of fruit)*

Microwave the butter in a microwave-safe mixing bowl for approximately 90 seconds on HIGH to melt it. Mix in the brown sugar, white sugar, vanilla, baking powder, baking soda, and salt. Stir until they're thoroughly blended.

Measure out the peanut butter. *(I spray the inside of my measuring cup with Pam so it won't stick.)* Add it to the bowl and mix it in. Pour in the beaten eggs and stir it all up. Add the chopped salted peanuts and mix until they're incorporated.

Add the flour in one-cup increments, mixing after each ingredient. Mix until all the ingredients are thoroughly blended.

Form the dough into walnut-sized balls with your impeccably clean hands and arrange them on a greased cookie sheet, 12 to a standard-sized sheet. *(If the dough is too sticky to form into balls, chill it for an hour or so, and then try again.)*

Make an indentation in the center of the dough balls with your thumb. Spoon in a bit of jam, making sure it doesn't run over the sides of the cookies.

Bake at 350 degrees F. for 10 to 12 minutes, or until the tops are just beginning to turn golden. Cool on the cookie sheet for 2 minutes, then remove to a wire rack to finish cooling.

Yield: Approximately 7 dozen cookies, depending on cookie size.

Hannah's Note: If you happen to run out of fruit jam and you have cookies left to fill, put a few chocolate chips in the indentation. You'll have to call those cookies PBCs, and they're wonderful!

Tracey likes her PBJs with strawberry jam, Andrea prefers apricot, Bill's wild about blueberry, and Mother loves them with peach. I prefer to eat one of each, just to test them, of course.

PEANUT BUTTER MELTS

Preheat oven to 375 degrees F., rack in the middle position.

1 cup melted butter *(2 sticks, 8 ounces, 1/2 pound)*

2 cups white *(granulated)* **sugar*****

2 teaspoons vanilla extract

1/8 cup molasses *(2 Tablespoons)*

1 teaspoon baking powder

1 and 1/2 teaspoons baking soda

1/2 teaspoon salt

1 cup peanut butter *(either smooth or crunchy, your choice)*

2 beaten eggs *(just whip them up in a glass with a fork)*

2 and 1/2 cups flour *(don't sift — pack it down when you measure it)*

Microwave the butter in your microwave-safe mixing bowl to melt it. Add the sugar, the vanilla extract, and the molasses. Stir until the mixture is thoroughly blended, then add the baking powder, baking soda, and salt. Mix well.

***For a sweeter cookie, add 1/2 cup white *(granulated)* sugar or roll dough balls in sugar before baking. If you want a real treat, add 2 cups of milk chocolate chips to the dough.

Measure out the peanut butter. *(I spray the inside of my measuring cup with Pam so it won't stick.)* Add it to the bowl and mix it in. Pour in the beaten eggs and stir until they're incorporated.

Add the flour in one-cup increments, mixing after each addition.

Form the dough into walnut-sized balls with your impeccably clean fingers and arrange them on a cookie sheet that's been greased, sprayed with Pam or another non-stick cooking spray, or covered with parchment paper. Place 12 cookies on a standard-sized sheet. *(If the dough is too sticky to form into balls, chill it for 20 or 30 minutes and then try again.)*

Flatten the balls with a fork in a crisscross pattern. *(If the fork sticks, either spray it with Pam or dip it in flour.)*

Bake at 375 degrees F. for 8 to 10 minutes, or until the edges are just beginning to turn golden. Cool on the cookie sheet for 2 minutes, then remove to a wire rack to finish cooling.

Yield: 4 to 5 dozen delicious cookies, depending on cookie size.

Hannah's Note: Bill's favorite PBJ snack is to spread jam on one cookie and stack another cookie on top. Mother likes PBFs better *(that's fudge frosting between the cookie layers)*.

PECAN CHEWS

Preheat oven to 350 degrees F., rack in the middle position.

1 cup butter *(2 sticks, 8 ounces, 1/2 pound)*
3 cups brown sugar
4 eggs, beaten *(just whip them up with a fork in a glass)*
1 teaspoon salt
1 teaspoon baking soda
3 teaspoons vanilla
2 cups finely chopped pecans
4 cups flour *(pack it down in the cup when you measure it)*

Melt the butter in a microwave-safe bowl. Add the brown sugar and mix well. Let the mixture cool to room temperature.

Add the beaten eggs and mix until they're thoroughly combined.

Mix in the salt, baking soda, vanilla extract, and pecans. Stir until everything is thoroughly combined.

Add the flour in one-cup increments, mixing after each addition. Continue mixing until the flour is thoroughly distributed.

Form the dough into walnut-sized balls with your impeccably clean fingers. Place the dough balls on a greased cookie sheet, 12 cookies to a standard-sized sheet. *(You can also spray the cookie sheet with non-stick cooking spray, or line it with parchment paper.)* Press the dough balls down with the back of a metal spatula.

Bake at 350 degrees F. for 10 to 12 minutes.

Let the cookies set up on the sheet for 2 minutes, then remove them to a wire rack to finish cooling.

Hannah's Note: There's no need to keep brown sugar in stock. It can be easily made with white sugar and molasses, 1/8 cup molasses for every 3 cups of white sugar. *(That's how they manufacture it, really. And it'll save you from having to deal with all those lumps.)* Just add the molasses to the white sugar and stir until it is thoroughly and evenly mixed. There's no problem if your recipe calls for dark brown sugar, or light brown sugar. Just mix in molasses until it's the right color.

Yield: 8 to 10 dozen, depending on cookie size.

PECAN DIVINES

(ANDREA'S FAVORITES)

Preheat oven to 350 degrees F., rack in the middle position.

2 cups melted butter *(4 sticks, one pound)*
3 cups white sugar
1 and 1/2 cups brown sugar
4 teaspoons vanilla extract
2 teaspoons baking soda
2 teaspoons salt
4 beaten eggs
5 cups flour *(don't sift — pack it down in the cup when you measure it)*
3 cups chocolate chips
4 cups chopped pecans

Melt the butter. *(Microwave it for 3 minutes on HIGH in a microwave-safe container, or in a saucepan on the stove.)* Mix in the white sugar and the brown sugar. Add the vanilla extract, baking soda, and salt. Mix thoroughly.

Feel the bowl. If it's not so hot the mixture will cook the eggs, add them now. Stir thoroughly.

Add half of the flour, the chocolate chips, and the chopped pecans. Stir well to incorporate. Then add the rest of the flour and mix thoroughly.

Drop by teaspoons onto greased cookie sheets, 12 cookies to a standard-sized sheet. You can also spray your cookie sheets with Pam or another nonstick cooking spray or line them with parchment paper. *(If the dough is too sticky to handle, chill it for 20 to 30 minutes and try again.)*

Bake at 350 degrees F. for 10 to 12 minutes or until nicely browned.

Let the cookies cool 2 minutes, then remove them from the baking sheet with a metal spatula, and transfer them to a wire rack to finish cooling.

Yield: Approximately 10 dozen.

Hannah's Note: These are Andrea's very favorite cookies. She says they're the best cookies she's ever tasted and I saved her life by baking them.

PINEAPPLE DELIGHTS

Preheat oven to 350 degrees F., rack in the middle position.

- 2 cups butter, melted *(4 sticks, 16 ounces, 1 pound)*
- 2 cups brown sugar *(pack it down in the cup when you measure it)*
- 2 cups white *(granulated)* sugar
- 4 eggs — beaten *(just whip them up in a glass with a fork)*
- 1 teaspoon baking powder
- 1 teaspoon baking soda
- 1 teaspoon salt
- 2 teaspoons pineapple extract *(if you can't find it, you can use vanilla)*
- 4 cups flour *(pack it down in the cup when you measure it)*
- 2 and 1/2 cups chopped, sweetened, dried pineapple *(measure AFTER chopping — if you can't find pineapple, you can substitute any dried fruit chopped in chocolate-chip-sized pieces)*

1/2 cup chopped coconut flakes *(measure AFTER chopping)*
3 cups rolled oats *(uncooked oatmeal — I used Quaker Quick-1 Minute in the round paper container that you save, but you don't know why)*

Melt the butter in a large microwave-safe bowl. *(About 3 minutes on HIGH.)* Add the sugars and let it cool to room temperature.

When the mixture is not so hot it'll cook the eggs, add the beaten eggs, baking powder, baking soda, salt, and pineapple extract, mixing after each addition.

Add the flour, one cup at a time, mixing after each addition. Then add the chopped pineapple, chopped coconut, and rolled oats, mixing them in thoroughly. The resulting dough will be quite stiff.

Drop by teaspoon onto a greased cookie sheet, 12 to a standard-sized sheet. *(I form mine into a ball so the cookies turn out nice and round.)*

Bake at 350 degrees F. for 12 to 15 minutes. Cool on the cookie sheet for 2 minutes, and then remove them to a wire rack to cool completely.

Hannah's Note: These cookies freeze really well if you roll them in foil and put them in a freezer bag.

Yield: Approximately 10 dozen, depending on cookie size.

PRALINE CHARLOTTES

Preheat oven to 350 degrees F., rack in the middle position.

1 and 1/2 cups melted butter *(3 sticks, 12 ounces, 3/4 pound)*
1 and 1/2 cups brown sugar
2 teaspoons vanilla
1 teaspoon baking powder
1 and 1/2 teaspoons baking soda
1 teaspoon salt *(decrease to 1/2 teaspoon if you use salted pecans)*
1 and 1/2 cups finely ground pecans *(grind them up in your food processor with the steel blade and measure AFTER grinding)*
2 beaten eggs *(just whip them up with a fork)*
3 cups flour *(don't sift — pack it down in the cup when you measure it)*

Microwave the butter in a microwave-safe bowl to melt it. Add the sugar and vanilla extract. Stir until blended, and then add the baking powder, baking soda, and salt. Mix well.

Add the finely ground pecans to the bowl and mix them in.

Pour in the beaten eggs and stir until everything is thoroughly blended.

Add the flour in one-cup increments, mixing after each addition. Continue to mix until all the ingredients are thoroughly blended.

Let the dough sit for 10 minutes to firm up. Then form the dough into walnut-sized balls with your impeccably clean fingers, and arrange them on a greased cookie sheet, 12 dough balls for each standard sheet. *(You can also spray the cookie sheets with Pam or another nonstick cooking spray, or line them with parchment paper.)*

Hannah's 1st Note: If the dough is too sticky to form into balls, chill it for 20 to 30 minutes and then try again.

Flatten the dough balls with a fork in a crisscross pattern. *(If the fork sticks, either spray it with Pam or dip it in flour.)*

Bake at 350 degrees F. for 8 to 10 minutes or until the cookies are golden brown around the edges. Cool them on the cookie sheet for 2 minutes, then remove them to a wire rack to finish cooling. When they're cool, prepare the frosting.

PRALINE FROSTING:

3/4 cup butter *(one and a half sticks)*

2 teaspoons vanilla extract *(or 1 and 1/2 teaspoons vanilla extract and 1/2 teaspoon of maple extract)*

3 and 1/2 cups powdered sugar *(not sifted)*

1/3 cup cream

1/2 cup finely chopped pecans

approximately 6 dozen pecan halves for decoration *(optional)*

Before you start, arrange the cooled cookies on racks or on sheets of wax paper. Then heat the butter in a saucepan over medium heat, stirring occasionally, until it turns a medium shade of brown *(the color of peanut butter)*. Remove the pan from the heat and add the vanilla extract *(and the maple flavoring if you use it)*. Blend in the powdered sugar, the cream, and the finely chopped pecans. Stir the frosting with a spoon until it's well mixed, but don't let it cool completely.

Frost the cookies and place a pecan half *(optional)* on top of each cookie for decoration. *(Frosting these cookies is like spreading butter and you don't have to spread it all the way out to the edges.)* If your frosting hardens before you're through, scrape it into a microwave-safe bowl and heat it for 30 seconds to 1 minute on HIGH in the microwave to soften it so that you can spread it again.

Let the finished cookies rest on racks or on wax paper until the frosting has hardened for at least an hour. Then store the cookies in a cookie jar or other closed container.

Yield: Approximately 8 dozen, depending on cookie size.

Hannah's 2nd Note: These cookies, unfrosted, make a delicious "tea" cookie with a light, delicate flavor. The only changes you have to make are: roll the dough balls smaller and press them down with the heel of your impeccably clean hand. Bake them for about 8 minutes or until the edges begin to turn golden. They're EXCELLENT with hot chocolate.

RAISIN DROPS

Preheat oven to 350 degrees F., rack in the middle position.

Jo Fluke's Note: This recipe is from my good friend, Lois Brown.

1 and 1/2 cups raisins *(I've used regular raisins, and also golden raisins — they're both good.)*

1 and 1/2 cups water *(right out of the tap is fine)*

_____

3 and 1/2 cups all purpose flour *(don't sift — just scoop it out and level it off with a knife)*

1 teaspoon salt

1 teaspoon baking powder

1 teaspoon baking soda

_____

1 cup softened butter *(2 sticks, 8 ounces, 1/2 pound)*

1 and 1/2 cups white *(granulated)* sugar

3 eggs, beaten *(just whip them up in a glass with a fork)*

1 teaspoon vanilla extract

_____

1/2 cup white *(granulated)* in a small bowl to coat the dough balls

Hannah's 1st Note: Hank, the bartender

down at the Lake Eden Municipal Liquor Store, suggested that you could soften the raisins in brandy or rum, instead of water. *(I used water.)*

Put the raisins and the water in an uncovered saucepan. Simmer them on the stove until all the water is absorbed. *(This took me about 20 minutes.)*

Move the saucepan to a cold burner, or place it on a potholder on your counter, and cool the raisins for 30 minutes. *(If you're in a hurry, you can speed up this cooling process by sticking the pan in the refrigerator until the raisins are approximately room temperature.)*

In a medium-sized mixing bowl, combine the flour, salt, baking powder, and baking soda. *(I stir mine gently with a whisk so that everything's mixed together.)* Set the bowl aside.

Hannah's 2nd Note: I used an electric mixer for this part of the recipe. You can do it by hand, but it takes some muscle.

Mix the softened butter and sugar together on HIGH speed until they're light and fluffy.

Add the eggs and mix on MEDIUM speed

until the mixture is a uniform color.

Take your bowl out of the mixer and blend in the raisins and the vanilla extract by hand.

Fold in the flour mixture carefully. The object is to keep the dough fluffy.

Put approximately 1/2 cup sugar into a small bowl. Drop the dough from a teaspoon *(or Tablespoon if you want large cookies)* into the bowl of sugar. Form the drops into balls with your fingers and move them to a lightly greased cookie sheet *(I sprayed my cookie sheet with Pam)*, 12 cookies to a standard-sized sheet.

Bake the Raisin Drops at 350 degrees F. for 9 to 10 minutes, or until just lightly browned.

Lois Brown's Note: I bake just a few at first to make sure there's the right amount of flour. If they spread out too thin, add another Tablespoon or two of flour. I have been making this recipe for my family for 40 years.

Yield: 5 to 6 dozen deliciously soft raisin cookies.

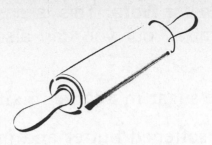

*Raspberry Vanilla Swirls

DO NOT preheat oven — cookie dough must chill before baking.

- 1 cup white *(granulated)* sugar
- 1 cup *(2 sticks, 8 ounces, 1/2 pound)* salted butter, softened
- 1 large egg
- 1/2 teaspoon salt
- 1/2 teaspoon baking powder
- 1/2 teaspoon vanilla extract
- 2 and 1/2 cups all-purpose flour *(scoop it up and level it off with a table knife — don't pack it down in the cup)*

- 1 teaspoon raspberry extract
- 1 teaspoon red food coloring
- 1 Tablespoon seedless raspberry jam
- 1/8 cup *(2 Tablespoons)* all-purpose flour *(that's in addition to the flour you added earlier)*

---

powdered sugar for rolling out the dough

Hannah's 1st Note: This is easy with an electric mixer, but you can also do it by hand.

Place the sugar in a large mixing bowl.

Add the softened butter and mix until it's light and fluffy.

Add the egg and mix well.

Sprinkle in the salt and the baking powder. Mix until they're thoroughly incorporated.

Add the vanilla extract. Mix it in well.

Add the flour by half-cup increments, mixing after each addition.

Scrape down the sides of the mixing bowl and give the dough a final stir by hand.

Place a sheet of wax paper on the counter. Dust the wax paper with powdered sugar.

Remove HALF of the cookie dough from your mixing bowl and place it on the wax paper. Pat it out like pie crust with your impeccably clean hands and then dust the top with more powdered sugar.

With a rolling pin, roll the dough into a rectangle that is approximately 1/4 inch thick. Cover the dough with another sheet of wax paper and store it in the refrigerator.

Go back to the dough in the mixer. This will be the raspberry part of your cookie pinwheels.

Turn the mixer on LOW and add the raspberry extract and the red food coloring. If you bought it in one of those little squeeze bottles, you don't have to measure out a teaspoonful. Just keep adding drops until you think it's the right color for your pinwheels.

Heat the Tablespoon of seedless raspberry jam in the microwave for a few seconds until it reverts to a liquid. Then add it to your mixing bowl and mix it in.

You've added more liquid to your cookie dough, so now you must add a bit more flour. Sprinkle in the additional eighth cup of flour and mix well.

Tear off a sheet of wax paper and spread it out on the counter. Dust it with powdered sugar and roll out the pink half of your dough. Again, form a rectangle that is approximately 1/4 inch thick.

Cover the raspberry half of your dough with another sheet of wax paper. Place it on top of your vanilla cookie dough in the refrigerator.

Chill both halves of your pinwheel cookie dough for at least 2 hours.

After your cookie dough has chilled for 2 hours, tear off another sheet of wax paper and spread it out on the counter. Dust it with powdered sugar. This will hold the cookie roll you're about to make.

Grasping the raspberry dough by the corners of the wax paper, carefully slide it off the vanilla dough and place it to the side on the counter. Then peel the top sheet of wax paper off the vanilla dough, working slowly and carefully so that it doesn't tear.

When the vanilla dough is bare on top, position the long end of the raspberry dough rectangle next to the long end of the vanilla dough rectangle. Peel the top layer of wax paper from your raspberry cookie dough.

Dust the bare top of your raspberry cookie dough with powdered sugar. Then cover it with the sheet of wax paper you tore off earlier. Grasping both sheets of wax paper, the one on the top and the one on the bottom, flip the raspberry dough over so that the side you dusted with powdered sugar is now on the bottom.

Hannah's 2nd Note: Believe me, this is harder to explain than it is to do. I wish I could just come over to your kitchen and show you!

Peel off the top sheet of wax paper and slide the raspberry dough on top of the vanilla dough. Working carefully and loosening the wax paper as you go, push your raspberry cookie dough off the wax paper and onto the bare vanilla cookie dough.

If the edges of the dough are uneven, trim them with a sharp knife. Use the pieces of dough you've trimmed for patches if there are any holes.

Working from the long side of the rectangle, roll up the dough so that it forms a log. This will create a pinwheel later when you slice the log into cookies.

Roll your cookie log in a piece of wax paper, twist the ends to keep the roll from coming undone, and refrigerate it for another 2 hours. ***(Overnight is fine, too.)***

Hannah's 3rd Note: At this point, you can even freeze the dough log if you put it into a large freezer bag that's airtight. Thaw it in the refrigerator 24 hours before you want to bake the cookies.

When 2 hours have passed, preheat your oven to 375 degrees F., rack in the middle position.

Line a cookie sheet with parchment paper or spray it with Pam or another nonstick cooking spray.

If your cookie roll has flattened in the refrigerator, you can roll it a bit on the counter to round it out.

Using a sharp knife, cut 1/4 inch slices from the cookie dough log. Cut only as many as you can bake at one time and return the log to the refrigerator between baking.

Place the Raspberry Vanilla Swirls on the cookie sheet, twelve to a standard-sized sheet.

Bake at 375 degrees F. for 8 to 10 minutes.

Remove the cookies from the oven and cool them on the cookie sheet for 2 minutes, then remove them to a wire rack to cool completely.

Yield: 4 to 6 dozen pretty and tasty cookies that everyone will love.

RED VELVET COOKIES

Preheat oven to 375 degrees F., rack in the middle position.

2 one-ounce squares unsweetened baking chocolate

1/2 cup butter *(1 stick, 4 ounces, 1/4 pound)* **at room temperature**

2/3 cup brown sugar, firmly packed

1/3 cup white *(granulated)* **sugar**

1/2 teaspoon baking soda

1/2 teaspoon salt

1 large egg

1 Tablespoon red food coloring

2 cups flour *(pack it down in the cup when you measure it)*

3/4 cup sour cream

1 cup *(6-ounce package)* **semi-sweet chocolate chips**

Line your cookie sheets with parchment paper. Spray the parchment paper with Pam or another nonstick cooking spray. *(If you don't have parchment paper, you can use foil, but leave little "ears" of foil sticking up on the ends, enough to grab later when you slide the whole thing on a wire rack to cool.)*

Unwrap the squares of chocolate and break them apart. Put them in a small microwave-safe bowl. *(I used an 8-ounce measuring cup.)* Melt them for 90 seconds on HIGH. Stir them until they're smooth and set them aside to cool while you mix up your cookie dough.

Hannah's 1st Note: Mixing this dough is easier with an electric mixer. You can do it by hand, but it takes some muscle.

Combine the butter, brown sugar, and white sugar in the bowl of an electric mixer. Beat them on MEDIUM speed until they're smooth. This should take less than a minute.

Add the baking soda and salt, and resume beating on MEDIUM speed for another minute, or until they're incorporated.

Add the egg and beat on MEDIUM speed until the batter is smooth *(an additional minute should do it)*. Add the red food coloring and mix for about 30 seconds.

Shut off the mixer and scrape down the bowl. Then add the melted chocolate and mix again for another minute on MEDIUM speed.

Shut off the mixer and scrape down the bowl again. At LOW speed, mix in half of the flour. *(That's one cup.)* When the flour is incorporated, mix in the sour cream.

Scrape down the bowl again and add the rest of the flour. *(That's the second cup.)* Beat until the flour is fully incorporated.

Remove the bowl from the mixer and give it a good stir with a spoon. Mix in the chocolate chips by hand. *(A firm rubber spatula works nicely.)*

Use a teaspoon to spoon the dough onto the parchment-lined cookie sheets, 12 cookies to a standard-sized sheet. *(If the dough is too sticky for you to work with, chill it for a half-hour or so, and try again.)*

Bake the cookies at 375 degrees F., for 9 to 11 minutes, or until they rise and become firm. *(Mine took exactly 9 minutes.)*

Slide the parchment paper from the cookie sheets and onto a wire rack. Let the cookies cool on the rack while the next sheet of cookies is baking. When the next sheet of cookies is ready, pull the cooled cookies onto the counter or table, and slide the parchment paper with the hot cookies onto the rack. Keep alternating until all the dough has been baked.

When all the cookies are cool, peel them off the parchment paper and put them on wax paper for frosting.

CREAM CHEESE FROSTING:

1/4 cup softened butter *(1/2 stick, 2 ounces, 1/8 pound)*

4 ounces softened cream cheese *(half of an 8-ounce package)*

1/2 teaspoon vanilla extract

2 cups powdered *(confectioner's)* sugar *(no need to sift unless it's got big lumps and then you should open a new package anyway)*

Mix the softened butter with the softened cream cheese and the vanilla extract until the mixture is smooth.

Hannah's 2nd Note: Do this next step at room temperature. If you heated the cream cheese or the butter to soften it, make sure it's cooled down before you continue.

Add the confectioner's sugar in half-cup increments until the frosting is of proper spreading consistency. *(You'll use all, or almost all, of the sugar.)*

A batch of Red Velvet Cookies yields about 3 dozen, depending on cookie size. They're soft, velvety, and chocolaty, and they'll end up being everyone's favorite cookie.

Hannah's 3rd Note: If you really want to

pull out all the stops, brush the tops of your baked cookies with melted raspberry jam, let it dry, and then frost them with the Cream Cheese Frosting.

REGENCY GINGER CRISPS

DO NOT preheat oven — dough must chill before baking.

- **3/4 cup melted butter** *(1 and 1/2 sticks, 6 ounces)*
- **1 cup brown sugar** *(pack it down when you measure it)*
- **1 large beaten egg** *(or two medium, just whip them up with a fork)*
- **4 Tablespoons molasses** *(that's 1/4 cup)****
- **2 teaspoons baking soda**
- **1/2 teaspoon salt**
- **2 teaspoons ground ginger**
- **2 and 1/4 cups flour** *(not sifted — pack it down when you measure it)*
- **1/2 cup white sugar in a small bowl** *(for coating the dough balls)*

Melt the butter and mix in the sugar. Let the mixture cool to room temperature.

Mix in the egg, molasses, baking soda, salt, and ground ginger. Stir it until everything is incorporated.

***To measure molasses, first spray the inside of a measuring cup with Pam so that the molasses won't stick to the sides of the cup.

Add the flour in one-cup increments, mixing after each addition. Scrape down the sides of the bowl and give it a final stir.

Chill the dough for at least 1 hour. *(Overnight is even better.)*

When you're ready to bake, preheat your oven to 375 degrees F., rack in the middle position.

Roll the dough into walnut-sized balls with your impeccably clean hands. Then roll the dough balls in the bowl of white sugar to coat them. Place them on greased cookie sheets *(or cookie sheets you've sprayed with Pam or another nonstick cooking spray)*, 12 dough balls to a standard-sized sheet. Flatten the dough balls with the back of a metal spatula.

Bake the cookies at 375 degrees F. for 10 to 12 minutes or until the Regency Ginger Crisps are nicely browned.

Remove the cookies from the oven. Cool them on the cookie sheets for 2 minutes and then remove them to a wire rack to finish cooling.

Hannah's 1st Note: If you leave these on the cookie sheets for too long, they'll stick.

One way to get around this problem is to line your cookie sheets with parchment paper and spray the paper with Pam or another nonstick cooking spray.

Yield: 5 to 6 dozen delightful cookies, depending on cookie size.

Hannah's 2nd Note: I served these at Mother's Regency Romance Club. They asked me for something from the Regency Period. Since they had all the ingredients back then, I figured why not?

SHORT STACK COOKIES

DO NOT preheat oven — dough must chill before baking.

- **1 and 1/2 cups melted butter *(3 sticks, 12 ounces)***
- **2 cups white *(granulated)* sugar**
- **2 large eggs, beaten *(just whip them with a fork)***
- **1/2 cup maple syrup*****
- **2 teaspoons baking soda**
- **1 teaspoon salt**
- **1 teaspoon vanilla extract**
- **4 cups all-purpose flour *(pack the flour down in the cup when you measure it)***
- **1/2 cup white *(granulated)* sugar for coating the dough balls**

Melt the butter and then mix in the sugar. Set the bowl aside on the counter to cool to room temperature.

Once the mixture is cool, add the beaten eggs. Mix everything thoroughly.

Mix in the maple syrup, baking soda, salt, and vanilla extract.

***To measure maple syrup, first spray the inside of the measuring cup with Pam so that the syrup won't stick.

Add the flour in one-cup increments, mixing after each addition.

Chill the dough for at least 2 hours before baking. **(Overnight is fine, too.)**

When you're ready to bake, preheat the oven to 350 degrees F., rack in the middle position.

Place 1/2 cup white sugar in a shallow bowl. You'll use this to coat your dough balls.

Roll the dough into walnut-sized balls with your impeccably clean hands.

Roll the dough balls in the bowl of sugar to coat them and then place them on greased cookie sheets, 12 cookies to a standard-sized sheet. **(You can also use Pam or another nonstick cooking spray, or line the cookie sheets with parchment paper.)**

Flatten the dough balls with the back of a metal spatula.

Bake the cookies at 350 degrees F. for 10 to 12 minutes or until they are nicely browned.

Take the cookies out of the oven. Cool them on the cookie sheets for 2 minutes, and then remove them to a rack to finish cooling.

(If you leave them on the cookie sheets for too long, they'll stick.)

Hannah's Note: Edna Ferguson says these taste exactly like pancakes that are slathered with maple syrup and butter, and she wishes she could get away with serving them instead of real pancakes at the annual faculty breakfast.

SPICY DREAMS

Preheat oven to 350 degrees F., rack in the middle position.

Hannah's 1st Note: This recipe is from Lindy Frank and I'm glad she finally sent it to me. Her cookies disappear faster than a Popsicle on a hot day. Lindy calls these cookies "Ginger Cookies," but since we already serve a cookie by that name down at The Cookie Jar, we've renamed these "Spicy Dreams."

Hannah's 2nd Note: Lindy says to tell you that she makes these cookies festive by using colored sugar for holidays. She uses pink and red sugar for Valentine's Day, orange sugar for Halloween, green sugar for St. Pat's Day, red and green for Christmas, etc.

1 cup softened butter *(2 sticks, 8 ounces, 1/2 pound)*
1 pound and 6 ounces white *(granulated)* sugar *(2 and 2/3 cups)*
3 eggs
1 cup molasses
2 Tablespoons vinegar *(white will do just fine)*
2 Tablespoons baking soda
4 teaspoons ground ginger

1 teaspoon ground cinnamon

1 teaspoon ground cloves

1 teaspoon ground cardamom

1 pound and 12 ounces all-purpose flour *(6 cups — pack it down in the cup when you measure it)*

1/2 cup white *(granulated)* sugar *(or 1/2 cup colored decorator sugar, or 1/2 cup white and colored decorator sugar mixed together)*, for rolling dough balls***

Mix the butter and the sugar together and beat them with a mixer or a spoon until they look nice and fluffy. *(That's what the phrase "cream the butter and sugar" means if you see it in another recipe.)*

Add the eggs one at a time, mixing thoroughly after each addition.

Mix in the molasses and the vinegar. *(I always spray the inside of my measuring cup with Pam or another nonstick cooking spray before I pour in the molasses. Then it*

***Lindy uses white (and/or colored) granulated sugar for rolling the dough balls. Lisa and I use powdered sugar down at The Cookie Jar so that we won't get the Spicy Dreams mixed up with the Molasses Crackles when we serve them on the same day.

glops right out without sticking to the cup.)

Lindy sifts the flour, baking soda, ginger, cinnamon, cloves, and cardamom together before she mixes them in with the wet ingredients. *(She also weighs the flour and the sugar the way a true pastry chef would do.)* That means she's probably a better baker than I am, because I don't do any of that. I just mix in the baking soda first, and then the spices. I mix everything up thoroughly, and then I add the flour in one-cup increments, mixing after each cup is added.

Use your hands to roll the dough into walnut-sized balls. If the dough is too sticky, put it in the refrigerator for 20 to 30 minutes and then try again. Refrigeration stiffens the dough and makes it easier to work with.

Put the sugar in a small bowl and roll the balls in it. Place them on a greased cookie sheet *(I used Pam)*, 12 cookie balls to a standard-sized sheet. Press them down just a bit when you place them on the cookie sheet so they won't roll off when you carry them to the oven. You don't have to flatten them. They'll spread out all by themselves while they bake.

Bake the cookies at 350 degrees F., for 10

to 12 minutes. *(Mine took only 10 minutes.)*

Let the cookies cool for 2 minutes on the cookie sheet and then move them to a wire rack to finish cooling.

Yield: Approximately 10 dozen, depending on cookie size.

STRAWBERRY FLIPS

Preheat oven to 375 degrees F., rack in the middle position.

1 cup melted butter *(2 sticks, 8 ounces, 1/2 pound)*

1 cup white *(granulated)* sugar

2 beaten eggs *(just whip them up with a fork)*

1/3 cup seedless strawberry jam

1 teaspoon strawberry extract *(or vanilla extract if you can't find strawberry at your grocery store)*

1 teaspoon baking powder

1/2 teaspoon baking soda

1/2 teaspoon salt

1 and 1/2 cups chopped walnuts *(or pecans)*

3 cups flour *(don't sift — pack it down in the cup when you measure it)*

---

small bowl of powdered *(confectioner's)* sugar

1 bag frozen strawberries for garnish***

Melt the butter and stir in the white sugar. Set the bowl aside on the counter to cool.

***If fresh strawberries are available, they'll be fine as a garnish in this recipe.

When the butter/sugar mixture is not so hot it'll cook the eggs, add them and mix thoroughly. Then mix in the strawberry jam and stir until it's thoroughly incorporated.

Add strawberry extract, baking powder, baking soda, and salt. Mix everything up thoroughly. Then mix in the chopped walnuts.

Add the flour in one-cup increments, mixing after each cup. The resulting dough will be quite stiff.

Roll dough balls about 1 inch in diameter with your impeccably clean hands. *(If the dough is too sticky to roll, chill it for 20 to 30 minutes in the refrigerator and then try it again. You can even cover this dough and let It chill overnight in the refrigerator.)*

Roll the dough balls in the powdered sugar and place them on a greased cookie sheet, 12 to a standard sheet. *(You can also spray your cookie sheets with Pam or another nonstick cooking spray, or cover them with parchment paper.)* Make a deep thumbprint in the center of each cookie.

While the strawberries are still partially frozen, cut them in half lengthwise. *(If your berries are too large to fit on your cookie balls, cut them in quarters instead of halves.)* Flip the cut pieces over and place them skin side up in the thumbprint you've made on top of each cookie.

Bake the Strawberry Flips at 375 degrees F. for 10 to 12 minutes. Cool them on the cookie sheet for 2 minutes, then use a metal spatula to transfer them to a wire rack to finish cooling.

When the cookies are cool, dust them with powdered sugar and place them on a pretty platter to serve them.

Yield: 7 to 8 dozen cookies.

Hannah's 1st Note: The tart strawberry pieces are wonderful with the sweet cookie. Carrie Rhodes just adores these.

Hannah's 2nd Note: As a variant, you can also make these cookies with seedless raspberry jam and small whole raspberries on top. Of course then you'll have to call them Raspberry Flips instead of Strawberry Flips.

SURPRISE COOKIES

DO NOT preheat the oven — this dough must chill before baking.

1 cup melted butter *(2 sticks, 8 ounces, 1/2 pound)*
1 cup white *(granulated)* **sugar**
1/2 cup brown sugar *(pack it down in the cup when you measure it)*
2 beaten eggs *(just whip them up with a fork)*
1 teaspoon baking soda
1/2 teaspoon salt
1 teaspoon vanilla extract
2 Tablespoons water *(or coffee, if you have some left over from breakfast)*
3 cups flour *(not sifted — pack it down in the cup when you measure it)*
1 package Bridge Mix or assorted chocolate candies***
4 to 5 dozen walnut halves *(or pecan halves)*

Melt the butter and mix in the sugars. Set the mixture aside on the counter to cool to

***If I can't find Bridge Mix, I like to use Hershey's assorted miniature candy bars cut into four pieces. You can even use full-size chocolate candy bars if you cut them into small pieces.

room temperature.

When the mixture is not so hot it'll cook the eggs, add them and mix them in thoroughly. Then mix in the baking soda, salt, vanilla extract, and water *(or coffee if you used it)*.

Add the flour in one-cup increments, mixing after each addition. Give a final stir, cover the dough with plastic wrap, and place it in the refrigerator to chill for at least an hour *(overnight is fine, too)*.

When you're ready to bake, preheat the oven to 375 degrees F., rack in the middle position.

Scoop out a Tablespoon of dough *(use a Tablespoon from your silver drawer, not a measuring spoon)* and form the dough around a piece of Bridge Mix or a piece of cut-up candy bar.

Place the cookies on a greased cookie sheet, 12 cookies to a standard-sized sheet. *(You can also spray your cookie sheets with Pam or another nonstick cooking spray or line them with parchment paper.)*

Press a walnut half *(or pecan half)* on top of each cookie.

Bake your Surprise Cookies at 375 degrees F. for 10 to 12 minutes, or until they're golden brown.

Remove the cookies from the oven. Cool them on the cookie sheet for 2 minutes, and then use a metal spatula to transfer them to a wire rack to cool completely.

Yield: 8 to 10 dozen delicious cookies, depending on cookie size.

Hannah's Note: When I use Hershey's miniatures, Mother always tries to guess which cookies have the Krackel bars inside. If she gets one with a piece of Mr. Goodbar, she passes it to me.

SWEDISH OATMEAL COOKIES

Preheat oven to 350 degrees F., rack in the middle position.

1 cup butter *(2 sticks, 8 ounces, 1/2 pound)*
3/4 cup white (granulated) sugar
1 teaspoon baking soda
1 cup flour *(don't sift — pack it down in the cup when you measure it)*
2 cups oatmeal *(I used Quaker Oats — Quick-1 Minute)*
1 egg yolk *(use a large fresh egg)*

Melt the butter in a microwave-safe bowl on HIGH for approximately 1 and 1/2 minutes. Let it cool to room temperature. Mix in the white sugar.

Add the baking soda, flour, and oatmeal. Stir thoroughly.

Beat the egg yolk with a fork until it's thoroughly mixed and a lighter yellow in color. Add it to the bowl and stir until it's thoroughly incorporated.

Prepare to bake by greasing *(or spraying with Pam or another nonstick cooking spray)* a standard-sized cookie sheet. You can also use parchment paper if you wish.

Make small balls of dough with your fingers and place them on the cookie sheet, 12 to a standard-sized cookie sheet. Press them down with a fork in a crisscross pattern the way you'd do for peanut butter cookies.

Bake your Swedish Oatmeal Cookies at 350 degrees F. for 10 to 12 minutes or until they're just starting to brown around the edges. *(Mine took 10 minutes.)*

Remove the cookies from the oven, let them cool for 2 minutes on the cookie sheet, and then transfer them to a wire rack to complete cooling.

Yield: Approximately 5 dozen, depending on cookie size.

Hannah's Note: This recipe is from a lady I met in the park, Karen Lood. She told me it was important to use high-quality ingredients in these cookies, because their taste depends on the best in butter, flour, and oatmeal.

TWIN CHOCOLATE DELIGHTS

Preheat oven to 350 degrees F., rack in the middle position.

1 cup butter *(2 sticks, 8 ounces, 1/2 pound)*
2 and 1/2 cups white *(granulated)* **sugar**
1/2 cup cocoa *(unsweetened, for baking)*
2 teaspoons baking soda
1 teaspoon salt
2 teaspoons vanilla extract
4 beaten eggs *(just whip them up in a glass with a fork)*
3 cups flour *(no need to sift)*
1 cup chopped nuts *(optional — your choice of nut)*
2 cups chocolate chips *(a 12-ounce package)*

Melt the butter in a large microwave-safe bowl. Add the sugar and mix it in thoroughly. Then add the cocoa, baking soda, salt, and vanilla extract. Stir until the resulting mixture is smooth and well incorporated.

If the mixture is not so hot it'll cook the eggs, add them now. *(Otherwise, wait a few more minutes.)* Mix thoroughly so that the eggs are well incorporated.

Add the flour in one-cup increments, mixing after each cup. Then mix in the chopped nuts *(if you used them).*

Stir in the chocolate chips and mix thoroughly.

Place rounded teaspoonfuls of dough on a greased cookie sheet, 12 cookies to a standard-sized sheet. *(You can also spray your cookie sheet with Pam or another nonstick cooking spray or line it with parchment paper.)* You don't have to flatten the mounds of dough. They'll spread out all by themselves as they bake.

Bake your Twin Chocolate Delights at 350 degrees F. for 10 minutes. Cool them on the cookie sheet for 2 minutes, and then remove them to a wire rack to complete cooling.

Hannah's 1st Note: Mother loves these cookies. If I bake them when she's mad at me, she sweetens right up.

Hannah's 2nd Note: Twin Chocolate Delights should freeze well, but I can't swear to that — they never last long enough to try it.

Yield: Approximately 5 dozen chocolatey cookies.

VIKING COOKIES

Preheat oven to 350 degrees F., rack in the middle position.

- 2 cups butter *(4 sticks, 16 ounces, 1 pound)*
- 2 cups brown sugar *(pack it down when you measure it)*
- 2 cups white *(granulated)* sugar
- 4 eggs, beaten *(just whip them up in a glass with a fork)*
- 1 teaspoon baking powder
- 1 teaspoon baking soda
- 1 teaspoon salt
- 2 teaspoons vanilla extract
- 1/2 teaspoon cinnamon
- 1/4 teaspoon cardamom *(nutmeg will also work, but cardamom is better)*
- 4 and 1/2 cups flour *(pack it down in the cup when you measure it)*
- 3 cups white chocolate chips *(I used Ghirardelli)****

***Make sure you use real white chocolate chips, not vanilla chips. The real ones have cocoa butter listed in the ingredients. If you can't find them in your market, look for a block of white chocolate, one pound or a bit over, and cut it up in small pieces with a knife.

3 cups rolled oats (*uncooked oatmeal — I used Quaker's Quick-1 Minute*)

Melt the butter in a large microwave-safe bowl, or on the stove in a small saucepan. *(It should melt in about 3 minutes in the microwave on HIGH.)* Mix in the brown sugar and the white sugar, then set the bowl on the counter to cool.

Feel the bowl with the butter/sugars mixture. When it's not so hot it'll cook the eggs, add them and mix them in. Then add the baking powder, baking soda, salt, vanilla extract, and spices. Make sure everything is thoroughly combined.

Add the flour in half-cup increments, mixing after each addition. Then add the white chocolate chips *(or pieces of white chocolate if you cut up a block)* and stir thoroughly.

Add the rolled oats and mix. The dough will be quite stiff.

Drop by teaspoons onto a greased cookie sheet *(or sprayed with Pam or another non-stick cooking spray),* 12 cookies to a standard-sized sheet.

Flatten the cookies on the sheet with a greased metal spatula *(or with the palm of your impeccably clean hand)*. You don't have to smush them all the way down so they look like pancakes — just one squish will do it.

Bake at 350 degrees F. for 11 to 13 minutes or until the cookies are an attractive golden brown. *(Mine took the full 13 minutes.)*

Cool the cookies for 2 minutes on the cookie sheet, then remove them to a wire rack to cool completely.

Yield: 10 to 12 dozen delicious cookies, depending on cookie size.

These freeze well if you roll them in foil and put them in a freezer bag.

Hannah's Note: These cookies will go fast, even frozen. If you want to throw the midnight freezer raiders off the track, wrap the cookie rolls in a double thickness of foil and then stick them in a freezer bag. Label the bag with a food your family doesn't like. *(I use BEEF TONGUE, or PORK KID-NEYS, or even LUTEFISK. It works every time, even when Andrea's around.)*

WALNUT-DATE CHEWS

Preheat oven to 350 degrees F., rack in the middle position.

1 cup butter *(2 sticks, 8 ounces, 1/2 pound)*
3 cups brown sugar *(pack it down in the cup when you measure it)*
4 eggs, beaten *(just stir them up in a glass with a fork)*
1 teaspoon salt
1 teaspoon baking soda
1 Tablespoon *(3 teaspoons)* **vanilla extract**
2 cups finely chopped walnuts *(measure AFTER chopping)*
1 cup chopped dates***
4 cups flour *(don't sift — pack it down in the cup when you measure it)*

Melt the butter on HIGH in a microwave-safe container for 90 seconds, or in a small saucepan on the stove over low heat.

Transfer the melted butter to a large mixing bowl and add the brown sugar. Mix it well and let it cool to slightly above room temperature, just enough so that it won't cook the eggs when you add them!

***You can buy dates already chopped at the grocery store if you don't want to chop them yourself.

Mix in the beaten eggs. Stir until they're thoroughly incorporated.

Add the salt, baking soda, and vanilla extract. Mix it all up together.

Mix in the chopped walnuts and let the dough rest while you chop the dates.

You can chop your dates by hand with a knife, but it's a lot easier in a food processor or blender. If they're whole dates, pit them first *(of course)*, cut each one into two or three pieces with a knife, put them into the bowl of your food processor or blender, and sprinkle a little flour *(approximately 1/4 cup)* on top. The flour will keep them from "gumming up" when you process them.

Measure one cup of chopped dates and add them to your mixing bowl. Stir them in thoroughly.

Add the flour in one-cup increments, mixing after each addition. This dough will be fairly stiff.

Form the dough into 1-inch balls with your impeccably clean fingers. Place them on a greased cookie sheet, 12 to a standard-sized sheet. *(You can also spray the cookie sheet with Pam or another nonstick cook-*

ing spray, or line it with parchment paper.) No need to flatten the dough balls. They'll spread out when they bake.

Bake at 350 degrees F. for 10 to 12 minutes or until lightly browned. Let the cookies cool on the cookie sheet for 2 minutes, then use a metal spatula to remove them to a wire rack to complete cooling.

Hannah's Note: These were my father's favorites. Mother likes them, too. Lisa says her dad likes these best with a dish of vanilla ice cream.

Yield: Approximately 8 dozen tasty cookies, depending on cookie size.

WALNUTTOES

DO NOT preheat oven — this dough must chill before baking.

2 cups chocolate chips *(a 12-ounce bag)*
3/4 cup butter *(1 and 1/2 sticks, 6 ounces)*
1 and 1/2 cups brown sugar *(pack it down in the cup when you measure it)*
4 eggs
2 teaspoons vanilla extract
2 teaspoons baking powder
1 teaspoon salt
2 cups flour *(don't sift — pack it down in the cup when you measure it)*
2 cups finely chopped walnuts

----

approximately 1/2 cup white *(granulated)* **sugar in a small bowl**

Melt the chocolate chips with the butter either in a saucepan on the stovetop over LOW heat, or in a microwave-safe bowl in the microwave. *(Microwave on HIGH for 2 minutes, then stir until smooth.)* Mix in the sugar and let it cool to slightly above room temperature, just enough so that it won't cook the eggs when you add them!

Add the eggs, one at a time, mixing well after each addition.

Mix in vanilla extract, baking powder, and salt.

Add the flour, one cup at a time, mixing after each cup. Mix in the chopped walnuts and give the dough a final stir by hand.

Chill the dough for at least 4 hours. Overnight is even better.

When you're ready to bake, preheat the oven to 350 degrees F., rack in the middle position.

Roll 1-inch dough balls with your impeccably clean hands. *(This is messy — wear thin plastic gloves if you wish. If the dough becomes too warm and sticky, return it to the refrigerator and try again later!)*

Drop the dough balls into a small bowl with the white sugar and roll around to coat them. Then place them on a greased cookie sheet, 12 to a standard-sized sheet. *(You can also spray the cookie sheet with Pam or another nonstick cooking spray, or line it with parchment paper.)* Smush the dough balls down with a greased spatula.

Bake at 350 degrees for 12 to 14 minutes. Let the cookies cool on the cookie sheet for 2 minutes, then use a metal spatula to remove them to a wire rack to complete cooling. *(If you leave the cookies on the cookie sheet too long, they'll stick.)*

Yield: 4 to 5 dozen yummy cookies, depending on cookie size.

"There sure are a lot of cookie recipes!" Alice said, paging through them. "Have you baked all of them, Hannah?"

"Every one. And Lisa and I have served all of them down at The Cookie Jar at one time or another."

"I noticed that you serve different cookies almost every day," Bertie pointed out.

"That's right. We always bake at least ten kinds and that's not counting the bar cookies."

"But the bar cookies aren't here," Rose said, looking concerned. "I was looking for the Ooey Gooey Chewy Cookie Bar recipe."

Hannah reached over and flipped Rose's binder to the next section. "They're right here," she said. "You're not going to serve them down at the cafe, are you?"

"Of course not!" Rose looked slightly affronted. "I'd never do that without your permission. You don't serve cheeseburgers, and I won't serve Ooey Gooey Chewy Cookie Bars. It wouldn't be fair."

"That's the way I feel. When people want a roast beef sandwich and a slice of coconut cake, they come to you at the cafe. And when they want a Chocolate Chip Crunch Cookie or an Old Fashioned Sugar Cookie, they come to me."

"That's why Lake Eden's such a good place to live," Delores said. "We all look out for each other. And speaking of looking out, has anyone looked out the window lately? Rayne Phillips on KCOW was predicting another storm this morning."

"I'll check," Lisa said, heading for the kitchen to take a peek out the door to the parking lot. She was back a minute later, rubbing her hands together. "It's cold out there," she reported. "The wind's picked up and the snow is blowing across the parking lot. It's not that bad, though."

Delores looked relieved. "Good. Carrie and I have to go out to the hospital later to visit some patients."

"Earl's stopping by to pick me up in an hour," Carrie said. "If the roads are bad, he'll take us out there in the tow truck."

"Perfect!" Delores exclaimed.

Hannah exchanged shocked glances with Andrea and Michelle. Earl's tow truck had seen hard use this winter and it was far from the cleanest vehicle on the road. Their mother was dressed in a designer suit in a soft pale green material that was probably cashmere, and it would show even the tiniest speck of dirt. Their elegantly dressed mother had never ridden in a tow truck as far as Hannah knew, and Delores must have really wanted to get out to the hospital in order to agree to Carrie's plan. Had their mother, who'd never been known for her charity work, experienced a change of heart now that she'd organized the Rainbow Ladies? Or was there another reason Delores went to the hospital almost every day?

APPLE ORCHARD BARS

Preheat oven to 375 degrees F., rack in the middle position.

1/2 cup butter *(1 stick, 4 ounces, 1/4 pound)*

1/2 cup white *(granulated)* sugar

1 cup brown sugar, firmly packed

1/2 teaspoon baking powder

1/2 teaspoon baking soda

1/2 teaspoon salt

2 teaspoons vanilla extract

1 teaspoon cinnamon

2 beaten eggs *(just whip them up in a glass with a fork)*

1/2 cup rolled oats *(uncooked oatmeal — I used Quaker Quick-1 Minute)*

1 cup peeled chopped apple *(I used 2 medium Gala apples, cored, peeled, and seeded of course)*

2 cups flaked coconut

1 and 1/2 cups all-purpose flour *(not*

Melt the butter in a microwave-safe bowl in the microwave, or in a small saucepan on the stovetop.

Place the white sugar and the brown sugar in a large mixing bowl. Pour in the melted butter and stir the mixture until it's smooth.

Add the baking powder, baking soda, salt, vanilla extract, and cinnamon. Mix it in thoroughly.

Feel the bowl. If the mixture is not so hot it'll cook the eggs, add them now. Mix well.

Add the rolled oats and the chopped apple. Mix thoroughly.

Measure out 1 and 1/2 cups ONLY of flaked coconut. Reserve the 1/2 cup that's left over to sprinkle on top of your pan when you're all through.

Add the flour, one cup at a time, mixing after each cup.

Grease a 9-inch by 13-inch cake pan *(or spray it with Pam or another nonstick cooking spray)*.

Spoon the dough into the pan and smooth the top with a rubber spatula.

Sprinkle the 1/2 cup coconut you reserved evenly on the top.

Bake the bars at 375 degrees F. for 25 to 30 minutes, or until the top is golden brown.

Take the pan out of the oven, and let the bars cool in the pan, on a wire rack, or on a cold stovetop burner.

To serve, cut the Apple Orchard Bars into squares like brownies.

Hannah's 1st Note: Bill likes these with hot chocolate — he says it brings out the taste of the apples.

Hannah's 2nd Note: Tracey's still trying to convince Andrea that these are health food and she should be allowed to have them for breakfast.

BLACK FOREST BROWNIES

Preheat oven to 350 degrees F., rack in the middle position.

4 one-ounce squares semi-sweet chocolate *(or the equivalent — 3/4 cup semisweet chocolate chips will do just fine)*
3/4 cup butter *(1 and 1/2 sticks, 6 ounces)*
1 and 1/2 cups white *(granulated)* **sugar**
3 beaten eggs *(just whip them up in a glass with a fork)*
1 teaspoon vanilla extract *(or cherry extract)*
1 cup flour *(pack it down in the cup when you measure it)*
1/2 cup pecans
1/2 cup dried cherries *(OR 1/2 cup well drained maraschino cherries)****
1/2 cup semi-sweet chocolate chips *(I used Ghirardelli)*

Prepare a 9-inch by 13-inch cake pan by lining it with a piece of foil large enough to flap over the sides. Spray the foil-lined pan with Pam or other nonstick cooking spray.

***I used dried Bing cherries in one batch, and maraschino cherries in a second batch. People loved both batches, but all agreed that the ones with the dried cherries were chewier.

Microwave the chocolate squares and butter in a microwave-safe mixing bowl for one minute. Stir. *(Since chocolate frequently maintains its shape even when its melted, you have to stir to make sure.)* If it's not melted, microwave for an additional 20 seconds and stir again. Repeat if necessary.

Stir the sugar into the chocolate mixture. Feel the bowl. If it's not so hot it'll cook the eggs, add them now, stirring thoroughly. Mix in the flavor extract *(vanilla or cherry)*.

Mix in the flour and stir just until it's moistened.

Put the pecans and dried cherries in the bowl of a food processor and chop them together with the steel blade. If the dried cherries stick to the blades too much, add a Tablespoon of flour to your bowl and try it again. *(If you don't have a food processor, you don't have to buy one for this recipe — just chop everything up as well as you can with a sharp knife.)*

Mix in the chopped nuts and cherries, add the chocolate chips, give a final stir by hand, and spread the batter out in your prepared pan.

Bake at 350 degrees F. for 30 minutes. DO

NOT OVERBAKE.

Cool the Black Forest Brownies in the pan on a wire rack or on a cold stovetop burner.

When the brownies are completely cool, grasp the edges of the foil and lift the brownies out of the pan. Put them facedown on a cutting board, peel the foil off the back, and cut them into brownie-sized pieces.

Place the squares on a plate and dust lightly with powdered sugar if you wish.

Jo Fluke's Note: A big thank you to the ladies at Delta Kappa Gamma. After I spoke to them in Camarillo, California, they gave me a huge box of dried fruit that included the dried Bing cherries that I used in these brownies.

Hannah's Note: If you really want to be decadent, frost these brownies with Neverfail Frosting!

BLONDE BROWNIES

Preheat oven to 350 degrees F., rack in the middle position.

4 one-ounce squares white chocolate *(or the equivalent — 3/4 cup white chocolate chips will do fine)*

3/4 cup butter *(1 and 1/2 sticks, 6 ounces)*

1 and 1/2 cups white *(granulated)* **sugar**

3 beaten eggs *(just whip them up in a glass with a fork)*

1 teaspoon coconut extract *(or vanilla extract)*

1 cup flour *(pack it down in the cup when you measure it)*

1/2 cup pecans

1/2 cup coconut

1/2 cup white chocolate chips*** *(I used Ghirardelli)*

Prepare a 9-inch by 13-inch cake pan by lining it with a piece of foil large enough to flap over the sides. Spray the foil-lined pan with Pam or another nonstick cooking spray.

***If you used 3/4 cup white chocolate chips for the first ingredient in place of the 4 one-ounce squares of white chocolate, don't be confused. This half-cup of white chocolate chips is additional and will be used later in the recipe.

Microwave the white chocolate and butter in a microwave-safe mixing bowl for one minute. Stir. *(Since chocolate frequently maintains its shape even when melted, you have to stir to make sure.)* If it's not melted, microwave for an additional 20 seconds and stir again. Repeat if necessary.

Stir the sugar into the white chocolate mixture. Feel the bowl. If it's not so hot it'll cook the eggs, add them now, stirring thoroughly. Mix in the coconut extract.

Mix in the flour and stir just until it's moistened.

Put the pecans, coconut and the half-cup of white chocolate chips in a food processor. Chop them all together with the steel blade. *(If you don't have a food processor, you don't have to buy one just for this recipe — chop everything up as well as you can with a sharp knife.)*

Mix in the chopped ingredients, give a final stir, and spread the batter out in your prepared pan.

Bake at 350 degrees F. for 30 minutes. DO NOT OVERBAKE.

Cool the Blonde Brownies in the pan on

a wire rack. When they're thoroughly cool, grasp the edges of the foil and lift the brownies out of the pan. Put them facedown on a cutting board, peel the foil off the back, and cut them into brownie-sized pieces.

Place the squares on a plate and dust lightly with powdered sugar.

Jo Fluke's Note: I developed these Blonde Brownies for Laura Levine's party when she launched the third book in her Jaine Austen mystery series, **Killer Blonde**.

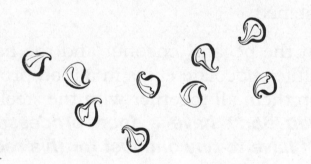

*Bourbon Brownies

Preheat the oven to 325 degrees F., rack in the middle position.

1 package of family style brownie mix *(the kind that makes a 9-inch by 13-inch cake pan or TWO packages that make 8-inch by 8-inch pans of brownies)****
1/2 cup chopped nuts *(walnuts, pecans, whatever you like)*
1/3 cup bourbon

1/2 cup butter, softened *(1 stick, 4 ounces, 1/4 pound)*
2 cups sifted powdered *(confectioner's)* **sugar**
3 Tablespoons bourbon

Hannah's 1st Note: Of course you can use your favorite brownie recipe and make your own if you wish.

Hannah's 2nd Note: Bertie says to use a good brand of bourbon in these brownies. They'll taste a lot better.

Grease and flour *(or spray with Pam or*

***If this confuses you, read the section that's titled, "A Not So Scientific Study of Pan Size" following the Bar Cookie section.

another nonstick cooking spray) a 9-inch by 13-inch cake pan.

Mix up the brownies, following the directions on the package.

Add the nuts and bake at 325 degrees F. for 35 to 40 minutes.

When the baking time is up, remove the pan from the oven and cool the brownies in the pan on a wire rack or set them on a cold burner on the stovetop to cool.

When the brownies are completely cool, use a hatpin, a wooden skewer, a metal cake tester, or anything you can find that has a thin, sharp point. Poke approximately 50 holes down through the brownies in the pan.

Measure out the 1/3 cup good bourbon and brush it or carefully pour it over the top of the brownies, letting it soak into all the holes.

Cover the pan with plastic wrap or aluminum foil, and refrigerate it for one hour.

When an hour's gone by, combine the softened butter, powdered sugar, and the 3 Tablespoons of bourbon in a bowl. Beat the mixture until it's smooth and is the consistency of frosting.

Hannah's 3rd Note: If you think your frosting is too thin to spread, add a little more powdered sugar. If you think it's too thick, add a little more bourbon.

Spread the frosting on top of the brownies as evenly as possible.

Sneak one brownie just for you and then cover the pan with foil or plastic wrap. Return it to the refrigerator until you're ready to serve the Bourbon Brownies.

To serve, cut into brownie-sized pieces and arrange them on a pretty platter.

Hannah's 4th Note: You'd better have plenty of strong coffee to serve with these!

CHOCOLATE HIGHLANDER COOKIE BARS

Preheat the oven to 350 degrees F., rack in middle position.

1 cup softened butter *(2 sticks, 8 ounces, 1/2 pound)*

1/2 cup powdered sugar *(don't sift)*

1/4 teaspoon salt

2 cups flour *(don't sift — pack it down in the cup when you measure it)*

---

1 cup melted butter, cooled to room temperature *(2 sticks, 8 ounces, 1/2 pound)*

1 cup white *(granulated)* sugar

4 beaten eggs *(just whip them up in a glass with a fork)*

1 teaspoon baking powder

1/4 teaspoon salt

1/2 cup flour *(don't sift — pack it down in the cup when you measure it)*

2 and 1/2 cups chocolate chips

1/3 cup powdered *(confectioner's)* sugar to sprinkle on top of the pan

FIRST STEP: Prepare a 9-inch by 13-inch cake pan by lining it with a piece of heavy duty foil large enough to flap over the sides. Spray the foil-lined pan with Pam or another nonstick cooking spray.

SECOND STEP: Mix the softened butter with the powdered sugar and the salt. Beat them until they're light and fluffy. Add the flour, one cup at a time, mixing after each cup. Dump the mixture into your prepared pan and pat it smooth with your impeccably clean hands.

Bake at 350 degrees F. for 15 minutes. This is the shortbread crust. Remove the pan from the oven and place it on a wire rack or a cold stovetop burner. *(Don't turn off oven!)*

THIRD STEP: Combine the melted butter with the white sugar in your original mixing bowl. *(No need to wash it.)* Mix in the beaten eggs. Add the baking powder, salt, and flour. Mix thoroughly. *(A hand mixer will do the job if you're tired of stirring.)*

Melt the chocolate chips in a saucepan on the stovetop over LOW heat, or place them in a small microwave-safe bowl and cook for 3 minutes on HIGH. *(Be sure to stir after 3 minutes — chips may maintain their shape even after they're melted.)*

Add the melted chocolate chips to your bowl and mix them in thoroughly.

Pour this mixture on top of the shortbread crust you just baked and tip the pan so that it's evenly distributed. Stick the pan back into the oven and bake it at 350 degrees F. for another 25 minutes. Then remove the pan from the oven and sprinkle on additional powdered sugar.

Let the Chocolate Highlander Cookie Bars cool thoroughly and then tip them out of the pan, pull the foil from the back, flip them right side up again, and cut them into brownie-sized pieces. You can refrigerate these, after you cut them.

Hannah's Note: Andrea said these were so rich, no one could eat more than one, but I watched her eat three when she thought I wasn't looking.

CHOCOLATE OVERLOAD COOKIE BARS

Preheat oven to 350 degrees F., rack in the middle position.

FOR THE CRUST:

1 and 1/2 cups all-purpose flour *(don't sift — pack it down in the cup to measure it)*
1/4 cup cocoa powder *(unsweetened, for baking)*
3/4 cup white *(granulated)* sugar
3/4 cup softened butter *(1 and 1/2 sticks, 6 ounces)*

Mix the flour, cocoa powder, and white sugar together and then cut in the softened butter. *(You can also do this with a food processor with a steel blade, using chilled butter that's been cut into chunks.)*

Spread the mixture out in the bottom of a greased 9-inch by 13-inch cake pan and press it down with a spatula.

Bake at 350 degrees F. for 15 minutes. Take the crust out of the oven, but DON'T SHUT OFF THE OVEN. You'll need to bake the filling.

FOR THE FILLING:

2 eight-ounce packages softened cream

cheese *(the block type, not the whipped type)*
1 cup mayonnaise *(I used Hellmann's)*
1 cup white *(granulated)* sugar
4 eggs
2 cups chocolate chips *(a 12-ounce bag)*
2 teaspoons vanilla extract

You can do these cookie bars by hand, but it's a lot easier with an electric mixer. Place the softened cream cheese in a bowl and beat it with the mayonnaise until it's smooth. Gradually add the white sugar.

Add the eggs, one at a time, beating after each addition.

Melt the chocolate chips in a microwave-safe bowl for 3 minutes. *(Chocolate chips may retain their shape, so stir them to see if they're melted.)* Let them cool for a minute or two, and then gradually add the melted chocolate to the cream cheese mixture.

Mix in the vanilla extract, and pour the chocolate mixture on top of the crust you just baked.

Bake at 350 degrees F. for 35 additional minutes. Let the Chocolate Overload Cookie Bars cool to room temperature and then chill for at least 4 hours.

Cut into brownie-sized bars. Garnish the bars with strawberries, sweetened whipped cream, or powdered sugar if desired.

LOVELY LEMON BAR COOKIES

Preheat the oven to 350 degrees F., rack in the middle position.

1 cup cold butter *(2 sticks, 8 ounces, 1/2 pound)*

2 cups flour *(don't sift — pack it down in the cup when you measure it)*

1/2 cup powdered sugar *(not sifted)*

---

4 beaten eggs *(just whip them up in a glass with a fork)*

2 cups white *(granulated)* **sugar**

8 Tablespoons lemon juice *(1/2 cup)*

1 teaspoon or so of lemon zest *(zest is finely grated lemon peel)*

1/2 teaspoon salt

1 teaspoon baking powder

4 Tablespoons flour *(that's 1/4 cup — don't sift)*

FIRST STEP: Cut each stick of butter into eight pieces. Zoop it up with the flour and the powdered sugar in a food processor until it looks like coarse cornmeal. Spread it out in a greased 9-inch by 13-inch pan, and pat it down with your hands.

Bake at 350 degrees F. for 15 to 20 minutes, or until golden around the edges. Remove the pan from the oven, set it on a wire rack or a cold stovetop burner, but DON'T SHUT OFF THE OVEN.

SECOND STEP: Mix the eggs with the white sugar. Add the lemon juice and the zest. Add the salt and baking powder. Mix thoroughly. Add the flour and stir until everything is combined.

Hannah's Note: This filling will be runny — it's supposed to be.

Pour the filling over the crust you just baked and stick it back into the oven. Bake it at 350 degrees F. for another 30 to 35 minutes. Then remove the pan from the oven and sprinkle on powdered sugar if you wish.

Set the pan on a wire rack or on a cold stovetop burner. Let the bars cool thoroughly and then cut them into brownie-sized pieces.

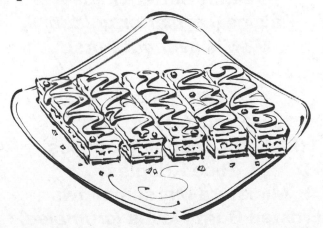

MULTIPLE CHOICE COOKIE BARS

Preheat oven to 350 degrees F., rack in the middle position.

1/2 cup butter *(1 stick, 4 ounces, 1/4 pound)*
1 can *(14 ounces)* **sweetened condensed milk**

COLUMN A
(1 and 1/2 cups of)
Graham Cracker Crumbs
Vanilla Wafer Crumbs
Chocolate Wafer Crumbs
Animal Cracker Crumbs
Sugar Cookie Crumbs

COLUMN B
(2 cups of)
Chocolate Chips
Butterscotch Chips
Peanut Butter Chips
Raisins *(regular or golden)*
M&M's *(without nuts)*

COLUMN C
(1 and 1/2 cups of)
Flaked Coconut *(5 ounces)*
Rice Krispies
Miniature Marshmallows
Frosted Corn Flakes *(crumbled)*

COLUMN D
(1 cup of)
Chopped Walnuts
Chopped Pecans
Chopped Peanuts
Chopped Cashews

Melt the butter and pour it into a 9-inch by 13-inch cake pan. Tip the pan to coat the bottom.

1. Evenly sprinkle one from Column A over the melted butter.
2. Drizzle sweetened condensed milk over the crumbs.
3. Evenly sprinkle one from Column B on top.
4. Evenly sprinkle one from Column C on top of that.
5. Evenly sprinkle something from Column D over the very top.

Press everything down with the palms of your impeccably clean hands. Bake at 350 degrees F. for 30 minutes. Cool thoroughly on a wire rack and cut into brownie-sized pieces.

Hannah's 1st Note: Make sure you cut these cookie bars before you refrigerate them. They harden in the refrigerator and they'll be very difficult to cut.

Hannah's 2nd Note: Kids love to help make these cookie bars when they get to choose the ingredients.

OOEY GOOEY CHEWY COOKIE BARS

Preheat the oven to 350 degrees F., rack in the middle position.

1/2 cup white *(granulated)* sugar

3/4 cup all-purpose flour *(not sifted — pack it down in the cup when you measure it)*

1/4 teaspoon salt

1/3 cup unsweetened baking cocoa* *(I used Hershey's)***

1/2 stick salted butter, melted *(1/4 cup, 2 ounces, 1/8 pound)*

2 cups milk chocolate chips *(I used a 12-ounce package of Ghirardelli milk chocolate chips)*

3 cups miniature marshmallows *(pack them down in the cup)*

1 and 1/2 cups flaked coconut *(pack it down in the cup when you measure it)*

1 cup chopped nuts *(I use either pecans, or walnuts)*

***You can find unsweetened baking cocoa in the baking aisle of your grocery store. Make sure you get an American brand. Some of the others are Dutch process and they won't work in this recipe. Also be careful not to get cocoa mix, the kind you'd use to make hot chocolate or chocolate milk.

1 can sweetened condensed milk *(14 ounces)*

Mix the white sugar, flour, salt, and cocoa together in a medium-sized bowl. Drizzle the melted butter over the top of the bowl and mix it in with a fork. When the butter is incorporated, the mixture will resemble small beads. *(You can also do this in the bowl of a food processor, using chunks of chilled butter and the steel blade.)*

Spray a 9-inch by 13-inch cake pan with Pam *(or other nonstick cooking spray)*, and dump the crust mixture in the bottom. Gently shake the pan to distribute the mixture and then press it down a bit with a metal spatula.

Sprinkle the milk chocolate chips evenly over the crust layer. Sprinkle the marshmallows over that. Sprinkle the flaked coconut on next, and then sprinkle on the chopped nuts. Press everything down with the back of a metal spatula. Pour the sweetened condensed milk over the very top as evenly as you can.

Bake the Ooey Gooey Chewy Cookie Bars at 350 degrees F. for 25 to 30 minutes, or until the bars are nicely browned on top.

Let the bars cool on a wire rack or on a cold stovetop burner. When they're cool, cut them into brownie-sized pieces.

WARNING: DON'T REFRIGERATE THESE COOKIE BARS WITHOUT CUTTING THEM FIRST — THEY'RE VERY DENSE AND SOLID WHEN CHILLED.

A Note From Edna Ferguson, the Queen of "Cheat" recipes: If you want a shortcut for the crust, just buy a chocolate cake mix and use half of it dry, mixed with the melted stick of butter. Keep the rest of the cake mix in an airtight bag and you can use it for the next batch you bake.

Hannah's Note: Kids love the name of these cookie bars.

PINEAPPLE RIGHT-SIDE-UP COOKIE BARS

Preheat oven to 350 degrees F., rack in the middle position.

Hannah's Note: This recipe has a crust you don't have to roll out. Don't you just love it?

1/2 cup frozen concentrated pineapple juice

1 can crushed pineapple *(you'll be measuring it AFTER you drain it)*

---

1 cup softened butter *(2 sticks, 8 ounces, 1/2 pound)*

1/2 cup white *(granulated)* **sugar**

2 cups flour *(don't sift — pack it down in the cup when you measure it)*

---

4 beaten eggs *(just whip them up in a glass with a fork)*

1/2 cup white *(granulated)* **sugar** *(not a misprint — you'll use a total of 1 cup white sugar in this recipe)*

1 teaspoon baking powder

1/2 teaspoon salt

4 Tablespoons flour *(that's 1/4 cup — don't sift)*

Set the frozen concentrated pineapple juice out on the counter to thaw.

Dump the crushed pineapple into a strainer and let it drain while you make the crust.

Mix the cup of softened butter with 1/2 cup white sugar until it's light and fluffy. Add the 2 cups of flour. Mix thoroughly.

Hannah's 1st Note: You can also do this in a food processor with cold butter cut into 1/2 inch chunks, and the steel blade. Just put the sugar in the bowl of your food processor, place the chunks of butter on top of the sugar, and cover the butter with the flour. Process with an on-and-off motion until the resulting mixture looks like coarse sand.

Spread the mixture out in a greased 9-inch by 13-inch pan. ***(You can also spray the pan with Pam or another nonstick cooking spray.)*** Shake the pan to spread out the mixture evenly, and then press it down with your impeccably clean hands.

Bake the crust at 350 degrees F. for 15 to 20 minutes or until it's starting to turn golden around the edges. Remove the pan from the oven, but don't shut off the oven!

In a medium-sized mixing bowl, combine the 4 beaten eggs with the second 1/2 cup of white sugar. Stir in the 1/2 cup of pineapple concentrate. *(If it's not completely thawed, just spoon it into a half-cup measure, level it off, and stir it into your bowl.)*

Use the back of a spoon to press all the juice out of the drained pineapple in the strainer. When it's as juice-free as you can make it, measure out 1/2 cup of crushed pineapple and add it to your bowl. Mix it in thoroughly.

Add the baking powder and the salt. Mix them in until they're thoroughly combined.

Stir in the 4 Tablespoons of flour. Mix it in thoroughly.

Hannah's 2nd Note: This mixture will be runny. Don't worry, it's supposed to be that way. It's like a baked custard and it will "set up" in the oven when the eggs cook.

Pour this mixture on top of the crust you just baked. Stick it back into the oven and bake it at 350 degrees F. for an additional 50 minutes.

When the baking time is up, remove the pan from the oven and let it cool on a wire rack or a cold stovetop burner. Once your pan of Pineapple Right-Side-Up Bars has cooled thoroughly, sprinkle the top with powdered sugar and refrigerate them until you want to serve them.

To serve, cut the pan of bars into brownie-sized pieces and arrange them on a pretty platter.

ROCKY ROAD BAR COOKIES (S'MORES)

Preheat the oven to 350 degrees F., rack in the middle position.

24 graham crackers *(12 double ones)*

2 cups miniature marshmallows *(white, not colored)*

6-ounce package semi-sweet chocolate chips *(1 cup)*

1 cup salted cashews

1/2 cup butter *(1 stick, 4 ounces, 1/4 pound)*

1/2 cup brown sugar, firmly packed

1 teaspoon vanilla extract

Spray a 9-inch by 13-inch cake pan with Pam or another nonstick cooking spray. *(If you like, buy a disposable foil pan in the grocery store, place it on a cookie sheet to support the bottom, and then you won't have to clean up.)*

Line the bottom of the pan with a layer of graham crackers. *(It's okay to overlap a little.)*

Sprinkle the graham crackers with the marshmallows.

Sprinkle the marshmallows with the chocolate chips.

Sprinkle the chocolate chips with the cashews.

In a small saucepan over LOW heat, combine the butter and brown sugar. Stir the mixture constantly until the sugar is dissolved.

Turn off the heat, move the saucepan to a cool burner, and stir in the vanilla.

Drizzle the contents of the saucepan evenly over the contents of the cake pan.

Bake at 350 degrees F. for 10 to 12 minutes or until the marshmallows are golden on top. Cool in the pan on a wire rack or on a cool stovetop burner.

When the Rocky Road Bar Cookies are cool, cut them into brownie-sized pieces and serve.

If there are any leftovers *(which there won't be unless you have less than three people)*, store them in the refrigerator in a covered container. They can also be wrapped, sealed in a freezer bag, and frozen for up to two months.

Hannah's Note: If you freeze these bars, make sure you put on a label that describes something your family doesn't like. I thought I was safe with SMELT, but it turns out that Mike actually likes them if they're deep fried in beer batter!

A Not So Scientific Study of Pan Size

by Grandma Knudson

Sometimes the size of a pan is hard to tell because they don't seem to stamp it on the bottom anymore. And if they do, the chances arc it's in centimeters. In my day, they . . . well . . . never mind about that. I'll help you with your pan size as best I can.

Find a tape measure. If you have a sewing box, you might have one in there. Chances are, you don't. Look around to see if one of your kids left a ruler out somewhere. And if that doesn't work, go out to the garage and look for one of your husband's tape measures. All you have to do is tip the pan over and measure the bottom.

To make things even easier, a 9-inch by 13-inch pan is a cake pan, the kind you use in a home kitchen. It's easy to spot, even in a cluttered cupboard. You probably got one for a wedding present with a clear plastic lid that cracked right away. Chances are you threw the lid away, but I'll bet you kept the pan.

Baking cookie bars is easy if you have the right size pan, but what if you don't and it's snowing outside? You surely don't want to scrape off your windshield and drive to CostMart to buy one. As long as you can remember your times tables and you can do some simple arithmetic, you can get around that problem by using a pan you already have.

Say the recipe calls for an 8-inch by 8-inch square pan and you don't have anything even approaching that size. Just multiply the two numbers together. Eight times eight is sixty-four. Write it down so you won't forget it. Just dig a little deeper in the back of the cupboard and see if you've got a 7-inch by 9-inch pan. Pyrex used to make those and it's entirely possible you still have your great-grandma's set of baking pans. If you find it, do the math. Seven times nine is sixty-three and sixty-three is more than close enough to sixty-four. My rule of thumb is that if you can find a pan that's six or less off the total inches you need, you should use it.

"This candy section is exactly what I need," Claire said, flipping through the recipes. "I think I can make almost every recipe here."

"Almost?" Hannah questioned her.

"Yes. The Brown Sugar Drops call for a candy thermometer."

"I'll help you with those," Grandma Knudson offered. "Then you'll see how easy it is to use one."

"Thanks." Claire turned to smile at her. "There's one more I can't make. I shouldn't give the kids Kitty's Jamaican Rum Balls. They've got real rum in them."

Hannah came over to Claire to glance at the recipe. "You can make them for the kids. Just think up another name and substitute some kind of juice for the rum. They'd be good with orange juice or pineapple juice."

"The kids will like those. And you could make them with the rum for the church board," Grandma Knudson suggested, and Hannah noticed that she had a twinkle in her eye. "It might make them cough up the money for a new furnace."

"Grandma!" Claire sounded shocked, but her lips were twitching with laughter.

The matriarch of Holy Redeemer Lutheran Church gave a ladylike shrug. "I'm just teasing, Claire. If you can't say outrageous things at my age, when can you?"

Candy

AUNT KITTY'S JAMAICAN RUM BALLS

4 cups finely crushed vanilla wafers *(a 12-ounce box is about 2 and 1/2 cups crushed — measure after crushing)*

1 cup chopped nuts *(measure after chopping — I use pecans, but that's because I really like them — I've also used macadamia nuts, walnuts, and cashews)*

1/2 cup Karo syrup *(the clear white kind)*

1/2 cup excellent rum *(or excellent whiskey, or excellent whatever)*

2 Tablespoons sweetened dry cocoa *(I'm going to use Ghirardelli sweet Ground Chocolate & Cocoa the next time I make them)*

1 Tablespoon strong coffee *(brewed — liquid)*

COATINGS:

Dry cocoa
Powdered *(confectioner's)* sugar
Chocolate sprinkles

If you haven't already done so, crush the vanilla wafers in a food processor, or put them into a plastic bag and crush them with a rolling pin. Measure them and pour 4 cups into a mixing bowl.

Chop the nuts finely with a food processor or with your knife. Measure and add 1 cup to your bowl.

Mix in the Karo syrup, rum *(or substitute)*, sweetened dry cocoa, and strong coffee. Stir until thoroughly blended.

Rub your hands with powdered sugar. Make small balls, large enough to fit into a paper bonbon cup. Dip the balls in cocoa, or powdered sugar, or chocolate sprinkles to coat them. Do some of each and arrange them on a plate — very pretty.

Refrigerate these until you serve them. They should last for at least a month in the refrigerator. *(I've never been able to put this to the test, because every time I make them, they're gone within a week.)*

Yield: At least 5 dozen, depending on how large you roll the balls.

Aunt Kitty's Jamaican Rum Balls make great gifts when they're packaged like fine candy. Most cake decorating stores stock a variety of frilly bonbon cups and decorative candy boxes for you to use.

Hannah's 1st Note: To make these non alcoholic, use fruit juice in place of the rum.

This should work just fine, but make sure you refrigerate them and eat them within a week. You'll have to change the name to "No Rum Balls," but that's okay. Choose a fruit juice that'll go well with the chocolate, like peach, orange, or pineapple.

Hannah's 2nd Note: I've always wanted to try these dipped in melted chocolate. I bet they'd be fantastic!

BROWN SUGAR DROPS

Hannah's 1st Note: The original name of this recipe was "Browned" Sugar Drops. Over the years, it got shortened to Brown Sugar Drops, even though there's no brown sugar in the recipe.

To make this candy, you will need a candy thermometer. I use the kind with a glass tube and a sliding metal clamp that attaches to the side of a saucepan. And even though the recipe calls for a 3-quart saucepan, I always use my 4-quart saucepan. That way I don't have to worry about the candy foaming up over the sides.

1 cup buttermilk
2 and 1/2 cups white *(granulated)* sugar
1 teaspoon baking soda
2 Tablespoons *(1/8 cup)* white Karo syrup
1/2 cup butter, room temperature *(1 stick, 4 ounces, 1/4 pound)*

Before you start, get out a 3-quart saucepan ***(or a 4-quart saucepan)*** and your candy thermometer. Place the thermometer inside the saucepan with the sliding clamp on the outside. Slide the thermometer through the clamp until it's approximately 1/2 inch from the bottom of the pan. ***(If the bulb touches*** *the bottom of the pan, your reading will be wildly off.)*

On a cold burner, combine the buttermilk, sugar, baking soda, and white Karo syrup in the saucepan. Stir the mixture until it's smooth.

Turn the burner on MEDIUM HIGH heat. STIR the candy mixture CONSTANTLY until it boils. *(This will take about 10 minutes, so pull up a stool and get comfortable while you stir.)*

Move the saucepan to a cold burner, but don't turn off the hot burner. You'll be getting right back to it.

Drop the butter into the candy mixture and stir it in. *(This could sputter a bit, so be careful.)* Slide the saucepan back on the hot burner and watch it cook. STIRRING IS NOT NECESSARY FROM THIS POINT ON. Just give it a little mix when you feel like it. Pull up your stool again and relax. Enjoy a cup of Swedish Plasma coffee *(strong black coffee)* and one of those yummy cookies you baked last night while you wait for the candy thermometer to come up to the 240 degree F. mark.

When your thermometer reaches 240 degrees F., give the pan a final stir, turn off the burner, and take your candy from the heat. Let it cool on a wire rack or a cold burner until it returns to almost room temperature. Then stir it with a wooden spoon until it looks creamy.

Lay out sheets of wax paper. Drop the Brown Sugar Drops by spoonfuls onto the paper. Don't worry if your "drops" aren't of uniform size. Once your guests taste them, they'll be hunting for the larger pieces.

Hannah's 2nd Note: If the time gets away from you and your candy hardens too much in the pan, you can stick it back on the burner over very LOW heat and stir it constantly until it's the proper creamy texture again.

Lisa's Note: This candy reminds me of the kind that's shaped like maple leaves. Dad used to bring it back from Vermont when he went back to visit Uncle Fritz. I loved that candy. Just for fun, I tried adding a teaspoon of maple extract right after I added the butter, and it was really good that way!

Yield: 3 dozen pieces of delicious candy.

CHOCOLATE PECAN ROLL

Hannah's 1st Note: You don't need a candy thermometer to make this candy.

8-ounce package dried apricots*** *(or pineapple, or cherries, or whatever)*
1 and 1/2 cups roughly chopped pecans *(measure AFTER chopping)*
2 one-ounce squares of unsweetened chocolate *(I used Baker's)*
14-ounce can sweetened condensed milk *(NOT evaporated milk)*
2 and 1/2 cups semi-sweet chocolate chips
1 teaspoon butter
1 teaspoon vanilla extract
pinch of salt

Hannah's 2nd Note: You don't absolutely positively have to use unsweetened chocolate squares. If you don't have them on hand, just use three cups of semi-sweet chocolate chips instead of 2 and 1/2 cups and it'll work out just fine.

***You can use almost any dried fruit in this candy. Lisa tried it with dried sweetened pineapple and pineapple extract, and it was delicious. If there's an extract that matches your fruit, you can use it instead of the vanilla.

Chop the dried fruit into pea-sized pieces. Then chop the pecans and measure out one and a half cups. *(This is easy to do if you have a food processor, but a knife and chopping board will work also.)*

Chop the squares of unsweetened chocolate into chip-sized pieces. *(They'll melt faster that way.)* Empty the can of sweetened condensed milk into a 2-quart saucepan. Add the unsweetened chocolate pieces and the semi-sweet chocolate chips.

Stir the mixture over LOW heat until the chocolate has melted. Give a final stir and take the pan from the heat.

Mix in the butter, flavor extract, salt, and the dried fruit. *(Don't add the nuts yet — they're for later when you make the rolls.)*

Put the saucepan in the refrigerator and chill the candy for 30 to 40 minutes.

Take the pan out of the refrigerator and divide the candy in half. Place each half on a two-foot-long piece of wax paper.

Shape each half into a roll that's approximately a foot and a half long and about 1 and 1/2 inches thick.

Roll the candy logs in the chopped nuts,

coating them as evenly as you can. Press the nuts in slightly so they'll stick to the outside of the roll.

Roll the finished logs in clean wax paper, twist the ends closed, and place them in the refrigerator for at least 2 hours to harden.

Cut the candy rolls into half-inch slices with a sharp knife.

Yield: Makes about 48 slices of delicious candy.

CHOCOLATE TRUFFLES

6 Tablespoons chilled butter *(3/4 stick, 3 ounces)*

12-ounce package semi-sweet chocolate chips *(I used Ghirardelli)*

1/2 cup firmly packed powdered sugar *(confectioner's sugar)*

6 egg yolks

1 Tablespoon rum, brandy, flavored brandy, or vanilla extract

Put an inch or so of water in the bottom half of a double boiler and heat it to a gentle boil. Cut the butter in chunks and place them in the top half of the double boiler. Add the chips and then the powdered sugar and set the top half over the bottom half. Put on the cover and let everything melt while you . . .

Beat the egg yolks in a small bowl with a whisk. Whisk until they're thoroughly combined, but stop before they get fluffy or lighter in color.

Stir the chocolate until it's completely melted. It will be thick, almost like fudge. Remove the top half of the double boiler and set it on a cold burner.

Stir several spoonfuls of beaten egg yolk into the chocolate mixture. When that's incorporated, stir in several more spoonfuls. Keep adding egg yolk in small amounts, stirring constantly, until all the egg yolks have been incorporated and the chocolate mixture is smooth and glossy.

Stir in the rum, brandy, or vanilla. Put the lid back on the top of the double boiler and refrigerate the chocolate mixture for 3 hours.

To Decorate Truffles:

**finely chopped nuts
powdered *(confectioner's)* sugar
chocolate sprinkles
shaved chocolate
cocoa powder
finely shredded coconut**

Warning: This next step is fairly messy. If you like, wear disposable plastic food-server gloves. You can also lightly grease your hands, or spray them with Pam or other nonstick cooking spray so the chocolate won't stick to your fingers.

Form small balls of chilled chocolate with your hands and roll them in bowls of the above ingredients. You can mix and match, or give all of your truffles the same coating. Place the truffles in ruffled bonbon papers and store them in an airtight container in the refrigerator.

These are incredibly delicious candies. They're super easy to make, but let's keep that a secret. It can't hurt to let people assume that you went to a lot of trouble, just for them.

Yield: 4 to 5 dozen, depending on truffle size.

IBBY'S METAPHYSICAL ENGLISH TOFFEE

Preheat the oven to 350 degrees F., rack in the middle position.

16-ounce box Club Crackers*** *(Mine were made by Keebler)*
1 cup butter *(2 sticks, 8 ounces, 1/2 pound)*
1 cup brown sugar *(tightly packed)*
2 cups milk chocolate chips *(12-ounce bag)*
2 cups chopped pecans *(salted or un-salted, it really doesn't matter — measure AFTER chopping)*

Line a 10-inch by 15-inch cookie sheet with foil. If you have a jellyroll pan, that's perfect. If you don't, turn up the edges of the foil to form sides.

Spray the foil with Pam or another non-stick cooking spray. *(You want to be able to*

***There are three packets in a 16-ounce box of Club Crackers. You'll use only one packet. You can buy a smaller box if you can find it, but you can always use extra crackers, right? If you can't find Club Crackers at your store, you can use any brand of salted soda crackers. Your goal is to cover the bottom of the pan as completely as you can with something both crispy and salty.

peel it off later, after the candy hardens.)

Line the pan completely with crackers, salt side up. Cover the whole bottom. *(You can break the crackers in pieces to make them fit if you have to.)* Set the cracker-lined jelly-roll pan or cookie sheet aside while you cook the toffee mixture.

Hannah's 1st Note: You don't need a candy thermometer to make this candy.

Combine the butter with the brown sugar in a saucepan. Bring it to a boil over medium high heat on the stovetop, stirring constantly. Boil it for exactly five minutes, stirring it constantly. If it sputters too much, you can reduce the heat. If it starts to lose the boil, you can increase the heat. Just don't stop stirring.

Pour the mixture over the crackers as evenly as you can.

Hannah's 2nd Note: I start by pouring the mixture in lines from top to bottom over the length of the pan. Then I turn it and pour more lines over the width of the pan. Once the whole pan is crosshatched with the hot toffee mixture, I pour any that's left where it's needed. If it doesn't cover the crackers completely, don't worry — it'll spread out quite a bit in the oven.

Slide the pan into the oven and bake the toffee at 350 degrees F. for 10 minutes.

Remove the pan from the oven and sprinkle the milk chocolate chips over the top. Give the chips a minute or two to melt and then spread them out as evenly as you can with a heat-resistant spatula, a wooden paddle, or a frosting knife.

Sprinkle the chopped pecans over the top of the chocolate and refrigerate the pan.

When the toffee has thoroughly chilled, peel it from the foil and break it into random-sized pieces.

Hannah's 3rd Note: Ibby used her toffee as a reward for high quiz scores. Once you taste it, you'll know why I can still recite at least one stanza from each of the Meta-physical Poets.

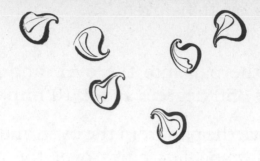

THREE-WAY FUDGE

Hannah's 1st Note: You don't need a candy thermometer to make this fudge. If you've got a microwave, you don't even need a STOVE to make this fudge.

1 cup *(6-ounce pkg.)* semi-sweet chocolate chips *(I used Ghirardelli)*

1 cup *(6-ounce pkg.)* white chocolate chips *(I used Ghirardelli)*

1 cup *(6-ounce pkg.)* milk chocolate chips *(I used Ghirardelli)*

14-ounce can of sweetened condensed milk

1 and 1/2 sticks salted butter *(6 Tablespoons — this fudge has 3 layers, and that's 2 Tablespoons of butter for each layer you'll make)*

Line an 8-inch square pan with wax paper, OR line it with foil and spray the foil with Pam or another nonstick cooking spray.

You can make this fudge on the stovetop or in the microwave. Either way will work just fine.

If you choose the stovetop method, use a heavy saucepan and stir constantly while you're melting the chocolate and other ingredients.

For the microwave, I combined my ingredients in a 2-cup Pyrex measuring cup and processed them for 70 seconds on HIGH. Remember that chocolate chips maintain their shape even after they're melted, so don't go by appearance. You'll have to stir them to be sure.

Hannah's 2nd Note: A 14-ounce can of sweetened condensed milk contains approximately one and a third cups. You're going to be dividing the can in thirds, so make each third a bit less than a half-cup and you'll come out all right.

MELT THE FOLLOWING TOGETHER FOR THE 1ST LAYER:

**1 cup semi-sweet chocolate chips
scant half-cup sweetened condensed milk
2 Tablespoons butter**

Stir to make sure everything's melted and then, spread the mixture out in the bottom of the 8-inch square pan you've prepared. Smooth it out with a rubber spatula, and let the pan sit on the counter until the fudge is cool and slightly hard to the touch. Then make the 2nd layer.

FOR THE 2ND LAYER, MELT THE FOLLOWING TOGETHER:

**1 cup white chocolate chips
scant half-cup sweetened condensed milk
2 Tablespoons butter**

Stir to make sure everything's melted and then spread the 2nd layer on top of the 1st layer, smooth it out with a rubber spatula, and let the pan sit on the counter until the 2nd layer is cool to the touch and slightly hardened. Then make the 3rd layer.

FOR THE 3RD LAYER, MELT THE FOLLOWING TOGETHER:

**1 cup milk chocolate chips
the remainder of the sweetened condensed milk
2 Tablespoons butter**

Spread this 3rd layer on top of the 2nd layer, smooth it out with a rubber spatula, and stick the pan in the refrigerator. Let your Three-Way Fudge harden in the refrigerator for at least two hours. *(Overnight is even better.)* Then turn it out on a cutting board and cut it into bite size squares.

Hannah's 3rd Note: Mike really likes this fudge when I add chopped macadamia nuts to the middle layer. Norman thinks it's best with chopped pecans in the bottom layer. I suppose that should tell me something about their personalities, but I have no idea what it is!

Claire looked very excited as she turned to Grandma Knudson. "Hannah's even got a recipe for fudge that you can make in the microwave. I ought to be able to do that, don't you think?"

"Oh, yes. Sometimes you sell yourself short, Claire. You're much more talented than you think."

"Thank you, Grandma. Is it all right if we stop at the Red Owl on the way home to get powdered sugar for rolling the rum balls? I want to try making those tonight."

"Of course it's all right. I'm running low on brown sugar, so I'll pick up a bag while we're there."

"Oh, good! Then I can make the English Toffee. That one's easy, too."

Florence shook her head. "I'm sorry, ladies, but I'm all out of brown sugar and I don't get another delivery until Monday. Everybody's doing their Christmas baking and

I sold the last bag this morning. The powdered sugar's gone too, except for the little bit that was left in the box that the Janowski twins opened."

"Why did they open the powdered sugar?" Lisa asked.

Florence shrugged. "I asked them and they said they wanted to make snowballs. I guess they thought that since it was white, it was like snow. All I know for sure is that they ended up dumping it all over each other while their mother was reading the nutritional label on a can of pork and beans."

Hannah turned to Claire who looked very disappointed. "You can still make the English Toffee. And you can make the rum balls, too. You have some molasses and some cornstarch, don't you?"

"Yes. Grandma keeps it in the pantry."

"Good. Then you can make your own brown sugar and your own powdered sugar."

"How do you do that?"

"If a recipe calls for a cup of brown sugar, put a cup of white sugar in the mixer. Just drizzle in a little molasses and mix it up until it's the right color. That's all brown sugar is anyway."

"Brown sugar is white sugar mixed with molasses?" Claire asked, sounding a bit doubtful.

"That's right. And you can make your own powdered sugar too, if you've got a blender."

Grandma Knudson gave a little nod. "We've got a blender," she said. "I knew about the brown sugar, but I've never heard of making your own powdered sugar."

"It's just white sugar with a little bit of cornstarch to keep it from sticking when you grind it into superfine crystals."

"It's right here in the recipe collection that Hannah gave us," Delores explained, holding up her binder. "It's the next section and it's called *Substitutions*. It even gives you a substitute for buttermilk."

"Perfect," Claire said with a smile. "That means Grandma and I can make the brown sugar drops and I can learn how to use that candy thermometer."

Substitutions

SUBSTITUTE FOR STORE-BOUGHT BROWN SUGAR

1 cup white, granulated sugar
2 Tablespoons dark molasses *(I use Brier Rabbit green label)*

Place the white, granulated sugar in a blender or a mixer.

With the mixer or blender running on low speed, drizzle in 2 Tablespoons of dark molasses.

Turn the mixer or blender on a higher speed and process until the white sugar has turned an even brown color.

If the brown sugar doesn't look dark enough, just add a little more molasses and mix it in well.

Hannah's Note: Using this method, you can make light brown sugar, regular brown sugar, and dark brown sugar. This means no more hard lumps in the brown sugar bag that's been sitting in your pantry for months. You don't have to keep brown sugar on hand as long as you have a jar of molasses and white sugar.

SUBSTITUTE FOR STORE-BOUGHT BUTTERMILK

1 Tablespoon fresh lemon juice *(OR white vinegar if you don't have fresh lemon juice)*

1 cup minus 1 Tablespoon whole milk at room temperature

Pour 1 Tablespoon of lemon juice *(or white vinegar)* into the bottom of a 2-cup measuring cup.

Fill the cup up to the 1-cup mark with whole milk.

Stir the mixture and let it stand on your kitchen counter for at least 5 minutes. This should cause it to sour and thicken slightly.

You can use the resulting mixture in any recipe that calls for buttermilk.

Hannah's 1st Note: You can also use this mixture in any recipe that calls for sour milk.

Lisa's Note: Florence has a cultured buttermilk powder in the baking aisle down at the Red Owl. It's specifically for cooking and baking and it's made by Saco. I bought a can, and I'm going to try it one of these days.

SUBSTITUTE FOR CAKE FLOUR

FOR ONE CUP OF CAKE FLOUR:

2 Tablespoons cornstarch
1 cup minus 2 Tablespoons all-purpose flour

Measure out 2 Tablespoons of cornstarch and put them in a 1-cup measure. Fill the measure with all-purpose flour.

You can stir this in a small bowl by hand or put it through a sifter. Do this for every cup of cake flour called for in the recipe.

If the recipe calls for a half-cup of cake flour, use 1 Tablespoon of cornstarch in the bottom of a half-cup measure. Fill the measure with all-purpose flour and you'll have one-half cup of cake flour.

SUBSTITUTE FOR CHOPPED NUTS IN COOKIES

If someone in your family is allergic to nuts, or if you thought you bought them at the store and you didn't, you can use another ingredient that will provide crunch and texture in your cookies. Try substituting an equal amount of:

Crushed corn flakes
Pretzels broken into small pieces
Crushed Cheerios
Crushed Chex cereal
M&Ms or another small chocolate candy with a sugar shell
Crushed toffee
Finely chopped coconut
Dry oatmeal
Dried chopped fruit including raisins and cranberries

SUBSTITUTE FOR EGGS

1 and 1/2 Tablespoons water
1 and 1/2 Tablespoons vegetable oil
1 teaspoon baking powder

Mix this up for each egg that is called for in a baking recipe.

Hannah's Note: This substitute is fine for cookies, but it doesn't work that well with cakes, especially the type of cake that is light and fluffy.

SUBSTITUTE FOR STORE-BOUGHT POWDERED (CONFECTIONER'S) SUGAR

1 cup white, granulated sugar for each cup of powdered sugar you need

2 Tablespoons cornstarch for each cup of powdered sugar you need

Hannah's 1st Note: You'll need a blender to make this. A mixer won't do.

Combine the white sugar and cornstarch in a blender.

Turn on the blender and blend until the resulting mixture is of powdery consistency.

Pour the mixture out of the blender and store it in an airtight container on the counter *(I use a Tupperware-type plastic container)*.

Hannah's 2nd Note: Someday I'd really like to know why I have more bowls than covers for my plastic storage containers. I think it's another mystery like the one that happens almost every washday in my laundry room. Seven pairs of socks go into the washer, and 13 socks come out of the dryer!

Let the mixture sit on your counter for 15 to 30 minutes and then it's ready to use.

Hannah's 3rd Note: Don't fill your blender too much when you're making powdered sugar. It needs space to blend.

Lisa's Note: Sometimes, down at The Cookie Jar, I add some colored decorating sugar to the blender so that I end up with pretty pastel powdered sugar that I use to make frostings.

SUBSTITUTE FOR STORE-BOUGHT SELF-RISING FLOUR

Hannah's 1st Note: I occasionally come across a recipe that calls for self-rising flour. Florence doesn't stock it at the Lake Eden Red Owl, but I found out how to make my own.

1 cup all-purpose flour
1/2 teaspoon baking soda
1/2 teaspoon salt

Sift together into a bowl for every cup of flour that's called for in the recipe. Work with whole cups only, and then measure out what you need. ***(If your recipe calls for 1 and 1/2 cups of self-rising flour, you'll make 2 cups but use only 1 and 1/2 cups of the mixture.)***

Hannah's 2nd Note: You can store your substitute for store-bought self-rising flour in a covered container for up to 3 months.

"Why don't you ever use unsalted butter?" Alice Vogel asked Hannah. "I've seen a lot of recipes that say you should use it."

Hannah gave a little shrug. "Nothing I bake really needs it. Take a good look at some of those recipes with unsalted or sweet butter. They usually list salt as one of the other ingredients. It seemed silly to me to use unsalted butter when you're just going to add salt to the recipe anyway."

Edna looked up. "How about eggs? You don't specify the size."

"They're not exactly standard, especially if you're living in a farm community. Two medium-sized eggs are supposed to equal half of a cup. But who's going to crack them into a cup and measure? If you're worried about it, you can just assume that my recipes call for eggs the size of the large eggs you can buy at a grocery store."

"How about flour?" Carrie asked her. "Is

it always all-purpose flour?"

"Yes. If a recipe needs cake flour I write it out on the list of ingredients. And I don't use recipes that call for wheat flour, or rye flour, or soy flour. They're just too specialized. Some of the special flours may work in my recipes, but you'd have to try them yourself to see."

"This section on substitutions is really helpful," Bertie said, paging through it again. "The last time I bought cake flour for a recipe, the rest of the box sat on my shelf forever. And then it got little bugs in it and I had to throw it away."

"You should have put the box in a freezer bag, and frozen it," Florence told her. "If you do that, you won't get flour weevils."

Hannah nodded and left it at that. What Florence said was accurate enough for their purposes. The eggs were still there in the box of cake flour. There was no way to avoid that. But they wouldn't hatch if the flour was frozen.

"One question," Edna announced, giving Hannah a smile. "You just gave us all those substitutes. Is there anything that *doesn't* have a substitute?"

"Just one thing. It's something that's in a class all by itself, and you either love it, or you hate it. As far as I know, there is no known substitute for rhubarb!"

Bertie laughed. "And that's the truth! What would we do without rhubarb? Everybody I know has at least a hundred recipes for rhubarb cakes, and pies . . ."

". . . and sauces, and cookies," Lisa continued the list when Bertie hesitated.

"And Jell-O," Andrea added. "I've got a really good recipe for rhubarb Jell-O. Bill even likes it and he hates rhubarb."

"You've got a rhubarb cake in here, but no cookies," Bertie pointed out to Hannah. "I think you should work on that. After all, rhubarb is practically Minnesota's state fruit . . . or vegetable . . . or whatever it is."

"It's like a weed," Florence said with such distain, everyone knew she was one of the people who hated it. "Once it grows in your back yard, you can't get rid of it. I tried."

Alice laughed. "I've got six cherry rhubarb plants in *my* back yard, and I wish I had more."

"You can have mine if you come over and dig them up," Florence offered, and then she turned to Hannah. "Where's the Minnesota Peach Cobbler? And the Lemon Cream Torte? Those are my absolute favorites!"

"Here," Hannah told her, flipping to another section in Florence's binder. "Some of my recipes didn't really fit anywhere, so I put them under *Other Sweet Treats*. If there's something you can't find, it's probably there."

Other Sweet Treats

APRICOT BREAD PUDDING

DO NOT preheat oven — the bread pudding must settle for 30 minutes before baking.

8 slices of white bread *(either homemade or "store bought")*
1 cup butter *(2 sticks, 8 ounces, 1/2 pound)*
1/3 cup white *(granulated)* **sugar**
1/2 cup chopped dried apricots *(not too fine, you want some chunks)*
3 beaten eggs *(just whip them up in a glass with a fork)*
2 and 1/4 cups top milk*** *(you can use light cream or half and half)*

Heavy cream, sweetened whipped cream, or vanilla ice cream for a topping

***"Top milk" is Great-Grandma Elsie's word for the cream that floated to the top of old-fashioned milk bottles.

Generously butter a 2-quart casserole. *(You can also spray the inside of the casserole dish with Pam or another nonstick cooking spray.)* Remove the crusts from the bread and cut each slice into 4 triangles. *(Just make an "X" with your knife.)* Melt the butter in a large bowl and put in the bread triangles, tossing them lightly with a spoon until they're coated with butter.

Arrange approximately a third of the triangles in the bottom of the casserole. Sprinkle on a third of the sugar and half of the chopped apricots.

Put down half of the remaining bread triangles, sprinkle on half of the remaining sugar, and add ALL of the remaining apricots.

Cover with the rest of the bread triangles. Scrape the bowl to get out any butter that remains in the bottom of the bowl and put that on top. Sprinkle with the last of the sugar and set aside.

Place the beaten eggs in the butter bowl and whisk in the light cream. Pour this over the top of the casserole and let it stand at room temperature for thirty minutes. *(This gives the bread time to absorb the egg-*

and-cream mixture.)

Preheat the oven to 350 degrees F., rack in the middle position.

When the oven has come up to temperature, bake the bread pudding uncovered, for 45 to 55 minutes, or until the pudding is set and the top is golden brown.

Let the Apricot Bread Pudding cool slightly *(10 to 15 minutes or so)* and then spoon it out into dessert dishes. Top it with heavy cream, sweetened whipped cream, or a scoop of vanilla ice cream.

You can make this with any dried fruit, including currants or raisins. Andrea likes apricots, Mother prefers dates, and Michelle thought it was "yummy" with dried pears. We didn't try it with prunes. Carrie Rhodes is the only person I know who likes prunes. *(And I'm not going to comment about that!)*

Yield: Serves 6 unless you invite the Swensens to dinner.

FRUIT POCKET FRENCH TOAST

DO NOT preheat the oven — this dish must "rest" before baking.

- 1/2 cup butter *(1 stick, 4 ounces, 1/4 pound)*
- 1 cup brown sugar, firmly packed
- 1/2 cup maple syrup
- 1 cup chopped pecans *(optional)*

- 1 loaf *(at least 12 slices)* of sliced bread *(white, egg, raisin, whatever)*
- 1/2 cup butter, softened *(1 stick, 4 ounces, 1/4 pound)*
- 2 cups canned or fresh fruit *(any kind except melon or grapes)*

- 8 eggs
- 3/4 cup white *(granulated)* sugar
- 2 teaspoons cinnamon
- 2 cups heavy cream *(whipping cream)*
- 2 teaspoons vanilla extract

- 1/2 cup butter *(1 stick, 1/4 pound)*

- Powdered *(confectioner's)* sugar to sprinkle on top before serving

Leave one stick of butter out on the counter to soften it, or unwrap it and heat it for a few seconds in the microwave.

If you're using canned fruit, open the can and dump the fruit in a strainer now.

Heat a second stick of butter, the brown sugar, and the maple syrup in a microwave-safe bowl on HIGH for 2 and 1/2 minutes *(I used a quart measuring cup)*, or in a pan on the stovetop, stirring constantly, until the butter is melted. Spray a 9-inch by 13-inch cake pan with Pam or another nonstick spray, and pour the syrup mixture in the bottom. Sprinkle with the chopped pecans, if you decided to use them.

Lay out twelve slices of bread. You're going to make fruit sandwiches.

Spread some softened butter on one slice of bread. Top it with well-drained fruit cut in very thin slices *(berries or pineapple can be crushed)*.

Spread more softened butter on a second slice of bread and use it to cover the fruit. Cut this fruit sandwich in half and place it in the pan on top of the syrup mixture. Make 5 more sandwiches, cut them in half, and then place them in the pan. You can crowd them a bit, but do not overlap the bread.

Press the sandwiches down with the back of a flat metal spatula. Squish that bread!

Beat the eggs with the sugar and the cinnamon. Add the cream and the vanilla, mixing thoroughly. Pour this mixture over the bread in the pan.

Cover the pan with plastic wrap or foil, and let it stand out on the counter for a minimum of twenty minutes. *(If you're having a fancy breakfast, you can also make this the night before and keep it in the refrigerator until it's time to bake it.)*

Preheat your oven to 350 degrees F., rack in the middle position.

Take off the plastic wrap that covers your pan. Melt the third stick of butter and drizzle it over the top of the fruit sandwiches.

When your oven has come up to temperature, bake the Fruit Pocket French Toast at 350 degrees F., uncovered, for approximately 45 minutes, or until the top has browned. Let the pan cool on a wire rack for at least five minutes.

To serve: Sprinkle the top of the pan with powdered sugar before you carry it to the table. This will make it much prettier. Dish

out the Fruit Pocket French Toast with a
metal spatula, and offer more syrup and
butter for those who want it. A half sandwich is one serving.

Yield: 12 half-sandwich servings.

Hannah's Note: If you want to make this
and you're really in a pickle because you
don't have any fruit, try spreading the
bread with a thick layer of fruit jam or mar-
malade. I haven't tried this, but I'll bet you
a batch of my best cookies that it'll work!

HAWAIIAN FLAN

Preheat the oven to 350 degrees F., rack in the center position.

1 cup white *(granulated)* sugar
1/2 cup water

---

6 eggs
1 can *(14-ounces)* sweetened, condensed milk *(don't use evaporated — it won't work)*
1/4 cup white sugar
1/8 teaspoon salt
1 and 1/2 cups pineapple juice

---

1 small can *(8 ounces)* crushed pineapple, well drained
Sweetened whipped cream for a topping *(optional)*

Find an 8-inch by 8-inch square pan *(either metal or glass)*, or any other oven pan that will hold 6 cups of liquid. Do not grease, butter or spray it with Pam or another nonstick cooking spray. Simply have it ready, next to the stovetop.

Combine one cup of white sugar with the half cup of water in a saucepan. Bring it to a boil, stirring at first and then swishing it around until the mixture turns golden brown. *(This gets as hot as candy syrup, so wear oven mitts.)*

Carefully pour the syrup into the pan you've chosen and tip it to coat the bottom and the sides. This is your caramel sauce. *(Be very careful. This is extremely hot.)* Run water in the saucepan you used and set it in the sink. Then set the baking pan aside while you make the custard.

WARNING: Be very careful! This is extremely hot. When the caramel begins to cool, you may hear cracking noises. Don't panic. It's the caramel cracking, not your pan. I know this because I threw away a perfectly good glass pan because I thought it had cracked. I looked at it later, and only the caramel had cracked, not the glass!

Beat the eggs until they're light yellow and thick. *(This will take a while if you don't have an electric mixer.)* Add the sweetened condensed milk, the sugar, the salt, and the pineapple juice, and beat thoroughly.

Get out a strainer and strain this mixture into your baking pan.

Find a larger baking pan that will contain your custard pan with at least an inch to spare on all four sides. Place the custard pan inside the larger pan. Slip both pans into the oven and then pour hot tap water into the large pan, enough to immerse your custard pan halfway up the sides.

Bake one hour, or until a knife inserted in the center comes out clean.

Remove the custard pan from the water and let it cool on a wire rack for at least 10 minutes. *(This custard can be served either warm, or cold.)*

To serve, turn the custard out in a flat bowl or a plate with a deep lip. *(This is so the caramel sauce won't overflow.)* Place slices of custard in a dessert dish and sprinkle some of the crushed pineapple over the top. Then spoon on some of the caramel sauce and top with sweetened, whipped cream if you wish.

Delores prefers this custard chilled. Andrea says it's best at room temperature, and I like it warm.

LEMON CREAM TORTE

Preheat the oven to 250 degrees F., rack in the middle position (NOT A MISPRINT — two hundred and fifty degrees F.).

Hannah's 1st Note: Try to choose a day when the humidity is low to bake this. Meringues don't crisp up as well if the air is too humid.

MERINGUE:

**4 egg whites *(reserve the yolks in a bowl for the filling)*
1 cup white *(granulated)* sugar
1/2 teaspoon vanilla extract**

Cover a cookie sheet with parchment paper. *(You can use brown parcel-wrapping paper, but parchment works best.)* Draw two 8-inch diameter circles on your paper, using a round 8-inch cake pan as a guide. DO NOT cut them out of the sheet of parchment paper.

Spray the inside of the circles you've drawn with Pam, or another nonstick cooking spray, and then sprinkle it lightly with flour. The circles you've drawn are a guide. You will be filling them with meringue.

Beat the egg whites on HIGH speed until

491

morning and locked them in her suitcase. And, even worse, she hid the key."

"That's because they would have been gone in no time at all," Carrie told him. And then she turned to the other ladies. "Earl's crazy about lemon. I baked Hannah's Lovely Lemon Bar Cookies for him on Tuesday morning, and they were gone by Tuesday night."

"So I don't even get to taste your Lemon Softies?" Earl asked, looking mournful.

"Of course you do. There's an extra dozen in the bottom of my suitcase. If you're really nice to me, I'll give you the key when we get home."

Once coffee had been poured and the extra pies and cheesecake had been served, Earl cleared his throat. "I don't want to make you nervous, but it's nasty out there. The snow's coming down really hard, the wind's picked up to over forty miles an hour, and the last weather report I heard said that with the wind chill factored in, it was already minus thirty-two."

Hannah shrugged. "That's not too bad. It sounds like Minnesota in December."

"Or January," Mike added.

Mayor Bascomb laughed. "February and March, too. And then there's that blizzard we had in May of seventy-five."

they are stiff enough to hold a soft peak. Add 2/3 cup of the sugar gradually, sprinkling it in and continuing to beat as you sprinkle. Pour in the vanilla extract and sprinkle in the rest of the sugar *(1/3 cup)*. Mix it in very gently *(on LOW speed)*, or fold in with an angel food cake whisk or a very clean *(not a speck of grease!)* rubber spatula until the meringue is smooth.

Spoon half the meringue neatly into one of the 8-inch circles. Smooth the top with your rubber spatula. It should be about 3/4 inch thick. Spoon the remaining meringue into the second circle and smooth the top of that one, also.

Bake at 250 degrees F. for one hour, or until slightly golden on top and the surface is hard when touched.

Cool the sheet of meringue circles completely on the cookie sheet on a wire rack.

When the meringues are cool, gently loosen them by peeling off the paper. Put them back on the paper, loose, and move them to a cool, dry place. *(A dark cupboard is fine, but the refrigerator is NOT FINE.)*

FILLING:

4 egg yolks *(the ones you reserved)*
1/2 cup white *(granulated)* sugar
3 Tablespoons lemon juice
2 teaspoons lemon zest *(finely grated lemon peel — just the yellow part)*

---

2 teaspoons vanilla extract
1/2 cup whipping cream *(heavy cream)*
1/4 cup white *(granulated)* sugar *(You'll use 3/4 cup total in the filling)*

Beat the egg yolks with the 1/2 cup sugar until smooth. Add the lemon juice and zest.

Cook this mixture in the top of a double boiler, over gently boiling water, until it's smooth and as thick as mayonnaise. *(That's a little thicker than gravy and takes about 3 minutes or so.)* Move the top part of the double boiler to a cold burner and let the mixture cool while you complete the rest of the recipe.

Pour the vanilla into the whipping cream. Whip the cream just until it holds a peak. Don't over beat. Beat in the remaining 1/4 cup of sugar. Slowly stir the whipped cream mixture into the warm lemon mixture until you have a light, smooth sauce. *(Lick the spoon — it's yummy!*) Cover it and refrigerate the sauce for at least 2 hours, or until you're ready to serve.

To assemble, get out the meringues and the lemon filling. Decide which meringue looks best and set that aside for the top. Place the other meringue on a cake plate.

Spoon half of the lemon filling over the top of the meringue on the cake plate. Spread it with a rubber spatula so it's almost out to the edge.

Put the best-looking meringue on top. Spoon the rest of the lemon filling on top of that meringue and spread it out with a rubber spatula.

To serve, cut pie-shaped wedges at the table and transfer them to dessert plates. This is a light, sugary but tart, totally satisfying summer dessert.

Yield: Serves 4 to 6 people *(unless you invite Carrie — she always has thirds)*.

Hannah's 2nd Note: This dessert is certainly yummy, but it's not gorgeous. When Sally serves it at the Lake Eden Inn, she slices it in the kitchen because the meringues tend to crumble. Then she puts it on a beautiful dessert plate or in a cut glass dessert bowl, tops it with a generous dollop of sweetened whipped cream, and places a paper-thin lemon slice on top to make it look fancy.

LEMON FLUFF JELL-O

1 large can *(20 ounces)* crushed pine-apple

2 cups water *(for boiling)*

3 small *(3 ounces each)* packages of Lemon Jell-O

2 cups COLD water***

1 small *(2-cup)* container thawed Cool Whip *(or any other frozen, whipped, nondairy dessert topping — you can thaw it overnight in the refrigerator the night before you plan to make the Lemon Fluff Jell-O)*

1 can *(enough to make an 8-inch pie)* lemon pie filling****

Drain the can of crushed pineapple in a

***This is approximate because it all depends on your can of crushed pineapple. You're going to drain the crushed pineapple and save the liquid. Then you'll add the cold water to the juice until it makes a total of 2 cups.

****If you can't find lemon pie filling in a can *(Andrea couldn't — Florence didn't have it at the Red Owl)*, you can use a 3.4 ounce package of lemon pudding and pie filling. Just follow the directions for pie filling and add it to your Jell-O mixture at the proper time.

strainer over a bowl. Save the liquid to use later.

Boil two cups of water in a small saucepan. Take it off the burner.

Empty the three packages of Lemon Jell-O powder into the recently boiled water. Stir until the Jell-O is dissolved. This step should take about 2 minutes. *(There's nothing worse than Jell-O powder that doesn't dissolve. It makes a layer of sweet lemon rubber at the bottom of your Jell-O mold and the mixture on top is runny. To tell if Jell-O powder is dissolved, reach in with your impeccably clean fingers and rub a bit of liquid between your thumb and your finger. If it's not gritty, it's dissolved.)*

When the Jell-O powder is dissolved, combine the pineapple juice with COLD water to make 2 cups of liquid. Add this to your saucepan and stir it in.

Refrigerate your saucepan until the Jell-O is partially set. *(This should take approximately 45 minutes.)*

Spoon the Jell-O mixture into a bowl and whip it with a whisk or an electric mixer until it's a little fluffy. *(Not too long or you'll beat warm air into it.)*

Fold in the thawed Cool-Whip.

Fold in the lemon pie filling. *(This is the time to make the instant pudding and pie filling and fold it into your Jell-O if you couldn't find canned pie filling.)*

Fold in the drained, crushed pineapple and blend just until it's mixed in.

Spray a 2-quart Jell-O mold, or a standard-sized Bundt pan with Pam or another nonstick cooking spray. You'll also need a second, much smaller bowl or mold to hold the Jell-O that won't quite fit in the first mold.

Transfer the Jell-O mixture to your molds and chill it in the refrigerator for at least 12 hours before serving.

MINNESOTA PEACH COBBLER

Preheat the oven to 350 degrees F., rack in the middle position.

Hannah's 1st Note: Don't thaw your peaches before you make this — leave them frozen.

Spray a 9-inch by 13-inch cake pan with Pam or another nonstick cooking spray.

10 cups frozen sliced peaches *(approximately 2 and 1/2 pounds)*
1/8 cup lemon juice *(2 Tablespoons)*
1 and 1/2 cups white *(granulated)* sugar
1/4 teaspoon salt
3/4 cup flour *(don't sift — pack it down in the cup when you measure it)*
1/2 teaspoon cinnamon
1/2 cup melted butter *(1 stick, 4 ounces, 1/4 pound)*

Measure out ten cups of peaches and put them in a large mixing bowl. Let them sit on the counter and thaw for 10 minutes. Then sprinkle them with lemon juice and toss so that they're all coated.

In another smaller bowl combine the white sugar, salt, flour, and cinnamon. Mix them together with a fork until they're evenly combined.

Pour the dry mixture over the peaches and toss them a second time. *(This works best if you use your impeccably clean hands.)* Once most of the dry mixture is clinging to the peaches, dump them into the cake pan you've prepared. If there is any dry mixture left in the bowl, sprinkle it on top of the peaches in the pan.

Melt the butter. Drizzle it over the peaches. Then cover the cake pan tightly with foil.

Bake the peach mixture at 350 degrees F., for 40 minutes. Take it out of the oven and set it on a heatproof surface, but DON'T TURN ~~OFF~~ THE OVEN!

Top Crust:

1 cup flour *(don't sift — pack it down in the cup when you measure it)*
1 cup white *(granulated)* sugar
1 and 1/2 teaspoons baking powder
1/4 teaspoon cinnamon
1/2 teaspoon salt

1/2 stick softened butter *(1/4 cup, 2 ounces, 1/8 pound)*

2 beaten eggs *(just whip them up in a glass with a fork)*

Combine the flour, sugar, baking powder, cinnamon, and salt in the smaller bowl you used earlier. Cut in the softened butter with a couple of forks until the mixture looks like coarse cornmeal. Add the beaten eggs and mix them in with a fork. For those of you who remember your school library with fondness, the result will resemble library paste but it'll smell a whole lot better! *(If you have a food processor, you can also make the crust using the steel blade and chilled butter cut into 4 chunks. You'll take the dry mixture out of the food processor and add the beaten eggs by hand.)*

Remove the foil cover from the peaches and drop on spoonfuls of the topping. Because the topping is thick, you'll have to do this in little dibs and dabs scraped from the spoon with another spoon, a rubber spatula, or with your freshly washed finger. Dab on the topping until the whole pan is polka-dotted. *(Don't worry if some spots aren't covered very well — the batter will spread out and fill in as it bakes and result in a crunchy crust.)*

Bake at 350 degrees F., uncovered, for an additional 50 minutes.

Hannah's 2nd Note: Minnesota Peach Cobbler can be eaten hot, warm, room temperature, or chilled. It can be served by itself in a bowl, or topped with cream, sweetened whipped cream, or ice cream.

STRAWBERRY CUSTARD SQUARES

Preheat the oven to 375 degrees F., rack in the middle position.

- 1 cup flour *(don't sift — pack it down in the cup when you measure it)*
- 1/2 teaspoon salt
- 1/2 cup chilled butter *(1 stick, 4 ounces, 1/4 pound)*
- 2 Tablespoons whipping cream *(1/8 cup)*
- 1/2 cup flour *(NOT A MISPRINT — you'll use 1 and 1/2 cups in this part of the recipe)*
- 1/2 cup white *(granulated)* sugar
- 3 cups sliced strawberries***

TOPPING:

- 1/2 cup white *(granulated)* sugar
- 1 Tablespoon flour
- 2 eggs, beaten *(just whip them up in a glass with a fork)*
- 1 cup whipping cream *(heavy cream)*
- 1 teaspoon vanilla extract *(or strawberry extract if you have it)*

Spray a 9-inch by 13-inch cake pan with Pam or another nonstick cooking spray.

***I've used sliced strawberries, peaches, or chopped dark cherries.

In a small bowl, combine 1 cup flour and the salt. Cut in the half cup of butter until the resulting mixture looks like coarse sand. *(You can do this in the food processor with the steel blade if you like.)* Stir in the cream and pat the dough into the bottom of your cake pan.

Combine the 1/2 cup flour and the sugar. Sprinkle it over the crust in the pan and put the sliced strawberries (or other fruit) on top.

For the topping, mix the 1/2 cup white sugar and the Tablespoon of flour. Stir in the eggs, cream, and vanilla extract. Pour the mixture over the top of the fruit in the pan.

Bake at 375 degrees F. for 40 to 45 minutes, or until the top is lightly browned. Cool on a rack, and then refrigerate in the pan.

Serve warm or chilled with sweetened whipped cream or ice cream. You can also serve this plain or with a light sprinkling of powdered sugar.

Yield: 10 to 12 dessert squares.

RUBY'S DEEP-FRIED CANDY BARS

oil for deep-frying *(I used Canola)*
6 or more assorted chocolate-covered candy bars***

Buy the candy bars the day before you intend to make these, and chill them in their wrappers in your refrigerator overnight.

Hannah's 1st Note: If the kids are around, hide the candy bars in your vegetable crisper — they'll never look there.

An hour and a half before you want to serve, mix up the batter from the following ingredients:

1 and 2/3 cups all-purpose flour *(not sifted — pack it down in the cup when you measure it)*
1/4 teaspoon salt
3/4 teaspoon baking soda

***Milky Way, Snickers, Mars Bars, or Almond Joy work well. You can use regular size candy bars (approximately 2 ounces) or the miniatures you buy in a bag to give out at Halloween. Ruby uses the regular size. If you choose to use the miniatures, they won't take as long to fry as the larger size.

1/2 teaspoon cream of tartar
2 Tablespoons white *(granulated)* sugar

---

1 egg
1 cup whole milk

Combine the flour, salt, baking soda, cream of tartar, and sugar in a medium-sized bowl. Mix it all up together.

In a separate small bowl *(I used a 2-cup measuring cup)*, whisk the egg with the milk until it's nice and smooth.

Dump the milk and egg mixture into the bowl with the flour mixture and stir until there are no lumps. *(The resulting batter is about twice as thick as pancake batter.)*

Cover your bowl with plastic wrap, and chill it in the refrigerator for at least an hour. *(Two hours is okay, but no longer than that.)*

Hannah's 2nd Note: You can use a heavy pan on the stove to deep-fry these sinful treats as long as you have a reliable deep-frying thermometer. If you do this, you'll have to keep a sharp eye on the temperature of the oil. It should remain at a fairly constant 375 degrees F. A deep fryer that regulates its own temperature is really preferable, but you don't have to run right out and buy one just to try this recipe. If you use a deep fryer, DO NOT use the basket. The battered candy bars will stick to it and you'll never get them loose.

Prepare for deep-frying by heating your oil to 375 degrees F.

Prepare a cooling and draining surface by setting a metal rack over a pan lined with paper towels.

Hannah's 3rd Note: You will fry these candy bars one at a time and serve them the same way. That's to keep them from sticking together in the hot oil. You'll probably find that eager dessert eaters will line up in the kitchen to receive their treats.

Take out a candy bar, unwrap it, and dip it in the chilled batter. Make sure it's completely covered by the batter. Slide it gently into the hot oil with your batter-covered fingers *(or with two forks)* and fry it for approximately two and a half minutes, (2 and 1/2 minutes), or until nicely browned. Use a slotted metal spoon, or a pair of tongs to remove the candy bar from the hot oil.

Set the candy bar on the rack to drain and leave it there for at least 1 minute to cool. Then transfer it to a dessert dish or plate and serve.

Hannah's 4th Note: If you want to be fancy, sprinkle a little powdered sugar over the top of the candy bar.

When all the candy bars have been fried and eaten, you may have batter left over. If you do, dump it into a plastic bag, cut off the bottom corner, and squeeze the batter into the hot oil in a circular pattern. If you haven't guessed by this time, you're making funnel cake. Once the funnel cake is nicely browned, remove it from the oil with a slotted metal spoon, set it on the rack to drain, and then sprinkle it with powdered sugar. Yum!

WARNING: NEVER LEAVE HOT OIL OR FAT UNATTENDED!!!

There was the sound of voices upstairs in the community center lobby, and Lisa began to smile. "Here come the men. Herb said they'd be here before the party broke up."

The first one down the stairs was Mike Kingston, one of the most eligible bachelors in Lake Eden and a man that Hannah dated on a semi-regular basis. He was the chief detective at the Winnetka County Sheriff's Department. Mike came straight over to Hannah to give her a kiss on the cheek.

"Why are you wearing your uniform?" Hannah asked him, admiring the way he looked in his smartly styled uniform of maroon and gold, Minnesota's state colors.

"Mayor Bascomb and I are picking up the cookies to take out to the Children's Home. Some of the kids are afraid of law enforcement, and that's understandable. If they're in the Home because their parents are in jail, they think something bad is going to happen when they see a uniform, especially the little kids."

"But when a cop in a uniform arrives with boxes of cookies for them, that changes the equation?" Hannah asked.

"That's what I'm hoping." Mike stepped back and gave the ladies a little salute. "Good afternoon, ladies." And then he turned back to Hannah again. "Is there any coffee left?"

"I figured you'd be here any minute, so I just put on a second pot."

"Count me in for a cup," Mayor Bascomb said, arriving at the table with Lisa's husband, who had stopped to give Lisa a little hug.

"I'll have a cup too," Norman Rhodes, the town dentist, chimed in. "Hannah makes the best coffee around."

"Thank you," Hannah responded, avoiding his eyes. Seeing Norman was uncomfortable these days. There was too much history between them, and the situation had changed with the man who'd once asked her to marry him.

"Look what Hannah gave us for Christmas," Carrie pointed to the binder of recipes on the table. "All Hannah's recipes are inside and she made one for each of us."

"They're not *all* my recipes," Hannah pointed out. "I've got more at home on my bookshelf that I haven't entered in the computer. And they're not all *mine*. Some of these recipes are from family, friends, neighbors, and people who don't even live in Lake Eden."

"When will we get the rest?" Edna asked.

"As soon as I get time to type them into the computer so I can print them out. Don't hold your breath. That could take a while."

"I'll do it," Andrea offered. "Tracey can read them to me and I can type them up."

"Thanks, Andrea. That sounds good to me." Hannah gave her a smile and then she turned to the men. "Sit down and join us."

That was Lisa's cue to help Hannah pass out cups of coffee. The men always joined them for the last half-hour or so, and it wouldn't be a party without them.

"Too bad we were such greedy piggies when it came to dessert," Delores said, gesturing toward the nearly empty cheesecake platter and the pie plate where only crumbs remained. That comment caused the ladies to smile. Everyone knew that Hannah and Lisa always baked an extra dessert for the men.

"Don't tell me we're out of luck today!" Earl, Carrie's new husband, teased. "Carrie wouldn't let me taste a single one of her Lemon Softies. She packaged them up this

There were murmurs of agreement. Everyone knew how unpredictable the winter weather could be.

"Earl's going to follow Hannah home in the tow truck before he takes us out to the hospital," Carrie told Delores.

Earl gave a nod. "That's right. Old Lake Road is a little iffy right now."

"You don't have to do that," Hannah protested. "You're going to get a lot of calls and I can make it on my own. My truck's pretty heavy and it'll plow through almost anything."

Earl thought about that for a moment and then he shrugged. "Okay. You can have it your way, but I want you to call me if you get stuck."

"Do you have your cell phone with you?" Norman asked.

Hannah gave him an exasperated look, even though she knew he was just looking out for her. "Yes, I've got my cell phone. It's in my purse."

"But is it charged?" Andrea asked the follow-up question. Everyone here knew that Hannah was more than a bit forgetful about charging her cell phone.

"Of course it's charged! I put it in the charger just last . . ." Hannah stopped speaking and frowned. "I don't remember exactly when it was, but I'm sure it's fine."

"Get it out right now and check it," Delores ordered in her best motherly tone. "I don't want to spend the whole night worrying about whether you're freezing in a ditch somewhere."

With a speed borne of desperation, Hannah thought back to the last time she'd charged her cell phone. It was a weekend. She was fairly sure of that. She just hoped that it was *last* weekend. This was getting embarrassing, especially since she was almost positive that she could make it home just fine.

"I'll call you the minute I get home," she compromised.

"That's not good enough," Mike said. "This is a really heavy snow and some of the phone lines in your area are bound to go down. You might get home just fine, but you couldn't call your mother. And then she'd worry. Just get your cell phone and turn it on to see if it's charged."

Hannah hurried to the kitchen, found her cell phone in her saddlebag-sized shoulder bag, and took it back out to the table. "Here it is," she announced, pressing the button to turn it on. But even though she waited for several seconds, absolutely nothing happened.

"Yes?" Andrea asked, noticing the unhappy expression on her older sister's face.

"It's just taking awhile. It'll come on any second."

"You probably forgot to charge it again," Delores said with a sigh that could be heard all the way to the kitchen, where Lisa was packing up the leftovers from the luncheon. "You're always forgetting to charge it, Hannah. And Andrea even got you an extra charger for work so you could plug it in at The Cookie Jar."

Before Hannah could marshal a defense to her mother's accusation, Andrea reached over and took Hannah's cell phone. "It shouldn't take *this* long to come on." She turned to Delores. "But don't worry, Mother. Some cell phone batteries have a reserve, and Bill taught me how to check for that. Hannah might have enough reserve left to make one call."

There was complete silence as Andrea pressed a couple of buttons. Several moments later, she turned to Hannah and shook her head. "It's toast, Hannah. I checked the battery reserve and even that's depleted. You're totally out of juice."

"Honestly, Hannah!" Delores sighed loudly again. "It must be more than a week since you charged it. I know you're busy and these little things take time, but you really . . ."

"If I can stay in your guest room, we can use my cell phone on the way home," Michelle interrupted what was sure to be a lecture from their mother. She pulled her cell phone out of her pocket, turned it on, and glanced at the display. "There's no problem with mine. It's fully charged."

"You know you're always welcome to stay with me," Hannah said giving her youngest sister a grateful smile.

Michelle leaned close, so that no one could overhear. "I figured I'd better do something fast. Mother looked loaded for bear."

"Thanks, Michelle."

"Not a problem. It was payback for Bruno."

"Our dog?"

"That's right. It's for the time I brushed Bruno's teeth with Mother's toothbrush, and you went out to buy her a new one before she got home."

Hannah glanced at her watch as they climbed the covered steps to her second-story condo. "That took us an hour and twenty minutes!"

"I know," Michelle answered from two steps below. "It took three times longer than it should have."

"That's because I was driving slowly and being really careful. And we *still* ended up in the ditch!"

"Blame that on the visibility. I don't think it was more than a foot or so, and you couldn't see the edge of the road. We're just lucky Eddy Eilers came along to pull us out."

Hannah waited until Michelle reached the landing. "Do you want to catch, or shall I?"

"You catch. I'll open the door."

Hannah stabilized her stance as Michelle inserted the key in the lock. Her feet were apart, one slightly ahead of the other so that she wouldn't fall backwards.

"Here goes," Michelle warned, opening the door, and a nanosecond later, an orange and white, twenty-three-pound cat hurtled into Hannah's waiting arms.

"Hi, Moishe. I'm glad to see you, too." Hannah followed Michelle inside and placed her cat on his favorite perch on the back of the couch. "What have you been doing while I've been . . . Oh, no! Not again!"

"It looks like it snowed in here," Michelle said, quite unnecessarily, since the entire living room carpet was covered in small white Styrofoam beads.

Hannah sighed. "He got the beanbag again. It's my fault."

"Why is it your fault?"

"Because I listened to the weather on KCOW this morning. and I forgot to put the beanbag away. Moishe always gets nervous when the snow rattles against the living room window."

"So he tears apart the beanbag?"

"Right. I really ought to get rid of it anyway. It's so sixties."

"Maybe, but it's retro." Michelle turned to look at the fake green leather sack crumpled in a heap on the rug. "Are you going to fix it?"

"I have to. If I don't put it back together, Moishe might destroy something else the next time we get a winter storm."

"Point taken. Do you want me to get a broom and start sweeping up the beads?"

"Just use the vacuum. I put in a new bag the last time I used it. I'll get out the sewing kit."

Michelle gestured toward the window where the snow was blowing so hard against the pane, it sounded like a roll on a snare drum. "Are you sure we shouldn't wait for a while? It's still really bad out there."

"It'll be fine. Moishe only does it when he's alone and it starts getting nasty outside. It probably has to do with what he had to go through before he ended up here."

"Lucky cat," Michelle said, pausing to give Moishe a scratch under the chin as she went down the hall to get out the vacuum. "You'd really be in trouble if your mommy didn't love you so much."

"So why did we bake when we already have two sets of twelve dozen cookies?" Michelle asked, pulling a pan of Candy Bar Bar Cookies out of the upper oven and stepping aside so that Hannah could remove her Strawberry Custard Squares.

"Because we needed to," Hannah answered, crossing to the coffee pot to pour herself another cup.

"Okay. I'll buy that. What's next?"

"You mean baking?"

"Or cooking. Whatever. You know we always have a kitchen-fest every time I come home from college and stay with you."

"And that's one of the reasons I love it." Hannah smiled at her youngest sister. "We could make candy, or cookies, or cakes, or . . ."

Both sisters turned toward the door as the doorbell rang.

"Or night lunch," Hannah said, guessing who was there. "It's either Mike or Norman. And whichever one's there, he's bound to be hungry."

"I'll put on the coffee. You get the door," Michelle said, heading for the nearly depleted coffee maker on the counter. "And then, if it's okay, I'm going straight to bed."

"It's fine," Hannah said, walking toward the door. When she opened it, two ambulatory snowmen were standing on the landing.

"Good heavens!" Hannah exclaimed.

"It's brutal out there!" Mike commented, brushing the snow off his parka before he stepped in.

"We walked here from the gate," Norman told her, also brushing off the snow before he entered her living room. "Everything's shut down. We won't be able to get out until morning."

Until morning. The words echoed in Hannah's ears as she took their parkas and hung them in the laundry room to dry off. Why had they driven all the way out here anyway? Delores wasn't worried. Michelle had called her the second they pulled into the garage.

"We were worried about you," Mike said, answering Hannah's unspoken question. "I couldn't get through to your mother at the hospital to see if you'd called her. The lines were down. So Norman hitched a ride with me and we drove out here."

"Thanks for checking up on us," Michelle said, coming out of the kitchen, "but we already called Mother and told her we were okay."

Norman looked slightly apologetic. "Oh. We'll . . . we weren't sure, so we . . ."

"As you can see, everything's fine," Hannah said, gesturing her sister off to bed.

"Sorry about this," Norman said, "but we're going to have to stay with you."

"Of course," Hannah responded immediately, her answer practically dictated by proper Minnesota winter etiquette.

Mike gave her one of his devilish grins. "But you've got only one bedroom left. You don't expect both of us to stay up all night, do you?"

Hannah took a deep breath. No way was she falling for *that* hackneyed line! "Sure I do! I'll stay up with you, and I'll even make a night lunch. We've got cookies, and bars, and some chicken salad left over from the luncheon that I'll make into sandwiches. We can play cards until the sun comes up. That should be fun."

Both men exchanged glances, and Hannah noticed that they didn't look happy.

"Are we playing for money?" Norman asked her.

"No. We're playing for points."

"But that's no fun," Mike objected. "We should play for something worthwhile, something great, something both of us . . . I mean, all three of us want."

"What did you have in mind?" Hannah asked him.

"Oh, I don't know. What do you think, Norman?"

Norman looked embarrassed, and Hannah guessed that he'd been coached by Mike.

"Norman?" Mike prodded.

"Oh. Well. It's been a long day. Maybe we should play for a comfortable place to sleep."

"Great idea, Norman!" Mike turned back to Hannah. "How about it, Hannah?"

"Sounds good to me. I agree."

"You *agree?*" Mike asked, looking stunned.

"You do?" The same stunned expression was mirrored on Norman's face.

Hannah gave a little shrug. "It's fine with me. I'll bunk in with Michelle and the winner gets my bed. It's nice and comfortable and you get to cuddle with Moishe. And the loser gets my softest sleeping bag on the couch."

"Told you," Norman said under his breath, nudging Mike.

"Yeah," Mike responded.

"How about night lunch?" Hannah asked them. "Are you hungry?"

"I am," Mike said.

"Me, too," Norman answered her. "Mike can get out the card table and get everything all set up. I'll throw catnip mice for the Big Guy to keep him out of the way."

"Good idea," Hannah said, turning at

the kitchen doorway with a smile. Norman had just moved over to pet Moishe and she could hear him purring all the way across the room. "Don't let him near the cards. He likes to chew on them."

There was a thump as the catnip mouse sailed down the hallway with Moishe in hot pursuit. As she went off to the kitchen to make their night lunch, Hannah wondered how simple life would be for someone who didn't have two men who both wanted to play cards for her bed.

RECIPES ALPHABETICALLY BY CATEGORY

(New recipes are preceded by ⋆)

CANDY

COOKIES

SALADS

SOUPS

SUBSTITUTIONS FOR SOME INGREDIENTS

BAKING CONVERSION CHART

These conversions are approximate, but they'll work just fine for Hannah Swensen's recipes.

VOLUME:

U.S.	*Metric*
1/2 teaspoon	2 milliliters
1 teaspoon	5 milliliters
1 Tablespoon	15 milliliters
1/4 cup	50 milliliters
1/3 cup	75 milliliters
1/2 cup	125 milliliters
3/4 cup	175 milliliters
1 cup	1/4 liter

WEIGHT:

U.S.	*Metric*
1 ounce	28 grams
1 pound	454 grams

OVEN TEMPERATURE:

Degrees Fahrenheit	Degrees Centigrade	British (Regulo) Gas Mark
325 degrees F.	165 degrees C.	3
350 degrees F.	175 degrees C.	4
375 degrees F.	190 degrees C.	5

Note: Hannah's rectangular sheet cake pan, 9-inches by 13-inches, is approximately 23 centimeters by 32.5 centimeters.

ABOUT THE AUTHOR

Joanne Fluke is a *New York Times* and *USA Today* bestselling author of the Hannah Swenson mysteries, which include *Apple Turnover Murder, Cream Puff Murder, Carrot Cake Murder* and the book that started it all, *Chocolate Chip Cookie Murder.* Like Hannah Swensen, Joanne Fluke was born and raised in a small town in rural Minnesota but she now lives in sunny Southern California. Readers are welcome to visit her website at www.MurderSheBaked.com.

The employees of Thorndike Press hope you have enjoyed this Large Print book. All our Thorndike, Wheeler, and Kennebec Large Print titles are designed for easy reading, and all our books are made to last. Other Thorndike Press Large Print books are available at your library, through selected bookstores, or directly from us.

For information about titles, please call:

(800) 223-1244

or visit our Web site at:

http://gale.cengage.com/thorndike

To share your comments, please write:

Publisher
Thorndike Press
10 Water St., Suite 310
Waterville, ME 04901